VIETNAM-PERKASIE

VIETNAM-PERKASIE

A Combat Marine Memoir

W. D. Ehrhart

Foreword by H. Bruce Franklin

University of Massachusetts Press / Amherst

"Guerrilla War" and "A Relative Thing," which appear in
H. Bruce Franklin's foreword, were first published in
A Generation of Peace (New York: New Voices, 1975) and
are reprinted by permission of W. D. Ehrhart.

Sections of this book, in much altered form, have appeared in
*The Virginia Quarterly Review, TriQuarterly, Vietnam Journal,
Win, Northwoods Journal, Another Chicago Magazine,
Syncline, The Pub,* and *Samisdat.*
The University of Massachusetts Press edition is printed by
arrangement with McFarland & Co., Inc., Publishers.
Copyright © 1983 by W. D. Ehrhart. All rights reserved.
Foreword copyright © 1995 by H. Bruce Franklin.
This book is published with the support and cooperation of the
University of Massachusetts Boston.

All rights reserved
Printed in the United States of America
ISBN 0–87023–957–0
LC 94–36918

Library of Congress Cataloging-in-Publication Data

Ehrhart, W. D. (William Daniel), 1948–
    Vietnam-Perkasie: a combat marine memoir / W.D.
  Ehrhart; foreword by H. Bruce Franklin.
      p.   cm.
    Originally published: Jefferson, N.C.: McFarland, 1983.
    ISBN 0–87023–957–0 (pbk.: alk. paper)
    1. Ehrhart, W. D. (William Daniel), 1948– . 2. Vietnamese
  Conflict, 1961–1975—Personal narratives, American.
  3. Soldiers—Vietnam—Biography. 4. United States Marine
  Corps—Biography.   I. Title.
  DS559.5.E37   1995
  959.704'38—dc20
  [B]   94–36918
                                                    CIP

British Library Cataloguing in Publication data are available.

For my mother & father
and for my wife
with love

Contents

Foreword

W. D. Ehrhart is gradually gaining recognition as one of the most distinguished poets to emerge from the Vietnam War, as the preeminent anthologist of Vietnam War poetry, and as the author of a series of autobiographical memoirs unsurpassed among veterans' prose writings in their potent combination of personal experience and historical understanding. Such a triple achievement is not only unique in Vietnam War literature but rare indeed in any literature.

Vietnam-Perkasie: A Combat Marine Memoir is basic to understanding Ehrhart's life, his poetry, and the trajectory of his succeeding three autobiographical memoirs: *Passing Time: Memoir of a Vietnam Veteran Against the War; Going Back: An Ex-Marine Returns to Vietnam;* and his most recent volume, *Busted: A Vietnam Veteran in Nixon's America.* It is a stunning chronicle of how a red-white-and-blue American boy from the model American small town—"where people left their homes unlocked at night" and "carolers strolled from house to house on Christmas Eve"—is transformed by the Vietnam War into a human powder keg filled with an explosive mixture of rage and guilt and shame about himself and his country. This is the book that gives the most complete account of Ehrhart's experience in the war itself, opening with his physical wounding in the ferocious 1968 battle to retake the city of Hue and closing with scenes back in the United States that dramatize his psychological wounding. The main narrative is an extended flashback that takes him from his upbringing in that idyllic Pennsylvania town of Perkasie and his ultrapatriotic enlistment in the U.S. Marines at age seventeen through boot camp, the nightmare of discovering his identity as an alien invader, a murderer, and an instrument of imperial policy in Vietnam, and his return to an America that has become for him also an alien place. This is a familiar story in the literature by Vietnam veterans, similar to that told as brutally realistic autobiography in Ron Kovic's *Born on the Fourth of July,* as the sometimes surreal fiction of Tim O'Brien and Larry Heinemann, or as interstellar science fiction in Joe Haldeman's *The Forever War. Vietnam-Perkasie* features one characteristic of Ehrhart's writing that distinguishes it from most, though not all, literature by Vietnam veterans (or anybody else): he reveals things about his own actions that very few of us are brave enough to disclose. As he relentlessly probes the moral significance of these actions in Vietnam, he begins to display their historical significance. This leads to what is most distinctive about *Vietnam-Perkasie,* Ehrhart's ability to shape the autobiographical memoir into his own special vehicle for exploring history through personal experience.

Even as a high-school student, Ehrhart was committed to the belief in a crucial relationship between American history and the role of each individual American. It was this belief that led him in 1964 at the age of sixteen to ride around Perkasie on the back of a flatbed truck "singing Barry Goldwater campaign songs" for he was "fed up with Lyndon Johnson and his refusal to stand up to the communists in Vietnam." *Vietnam-Perkasie* reprints his 1965 high-school editorial filled with detailed historical arguments supporting the U.S. role in the Vietnam War and concluding with this rebuke to those who say that Americans are "dying for no good reason" in Vietnam: "What more noble a cause can a man die for, than to die in defense of freedom?" A few days after writing this, he decided to enlist in the Marines so that he could fight in Vietnam to defend freedom and his country.

By describing in undiluted detail what he actually experienced in Vietnam, *Vietnam-Perkasie* presents the raw materials from which Ehrhart was to fashion most of his early poems. Like many other Vietnam veteran poets, he developed a strikingly plain style, remarkable for its concision and avoidance of the mannerisms that have made "poetry" seem like a coterie activity. For example, in the sixty-five words that constitute the poem "Guerrilla War," Ehrhart dramatizes the basic facts of life for U.S. ground troops in Vietnam, facts that demolish the entire argument of his patriotic high-school editorial:

It's practically impossible
to tell civilians
from the Vietcong.

Nobody wears uniforms.
They all talk
the same language,
(and you couldn't understand them
even if they didn't).

They tape grenades
inside their clothes,
and carry satchel charges
in their market baskets.

Even their women fight;
and young boys,
and girls.

It's practically impossible
to tell civilians
from the Vietcong;

after a while,
you quit trying.

If one had to choose a single brief text to teach the history of the U.S. war in Vietnam, could one do better than Ehrhart's "A Relative Thing"?:

We are the ones you sent to fight a war
you didn't know a thing about.

It didn't take us long to realize
the only land that we controlled
was covered by the bottoms of our boots.

When the newsmen said that naval ships
had shelled a VC staging point,
we saw a breastless woman
and her stillborn child.

We laughed at old men stumbling
in the dust in frenzied terror
to avoid our three-ton trucks.

We fought outnumbered in Hue City

while the ARVN soldiers looted bodies
in the safety of the rear;
the cookies from the wives of Local 104
did not soften our awareness.

We have seen the pacified supporters
of the Saigon government
sitting in their jam-packed cardboard towns,
their wasted hands placed limply in their laps,
their empty bellies waiting for the rice
some district chief has sold
for profit to the Vietcong.

We have been democracy on Zippo raids,
burning houses to the ground,
driving eager amtracs through new-sown fields.

We are the ones who have to live
with the memory that we were the instruments
of your pigeon-breasted fantasies.
We are inextricable accomplices
in this travesty of dreams:

but we are not alone.

We are the ones you sent to fight a war
you did not know a thing about.
Those of us that lived
have tried to tell you what went wrong.
Now you think you do not have to listen.

Just because we will not fit
into the uniforms of photographs
of you at twenty-one
does not mean you can disown us.

We are your sons, America,
and you cannot change that.

When you awake,
we will still be here.

The qualities that characterize *Vietnam-Perkasie* and Ehrhart's poetry—
the distinctive flat voice speaking in a deceptively plain style, the painful hon-
esty and insights, the visceral power, the rare fusion of personal and historical
vision—also drive his later prose narratives and make them identifiable as

uniquely his own. On the surface, each narrative seems fairly straightforward, but closer inspection reveals that Ehrhart is following the classic dictum that the greatest art lies in the concealment of art.

Vietnam-Perkasie is the most deceptively simple of his prose books, which may help explain why it has commanded the widest audience—and why it is easy to misinterpret. As Ehrhart once remarked to me, "Vets who believe we should have nuked Hanoi and roasted Jane Fonda on a spit think *Vietnam-Perkasie* tells their story." When a mass-market press put it out in a 1985 paperback aimed at the thrill-seeking readers of survivalist military adventure stories, with a cover picturing Ehrhart as a gung-ho Marine "toting an M-16 in the jungles of Vietnam" in front of a billowing U.S. flag, it sold tens of thousands of copies. It has been frequently adopted as a text in college courses, where it is taught to support a variety of views on the war.

But *Vietnam-Perkasie* does not project an ambiguous vision. What it does present is the experiential basis for Ehrhart's ever-deepening insights into America's war in Vietnam as an expression of what lurks concealed under Perkasie's idyllic red-white-and-blue surfaces. The title suggests that the life of this "combat marine" incarnates some form of fusion between Vietnam and Perkasie, and the narrative dramatizes the explosive and ominous implications of this mixture.

H. Bruce Franklin
Rutgers University—Newark
July 1994

Preface

In order to protect the privacy of living persons and of the families and relatives of the dead, I have changed the names of most people in this book. Conversations have been reconstructed from memory; I have tried to make them as true to the original as possible.

I am indebted to the Pennsylvania Council on the Arts, the Mary Roberts Rinehart Foundation, William D. Quesenbery, Donald P. Cassidy, John N. Ehrhart, Jan Barry, James Beloungy and Marie McHarry, David Bloom, and Dan Gleason for their assistance and support during the writing of this book.

I am also grateful to Robbie Franklin of McFarland & Company for his willingness to publish this book when no one else would, and to Paul Wright of the University of Massachusetts Press for this new edition.

W. D. Ehrhart
Newtown, Pennsylvania
November 1982
Revised: Philadelphia
June 1994

Chapter 1

All I wanted was a cup of coffee. I was just sitting there, waiting for the water to boil, taking an occasional potshot out the window — and suddenly the world was in pieces. I never heard the explosion. Only the impact registered.

Sprawled out on the floor in a confusion of dust and debris and shredded clothing, I couldn't understand why I hadn't heard anything. "I'm hit bad," I thought, "sonofabitch, they finally got me," while another part of my brain kept screaming, "Jesus fucking Christ, not now, not now, not after all I've been through, oh please not now!" I almost threw up.

I'd been in Vietnam nearly twelve months to the day, and I'd been through one hell of a lot of shit during a year in a Marine infantry battalion: fifteen major combat operations, battalion scouts, patrols and ambushes and night listening posts, rocket attacks and mortar attacks and firefights and even a month at Con Thien — and I hadn't gotten a scratch.

I didn't even have to be on this operation. I was too short, had too little time left in-country: I was due to go home in less than a month. "What the hell," I'd thought, "Can't do diddly-squat back in the rear but sit around on my thumbs and mark days off my short-time calendar. Might as well be with my buddies."

Every Marine sent to Vietnam was supposed to serve there for thirteen months, unless he got a million-dollar wound or a bullet in the head first. When you got down to around ninety days left to go, you got your hands on a *Playboy* centerfold and drew ninety little numbered squares on her body. Each day you filled in one of the little squares on your short-time girl, and when all the little squares were filled in, you were supposed to take your short-time girl back to The World and trade her in for a real one. The morning Captain Broderick told me I didn't have to go on this operation, I had about thirty-five days left on my calendar. "What the hell," I'd said, "Might as well be with my buddies."

It wasn't quite as simple as all that, I suppose. In Vietnam, there were few things worse than having time on your hands — time to think about what you'd been doing and what was going on around you; time to compare the America you'd enlisted for with the one you saw blowing up villages, and tearing up rice fields with tanks and amphibious tractors, and bullying old men and women, and generally running around with your rifle and your name shooting anything that moved; time to think about those articles you kept reading in *Time* and *Stars 'n' Stripes* about protest marches and Vietcong flags in Times Square and Allen Ginsberg trying to levitate the Pentagon; time to imagine what miniskirts looked like on real girls, and wonder if the high school sweetheart you'd gotten a Dear John letter from five months ago was wearing one while every filthy bearded hippie in Trenton fucked her eyeballs out, and her loving every minute of it with flowers in her hair. It could drive you stark raving bonkers. I was more afraid of slack time than I ever was of combat.

And I guess there was more than a little macho in it. You know: "I'm a Marine, I ain't scared of a good fight, and even if I am, you'll be the last one to know about it." Whistling in the dark. One more test.

And anyway, I wouldn't have felt right letting my buddies go without me. It's like when you were a kid and the whole gang trashes old Mr. Bowen's garage, and everybody gets caught but you, and they all have to clean up the garage — and you feel so guilty watching them from your hiding place that you clamber out of the bushes and shuffle over and pitch in without anybody saying a word. Besides, nobody realized it was going to be this bad.

We were just going to bail out the U.S. Army again. Our battalion had come down to Phu Bai three or four days earlier from up around the Demilitarized Zone. We'd just spent four straight months in the field, and we'd been sent to the rear to give us a chance to rest and refit. And then the army MACV compound in Hue City radios down to Phu Bai one morning that they're taking incoming small arms and light mortar fire, nothing heavy, but can we send up a relief column and check it out? So we saddled up two companies and a command group, loaded into trucks, and headed up Highway 1 toward Hue.

That was about 0430 hours on January 31, 1968. By the time any of the Americans in Vietnam realized that a major North Vietnamese assault was underway from one end of the country to the other, our little relief column had been caught in one outrageous motherfucker of an ambush barely half of us would survive. Jesus, what a set-up.

Hue is built in two parts, north and south, bisected by the River of Perfumes. As we approached the south side of the city, North Vietnamese Army regulars — NVA — opened up at point blank range from concealed positions on either side of the highway with rockets, mortars, recoilless rifles and heavy machineguns. Marines began dropping like Samoans on iceskates. A lot of them never got up. But I wasn't hit.

And I mean everybody was getting hit. Captain Braithewaite, Alpha Company commander, got a .50-caliber machinegun bullet through both thighs in the first burst of fire. Major Miles, the operations officer, got killed trying to load dead and wounded back onto the trucks. That first day, we lost almost half our fighting strength. It took us nearly fourteen hours to fight our way six blocks north from the edge of the city to the MACV compound one block south of the river — and when we got there, we had a few choice words for the goddamned Army and their goddamned light sniper fire.

We actually got across the river briefly, charging over the long narrow bridge behind our two quad-.50 machinegun trucks. But the quad-.50's got knocked out almost immediately, and we had to fall back to the south side before sundown while we still had anybody left alive. And even then I wasn't hit. Not that day, or the next day, or the next day, or the next day. And everybody was getting hit, some guys two or three times. One gunner from Alpha Company got hit three times in less than an hour.

After that first adrenalin charge across the bridge, most of the fighting in the next two weeks took place on the south side of the river, the side opposite the old city that contained the Citadel of the ancient Annamese emperors. It was the Citadel that later got all the coverage on the six o'clock news, but in the early going, we couldn't even get close to it. We had to set up operations in the MACV compound, a few hundred Marines in a tiny pocket of a city teeming with 2,000 well-dug-in NVA regulars. From there, we slowly began to extend our tenuous hold on the city, one building at a time.

By the third day, the battalion scouts had managed to take a

3

building right across the street from the MACV compound. It was kind of beat up at the moment, but it was a really nice house just the same: three-story concrete and stone construction, a big yard with a low stone wall around it, canopied beds, a wine cellar, oil paintings on the walls, iron bars on the windows to keep out satchel charges. Definitely not your run-of-the-mill Vietnamese hooch. Probably the mayor's residence or the provincial governor's mansion, it was altogether a fine place to set up shop for awhile.

Which was a lucky break for us because for the next two days we couldn't get any farther. Or rather, we couldn't hold anything we took. Come daylight, we'd dash across the street to the next block, fight our way through it house by house: kick open a door, flip in a grenade, leap in shooting, go on to the next floor, then on to the next house — the NVA giving ground slowly and stubbornly, just waiting for nightfall. Then all in one big push, with their overwhelmingly superior numbers, they'd drive us back through the block, across the street, and right back into the mayor's house. Net gain: nothing. Casualties: heavy.

After two days of this, the battalion commander finally decided, "Bullshit, this is crazy. Let's get some flame tanks and do this right." Hooray for the colonel. And we meant it.

That's why I wanted a cup of coffee. There wasn't much else to do on the morning of February fifth because the flame tanks were over by the stadium supporting Alpha Company, and we couldn't have them until they'd cooked all the NVA holding the stadium. So I was just relaxing. Passing time. Enjoying the pleasures of urban warfare.

For a whole year I'd fought in the boondocks. With a few exceptions like Hue, Danang and Saigon, all of Vietnam was the boonies. Thatched-roof hamlets set among rice fields, water buffalo, dirt trails, sand barrens, bamboo jungles, abandoned plantations long overgrown, mangrove swamps — right out of *National Geographic*.

Then, suddenly, a real city. Not New York or Philadelphia, but a city nonetheless, with paved streets and concrete houses, a university, a stadium, big cathedrals, shops and stores, and all the assorted goodies that accumulate in cities. We even found a beer store that hadn't been looted yet, and had warm Vietnamese beer coming out of our ears.

This house-to-house stuff was a new kind of fighting, and we paid dearly for our on-the-job training. But there definitely were amenities, and I was enjoying several of them that morning. Most notably the roof over my head and the overstuffed armchair I was sitting in while I waited for the water to boil. When I'd found out we

4

were going to stay put and do nothing for awhile, I just pulled that big easy chair over to a second-story window in the governor's mansion and sat down to watch the war. I hadn't had much sleep lately and I started getting drowsy. A nice cup of coffee was just what I needed.

Every C-ration meal comes with a lot of things, but five of the things you get are a packet of coffee, a can opener, a plastic spoon, a big can (maybe with crackers and jam and cocoa inside), and a little can (maybe bread or date pudding). To make coffee, you empty the big can (eat the contents if you're hungry, or put them in your pocket for later), bend the lid back into a handle, and fill it with water from your canteen. Then you take your can opener and make a few air holes around the bottom of the little can, which you've also emptied. You bend the little can slightly at the open top end so the big can will sit on it, and that's your stove. You're supposed to get a heat tab with each meal, but usually you don't, so you just take a little piece of C-4 plastic explosive—it won't blow up if it's not under pressure—put that in your stove instead, and light it. You get up-wind of it so the fumes from the C-4 don't kill half your brain cells, put the big can on top of the little can, and when the water boils, you pour in the packet of coffee and give it a good stir with your plastic spoon. I was just about ready to pour in the coffee when the world came apart. Things were fine. Then they weren't. Just like that.

Most of the casualties we took in Vietnam got it in their first few months in-country, or their last few months. Guys got it in their first few months because they simply hadn't yet learned enough to avoid getting it. But guys got it in their last few months because they got stupid in a way that the new guys never could.

Because they couldn't suppress just a little longer the intoxicating illusion that they were actually going to get out of the game ahead. Because they couldn't stop thinking about that big Freedom Bird full of plump stewardesses leaping off the runway out of Danang, next stop: The World. About Mom and Dad, and hot running water, and cold beer from the tap in the tavern down the street anytime you wanted it. About clean socks and clean sheets, and cruising through town in your own car on Saturday night, and never jerking off again because little Suzie Creamcheese is gonna sit on your face till the cows come home, and who knows what all the hell else can make a man who's come so far just that once forget completely everything he's ever learned about staying alive, plop himself down in a big easy chair like it was his own kitchen back on the block, shrug his shoulders, and try to fix a nice cup of coffee.

Chapter 2

I grew up in Perkasie, Pennsylvania, a small town between Philadelphia and Allentown. By the time I graduated from high school, Perkasie was beginning to show a terminal suburban sprawl, but when I was growing up, it was still just a quiet little country town. People left their houses unlocked at night, neighbors called to each other from large front porches on warm summer evenings, and kids went sledding on Third Street hill when it snowed in the winter. There were no traffic lights in town. The whole countryside around was dotted with small family farms, and you could get on your bicycle and in ten minutes be coasting between cornfields, or go down to Lake Lenape and catch painted turtles and water snakes. Carolers strolled from house to house on Christmas Eve, and Jimmy the shoe repairman knew the shoe size of everyone in town.

An almost nonexistent crime rate allowed the town's few part-time cops to serve primarily as dogcatchers and targets for adolescent snowballs and water balloons. The starting quarterback of the high school football team was a celebrity on a par with movie stars and statesmen, and coach Wayne Helman was a genuine folk hero. Our high school guidance counsellors actively discourages students from considering such schools as UCLA and Tulane—in fact, couldn't understand why anyone would want to go to college so far away from home—considering it a solemn duty to steer as many kids as possible to Millersville, Shippensburg, Kutztown, and West Chester. Traveling to New York City, ninety miles to the northeast, was an exotic and

6

rather dangerous venture to be planned months in advance and talked about for years after. Few people actually ever made the trip; those that did were considered daring, and perhaps a little eccentric. Rotary Club and church were well attended, and nothing much out of the ordinary ever happened except the occasional shotgun wedding that had saved more than one of my childhood friends from bastardy.

I don't recall anything resembling real poverty. Most folks worked hard and honestly for what they had, and most folks were comfortable. Life in America was good, and came as the direct result of the bounty and blessing of God, the wisdom of our Revolutionary Fathers, and the sacrifices of preceding generations.

In elementary school, I read books about John Paul Jones and Pecos Bill, and at Halloween I collected money for UNICEF to help the children in countries less fortunate than my own. Leaving food on a plate at mealtime brought a stern admonishment to remember the starving millions in China. Ike, the good soldier and fatherly statesman, was president, and each school day began with the Lord's Prayer and the Pledge of Allegiance, in that order. We learned about peasants in Bolivia, and William Penn and wampam belts, and sometimes we had atomic bomb drills where we would have to sit in rows in the halls, facing the wall and curling up with our heads between our knees and our hands clasped behind our necks. Every Memorial Day, I decorated my bicycle with red, white and blue crepe paper and rode in the town parade; and every year I could hardly wait for the twenty-one–gun salute fired by the uniformed members of the Hartzell-Crouthamel American Legion Post, and the playing of taps at the end of the salute that sent chills through my body and left everyone reverently silent for a moment like the end of a church service. I knew the Twenty-third Psalm and the Gettysburg Address by heart, and earned enough money selling newspapers to buy a subscription to a magazine called *Our Navy*. Elvis Presley was a scandalous and exciting sensation, and I had nightmares about the Russian sputnik.

Once, Jeff Alison and I sneaked into his father's bedroom and found the Silver Star cradled in velvet in a black box with gilt trim. When we finally screwed up enough courage to ask him how he'd earned it, his modestly vague response fired our ten-year-old imaginations to act out the most daring and heroic deeds. Playing war, we always argued over who would be the Japs or the Krauts or the Commies, always finally forcing the least popular playmates to be the bad guys, and my favorite Christmas toy was a "real" .30-caliber machine-gun mounted on a tripod stand, battery-powered, with simulated sound and flashing red barrel. I mowed down thousands with it. Everybody wanted to be on my side, until I broke my plastic miracle hitting the dirt too realistically. For a long time afterwards, I was regularly appointed a dirty Commie. It was almost unbearable.

I was in the tenth grade when John Kennedy was assassinated. Together with my oldest brother and his girlfriend, I stood in line from ten at night until six the next morning to see the casket lying beneath the great Capitol dome; and when I saw it, I cried. On the cover of my high school notebook for that year, I wrote, "Ask not what your country can do for you; ask what you can do for your country." Beneath that, I added, "Ich bin ein Berliner." The Cuban missile crisis was still recent history, and I can recall clearly the photograph in *Life* magazine of U.S. Army helicopters suspended in the air over the green rice fields of a country called Laos. Vietnam was beginning to appear more frequently in the news, and over it all loomed the sinister figure of Nikita Khrushchev, pounding his shoe and shouting, "We will bury you!"

That summer, I worked as a lifeguard at the municipal swimming pool. One night after hours, one of the older guards produced a six-pack of beer from the trunk of his car, offering to split it with the rest of us. I didn't like the taste of it, but I drank some anyway and got giddy and lightheaded on less than half a can. By the end of the summer, I learned how to kiss with my mouth open, and could drink almost a whole beer before I got silly.

In November of 1964, I rode around Perkasie one evening on the back of a flatbed truck singing Barry Goldwater campaign songs. I was fed up with Lyndon Johnson and his refusal to stand up to the communists in Vietnam. Goldwater carried Perkasie and the surrounding communities by a wide margin. I was sixteen. In English class that year, I wrote a story about a teenaged boy behind the Iron Curtain who tries to flee across the border to freedom. He is killed by border guards just as he reaches the wire, and the last sentence reads: "He doubled over and slipped to the ground, his mouth twisting into a smile."

I earned a varsity letter in track that spring, and was also elected to the National Honor Society. When the school year ended, a friend and I took off for California, neglecting to tell our parents in advance. It was a great adventure to be on our own in paradise for a whole summer, and when we returned to begin our senior year of high school, we were greeted with admiration and wonder by our friends.

By December of 1965, I had already been accepted for

8

admission to four different colleges; I had only to decide which one I wanted to attend. But with the communist insurgency in Vietnam commanding the headlines regularly, I began thinking about enlisting in the service instead. In a journalism class that spring, I wrote this editorial:

"The casualty rates in the war in Vietnam are rapidly rising. More American boys have been killed in the first four months of this year than were killed in all of 1965. Just this past week, more United States soldiers were killed than South Vietnamese.

"These are staggering realizations. But even more staggering are the anti-American demonstrations that are rocking every major city in South Vietnam. It appears that we are not welcome there. We are fighting a war to liberate a people who do not wish to be liberated. American boys are dying for no good cause.

"Yet is this true? We don't believe it is. The people of South Vietnam live in constant fear. No, perhaps not the city-dwellers, those who are doing most of the demonstrating. They have the security of the city to protect them. But the people who farm the thousands of rice fields, the people who live in the fishing villages, the mountain tribesmen, these people truly live in fear. Vietcong guerrillas roam the country controlling the fields, jungles, rivers, villages, roads and everything except the few small strongholds of United States Special Forces and Marines. The people are forced to hide VC from pursuers. Vietcong strongmen tax villagers heavily for food — food which they use to feed their guerrilla bands. Vietcong 'recruiters' take men and boys and forcibly impress them into the rebel army. All of this is done under threats of destruction of crops and villages, torture and death — and the VC have proven that they do not bluff.

"There is no freedom in South Vietnam. To have freedom, there must be free elections. Yet how can there be free elections in South Vietnam with such strong influences as the VC have on the vast majority of the people? And without free elections, how can there be freedom?

"As long as the Vietcong or any other subversive influences exist, there can never be a free country of South Vietnam. This, then, is the cause for which so many Americans have lost their lives.

"To those of you who feel that these boys are dying for no good reason, we say this: What more noble a cause can a man die for, than to die in defense of freedom?"

Within a few days of writing that editorial, I made up my mind to enlist — and of course, there was never any doubt about which service I would have to join. The Marines had the most colorful reputation and tradition. Marines were heroes by virtue solely of being Marines. Our high school had an Armed Forces Day assembly every spring during which representatives of all four branches of the military would address the students, and the Marine, in his dazzling dress blue uniform with red trouser stripes and gold piping, stood out like the Star of Bethlehem.

My parents, of course, were not exactly thrilled with the idea of my enlistment. Because I was only seventeen, they had to sign the enlistment contract, too — and they were reluctant to do so. After all, what parent wants a son to join the Marines when he could go to college? But we talked it over one night for a long time. Finally I asked, "Is this how you raised me? To let somebody else's kids fight America's wars?" That ended the discussion.

Once again, like the previous autumn when I'd returned from California, I was the center of attention. Mr. Diehl, my English teacher, suggested that I might be wise to go to college first, then become an officer if I still wanted to join. And Mrs. Geosits, my journalism teacher, advised me to take the summer months to think over my decision. But other teachers stopped me in the hall to shake hands and congratulate me and wish me luck. I got my picture in the local weekly, the Perkasie *News-Herald*, standing with my recruiter in front of the high school, and in the neighboring Quakertown *Free Press* as well. My high school sweetheart, Jenny, began wearing a Marine Corps eagle-globe-and-anchor pin on her blouse.

One day at school a few weeks before I graduated in June, 1966, Karen King came up to me. "You're really joining the Marines?" she asked.

"Yes."

"They'll send you to Vietnam. You could get killed."

"I know," I said, gazing past her shoulder into the distance.

"You're crazy," she said, "but I really admire you."

Chapter 3

We were all silent as the bus pulled up to the gate lit only by a few small spotlights. It was almost midnight, June 17, 1966. On the airplane from Philadelphia to Charleston, there'd been new friends made, strained camaraderie, and talk of homes and girlfriends and ambitions. But as the last miles of the journey rolled away beneath the shadowy arch of Spanish moss, the bus carried each man ever deeper into the black tunnel of his own mind. There was no conversation now, no sound but the mechanical grate and whine of the bus itself. Nervous anticipation — raw fear of the unknown — made thought impossible. I could see gold letters on a red brick wall illuminated by a spotlight: "Marine Corps Recruit Depot, Parris Island, South Carolina."

A uniformed guard waved the bus through. My stomach was the size of a golf ball, and getting rapidly smaller. I clutched the stack of folders on my lap nervously. At the Philadelphia airport, a Marine sergeant had entrusted me with the orders and records of all the recruits in our group. "You're in charge," he'd said right in front of my parents, younger brother, and girlfriend, and I'd swelled with pride. Already I'd been singled out as bright and capable. Well, why not? After all, I'd just graduated from high school with honors. I wasn't your typical dumb recruit, and the Marine Corps could see that. I squeezed the stack of folders over and over again with the reflex rhythm of a captive chimp picking at the bars of his cage. My stomach was doing somersaults as the bus rolled up to the only lighted building on the sleeping base.

The bus stopped. A lone figure in a khaki uniform and dark brown Smokey the Bear hat strode through the glare of a spotlight shining down from the side of the building. The driver opened the door, and the lone figure stepped onto the bus, causing the bus to list noticeably to the right. Now I know everyone who's ever written about Marine boot camp has tried to claim that the drill instructors are all eight and a half feet tall. And everybody knows that it just isn't true. But the DI who got onto that bus was eight and a half feet tall. And he was ugly. He blocked the huge windshield of the bus completely. His chest strained at the buttons on his shirt, so that they seemed about to fly off at any moment like buckshot from a scattergun. Standing there with his hands on his hips, he looked like a cross between Paul Bunyan, Babe the Blue Ox, and Godzilla.

"Who's got the records." It wasn't a question. I held them up to him with both hands, as though offering a goblet of holy water to a priest. He encircled the whole stack with a gargantuan hand, made them disappear, and that was that. No "Thank you." No "Well done, Marine." Nothing. I couldn't believe it. My ace in the hole had become a stone in a pit. My stomach took off after the stone.

It immediately changed directions, however, leaping into my mouth and trying to slither out between my teeth as the Voice of God shattered the silence: "There's four columns of yellow footprints painted on the deck in front of those steps over there," roared the DI, jerking a thumb in the general direction of the lighted barracks. "When I give the word, you filthy pigs have three seconds to get outta this bus and plant yourself on one of those sets of yellow footprints. I don't wanna see nothin' but assholes and elbows flyin'. You will not talk. You will not eye-fuck the area. You will keep your head and eyes front at all times. You will do everything you're told instantly, and you will do nothing else. I'll kill the first cocksucker that fucks it up. You scuzzy shitbirds are *mine*, ladies! And I don't like you. Now, MOVE! *Do it! Do it!*"

One moment I was sitting on the bus getting my eardrums pummeled raw; the next moment I was standing on a set of yellow footprints. Just like that. The footprints were painted so close together that my face and body were smashed up tight against the guy in front of me; the guy behind me was smashed up tight against me; and we were all rubbing shoulders with the columns on either side of us — a formation we would soon come to know as "asshole to bellybutton."

I'd wanted to be a Marine, and I couldn't deny it. But this?! Oh, no, this isn't at all what I'd had in mind. Standing in the midst of

12

that lump of crushed fear-crazed bodies in the hot Southern night with the Voice of God still pounding in my ears and my heart hammering to beat the band, I suddenly wanted to be anywhere but here. Anywhere! I wanted to pee. I wanted to throw up. I wanted to cry. I remember thinking very, *very* clearly: "I want Mommy. Please take me home, Mommy. I won't be bad anymore." It was the last clear thought I would have for days.

Again the Voice roared, "Get in the building!" Three or four more identical copies of Godzilla the Blue Bunyan materialized out of nowhere, all of them shouting, "Get in the building! Get in the building! Line up in front of the tables! Double time! Get in the building!" We began to surge forward frantically in one lump, bodies in back climbing over the ones in front of them like stampeded cattle, stumbling and falling and crawling on hands and knees and getting up and falling again.

Inside, naked lightbulbs glared bright white above two long rows of tables. "Face the tables! Eyes front! Stand at attention! Chin in! Chest out! Thumbs along the trouser seams! Don't move! Don't move!" Drill instructors were everywhere, shouting in recruits' faces at distances ranging from three to six inches: "Keep your head and eyes front, piggy! Don't even breathe, piggy! What're you lookin' at, sweetpea?! You eye-fuckin' me, sweetpea?! You wanna fuck me, scum?! Z'at it, shitbag?! You queer, piggy?! Fuck the deck, piggy! Down, piggy, hit the deck! Push-ups! One! Two! Three! Four! Lemme hear you squeal, piggy! *Squeal*, goddamn you!!" They had steel forge bellows for lungs.

"Empty your pockets onto the tables, wormies! Empty your dittybags onto the tables, wormies! Empty your wallets onto the tables, piggies! Put your wallets into the green bag in front of you! Put your money, jewelry, legal identification, draft card, driver's license into the green bag in front of you! No photographs! Nothing else! Is this your sweetheart, piggy? *Answer me*, shithead!!"

"Yes."

"*Yes, sir*, you filthy scumbag!"

"Yessir."

"I can't hear you!"

"Yessir!"

"Louder!"

"YES, SIR!"

"She looks like a whore, puke."

Nothing.

"I said she looks like a whore!"

"No, sir."

"You callin' me a liar?!"

"No, sir."

"I can't hear you, piggy!"

"No, SIR!"

"She looks like a whore!"

"YESSIR!"

"She's probably fucking your father right now."

"YESSIR!"

"Hey, nigger! Your mother a monkey?"

Nothing.

"You better answer me, you ape! I'll break your black ass a dozen ways to Sunday!"

In the meantime, everything else on the tables got swept into huge trash barrels by several volunteers: "Anybody here drive a truck?" — and the truck drivers were given big push-brooms and ordered to clear the tables: spare clothes, soap, toothbrushes, photographs, combs, electric razors, aftershave, shampoo, books, everything disappeared into the trash barrels.

Then a DI with stripes all up and down his arms got up on the tables and started pacing. "You boys wanna be Marines," he began in something very near a normal tone of voice. "We didn't ask for you; you came to us. It isn't easy to make a Marine because Marines are the best there is. You're going to hate it here. You're probably going to wish you were dead. But most of you won't die — unless you try to run. This is Parris Island. It's called an island because it is an island. It's surrounded by swamps, and the swamps are filled with poisonous snakes. The snakes work for the Marine Corps. The causeway you came in on is guarded day and night, so you can't get out that way. If you get through the swamps, you have to swim a two-mile channel against some of the strongest currents in the world. And if you don't drown, the MPs will be waiting to pick you up when you get to the mainland. And they'll bring you back, and you'll go to the brig for six months, and then you'll begin training all over again. Don't try to run. The easiest way to leave this island is to march out the front gate on graduation day. So do as you're told. Do your best, and you might make it."

The moment he finished talking, the decibel level shot back up to 232. "All right, hoggies, time to sheer the sheep! Bleat, bleat, little sheep. *I said bleat!*" We all began to bleat. "Louder!" We all bleated

14

louder. The DIs were everywhere, a flurry of motion you could just catch from the corners of your eyes — you didn't dare look right or left or up or down or anywhere but straight ahead. Anybody who did got nailed instantly, two or three DIs descending upon him like avenging angels, hounding him into jello.

"Double time! Double time! Through the hatchway — not *that* hatchway, you goddamned stupid gorilla! Column of twos! Asshole to bellybutton! Line up on the yellow footprints!" There were yellow footprints painted all over Parris Island. Several barber chairs and several sleepy barbers waited for us at the end of this particular line of yellow footprints. Each haircut took about twelve seconds: zip, zip, zip, and your skull was as smooth as an eggshell. While we stood there packed in line, the DIs assaulted anybody who had hair longer than an inch or two: "Hey, Goldilocks; hey, sweetheart; you like your hair, pretty lady?! We gonna cut it all off, and never give it back again. You like that, sweetpea? That make ya happy? *Answer me*, you dumb fuck! When I ask you a question, you better have an answer! I'll spread your pea-brain all over the wall!"

"Yessir!"

"I can't hear you!"

"YESSIR!"

"You look like a pussy, sweetpea! Are you a pussy?!"

"No, sir!"

"What?! You callin' me a liar?!"

"No, SIR!"

"You look like a pussy, puke."

"YESSIR!"

"Tell me what you are, puke."

"I'm a pussy, sir."

"I can't hear you!"

"I AM A PUSSY, SIR!"

We were herded off to the showers, looking like a bunch of freshly peeled onions. Finally, well into the early hours of the morning, we were herded upstairs into a large open bay lined with two rows of double-deck steel bunk beds. "Get in the rack! Lie at attention!" a DI commanded. Then, "Sleep!" The lights went out.

I disobeyed the DI's order: I didn't sleep. I don't think anyone else slept either, but I was too scared to look anywhere but straight up at the ceiling, so I don't know. I was terrified that I wouldn't wake up fast enough, and then I'd be killed instantly. My stomach was a churning cauldron of bile and acid. Someone inside my head was banging away with a sledgehammer, frantically trying to break out. With all my heart and soul, I did not want to be here. I couldn't understand how any of this had happened. I lay there for what seemed like hours in a kind of trance, staring at the ceiling, my mind in neutral and somebody flooring the accelerator. Jesus, Jesus, sweet Jesus, save me please.

The lights went on. A swarm of DIs charged into the bay banging the lids of garbage cans against the metal bedframes. "Get up! Get Up! Get up! Get in front of your racks! Stand at attention! Eyes front! Get up! Get up! Move, move, move! Time to slop the hogs, ladies! Everybody nice and hungry?! I asked you a question, goddamn it!"

"Yessir!" we all shouted in unison.

"Louder!"

"YESSIR!"

Still in civilian clothing, we were herded off, asshole to bellybutton, to our first breakfast in the Marine Corps.

The last thing I wanted to see was food. No way in hell I could eat anything. But I had this voice inside me, probably the guy with the sledgehammer, that kept saying if I didn't take everything that was given to me and eat everything I had taken, I would be killed instantly. So I went through the chowline with my metal tray outstretched, shoulder to shoulder with everyone else, eyes staring straight ahead and stomach screaming, "Please don't do this to me!" as the messmen heaped on eggs, grits, sausage, French toast, butter, syrup, hot cereal, cold cereal, sugar, milk, juice and a banana. I ate every bit of it, and every mouthful went down like rock salt. I had to swallow stuff two and three times because it kept coming up again. The banana was an unholy nightmare: it was three feet long and weighed thirty-eight pounds. I saved the banana for last, hoping it would go away, but it wouldn't. I knew I was going to die.

After breakfast, the pace quickened into a kaleidoscope of shouting, screaming, lifting, toting, sweating, running, waiting asshole to bellybutton, push-ups, squat thrusts, medical exams, dental checks, shot lines, written tests, forms, obscenities, screaming and shouting:

— Packing up the clothes we were wearing and addressing the packages to some place called home, casting off the last traces of another life and becoming Private Ehrhart, W.D., 2279361, Platoon 1005, dressed in oversized green utilities designed to make you feel puny and lost and awkward and identical to everyone around you.

— Trying to march and failing miserably and being informed

16

vociferously of the failure, watching with envy and humiliation while advanced platoons stepped by in perfect cadence and our own DIS roared, "You'll never march like that, you helpless, worthless shit-bags!"

— Receiving our issues of field gear, linen and blankets, seabags and extra clothing, and trying to drag it all across the sweltering parade deck without dropping any of it, and dropping it all over the place as DIS perforated your eardrums with their eyeteeth;

— Rifle issue, where a DI announced: "This is your life, ladies. The Marine Corps loves its rifles. The Marine Corps doesn't give a damn about you. The Marine Corps doesn't even like you. And if anything ever happens to your rifle, if it so much as gets a tiny little scratch on it, the Marine Corps will hate you forever and ever. And then you'll be in the hurt-locker, ladies, and you won't like that at all." I had no idea what the hurt-locker was, but I was certain I wouldn't like it.

Another DI told us: "The Marine Corps is your father and mother. The DI is your priest and your doctor and your lover. The Marine Corps will give you everything you'll ever need. If the Marine Corps doesn't give it to you, you don't need it. The Marine Corps will teach you everything you'll ever need to know. If the Marine Corps wants you to think, you'll be issued a brain. Don't think, ladies. Don't even try to think. Jump when you're told to, and don't come down till the Marine Corps tells you to."

The sequence of individual events was without order or logic or foundation. The raging DIS in Smokey the Bear hats never relaxed and never slept and never let up, and they would kill you instantly if you did anything wrong. And you were always, always, doing something wrong. And they never missed a thing.

After a few days — perhaps three or four, but maybe as many as six, I have no idea — three new DIS appeared in our barracks one morning. They were obviously in a foul mood. All DIS were always in foul moods; they claimed it was our fault. The three new DIS, we were abruptly informed, were our permanent DIS and we were about to begin our training cycle.

Jesus, Joseph and Mary! Begin our training cycle?! I thought we'd begun days ago. What in God's name were they going to do to me now?!

I had a religious rebirth in boot camp. My father is a minister in the United Church of Christ, and every Sunday for fifteen years I'd gone to Sunday School and church. In high school, however, I'd begun to find all sorts of things wrong with my own liberal Protestant faith

17

and became, in quick succession and with deep conviction, Taoist, Buddhist, Zen, Hindu, and Quaker. In my last few months of high school, I'd often accompanied my girlfriend, Jenny, to Catholic mass. But that was only to please her, for I'd finally determined that I was actually an agnostic.

But boot camp is one of the great missionary strongholds of Western civilization. Cut off from love and warmth, familiarity or any semblance of human kindness, surrounded by large angry DIS skilled in foreign languages and deviant behavior, in fear for your mortal life virtually every single moment, you find yourself yearning for anything stable and comforting to sustain you in your constant need.

Under such a strain, you become possessed of a vivid memory recalling every wrong you've ever committed in your entire life. You are riddled with guilt over the unconscionable way you always treated your mother and father, brothers, friends and strangers, your dog, your cats, and the local police chief. You try and try, but you can't recall a single good deed you've ever done or a kind word you've said. And you realize that if you died tomorrow, which was always a near-by possibility at Parris Island, you would go straight to Hell and burn there forever. An eternal boot camp.

I prayed every night. In fact, the whole eighty-man platoon shouted the Lord's Prayer in unison while lying in our beds at attention. Except when Sergeant Ellis was on duty. His nose had been broken six times, his left shoulder and left eye drooped, 100-proof bourbon flowed through his veins, and he didn't like the Lord's Prayer. The prayer he liked was: "Pray for war!" So when Staff Sergeant Olsen or Sergeant Benson was on duty, we shouted the Lord's Prayer in unison, and when Sergeant Ellis was on duty, we shouted, "Pray for war!"

But even after we'd offered up our platoon prayer and the DI had ordered, "Sleep!" and the lights had gone out, I prayed all by myself and without being ordered to. I asked God to forgive my sins, and to bring peace into the world, and to look after my family and Jenny, and to give comfort to all homeless, lonely and starving people, and to get me out of boot camp alive if He could possibly see fit to arrange it. I was always quick to add that His Will Be Done, but I fervently hoped in the silence of my heart that His Will didn't include my being eaten alive by a drill instructor in South Carolina.

And I went to church every Sunday. All recruits went to church every Sunday—and woe betide the recruit stupid enough ever to

18

suggest he didn't want to go to church. But everybody always wanted to go to church because it was the only hour in a 168-hour week when you weren't doing push-ups or close order drill or bayonet training while livid DIs swarmed all over you like horseflies. The chaplain spoke English like he was carrying on a conversation with a bank teller on a Tuesday morning in Perkasie. It sounded nice, I prayed in church, too. And took communion. And really sang the hymns.

One million push-ups, eleven hundred and eighty-six obstacle courses, and twelve thousand "Aye, aye, sirs" later, the good Lord did in fact deliver me, creating a lifetime convert in the process. As I stood in graduation formation on the parade deck, facing a replica of the statue of the Marines raising the flag at Iwo Jima, I thought back to that first night in June when I couldn't begin to conceive of this day. I burst into a broad grin, barely able to contain the pride struggling to get out of me in a mighty shout. In a few moments, I would be meritoriously promoted to Private First Class W.D. Ehrhart, United States Marine.

Home on leave a few weeks later, I escorted my mother to church where I sat in full dress uniform in the front pew while my father preached from the pulpit and the congregation beamed their collective approval. Then I hurried off to pick up Jenny and her parents and go with them to Catholic mass. Later that day, I even went to Quaker meeting with my friend Sadie Thompson, and afterwards everybody shook my hand and told me how glad they were that I'd come.

When Sadie and I got back to her house, she asked me to come in, but I said I couldn't because Jenny and I were going out to dinner.

"You really love Jenny, don't you?"

"Yes, I do. We're going to be married as soon as I get home from Vietnam."

"I guess I won't be seeing you again before you go," she said. "Please take care of yourself, Bill. And Bill," she added after a thoughtful pause, "try not to kill anybody."

Chapter 4

The first thing that struck me about Vietnam was the smell: a sharp, pungent odor compounded of cooking fires, fish sauce, rice fields fertilized with human and animal excrement, water buffalo, chickens, unwashed bodies, and I don't know what all else, but it clawed violently at my nose and caught fire in my lungs. It was awful. It permeated everything. I kept thinking, "Jesus Christ, these people don't even smell like human beings."

And they were so little. So *foreign*. Every now and then, you'd see a pair of young girls walking along the road hand in hand dressed in the flowing *ao dais* of travel posters and picture books, but most of the people, both men and women, wore loose nondescript two-piece outfits that looked like dirty pajamas, and everyone wore broad conical straw hats. Half-naked children played in the dirt or rode on the backs of huge grey water buffalo, the Vietnamese version of Bossie the Cow. South Vietnamese soldiers — ARVN — dressed in oversized green utilities and carrying no weapons of any kind, strolled casually along the highway, some of the men holding hands.

As the jeep I was riding in moved slowly down the rutted, pitted road that was the major north–south highway in Vietnam, rice fields hemming us in on both sides periodically gave way to small hamlets of a dozen or more thatched-roof huts. Some of the hamlets were set well back from the road, as though the road were an afterthought to the local geography. Those that actually fronted the highway included open-stalled shops selling canned Coca-Cola, brightly colored Oriental pajamas unlike anything worn by the Vietnamese, camouflage utilities and broad-brimmed camouflage bush hats. Sheets of corrugated tin and large squares of cardboard from C-ration cartons were ingeniously incorporated into the construction materials of many of the huts, so that the front door of a house might read, "Rations, Combat, Individual, 12 Meals," followed by a supply number, instead of "Welcome" or "The Smiths."

The most amazing things were the buses, high square contraptions of foreign make, probably French and probably dating from the French occupation. Each one that passed listed at an impossible angle and was loaded to an impossible capacity with people, chickens, bicycles, baskets of produce and pigs. More people and chickens and bicycles and baskets of produce and pigs perched precariously on the flat top, and still more people with bundles and baskets hung on to the runningboards and hood. Occasionally, we'd pass one of them broken down along the highway, the driver waving his arms wildly at the uncooperative engine, the passengers stoically clinging to their hard-won places, waiting for a miracle.

The one-hour cultural orientation class I'd had in processing on Okinawa only a few days earlier hadn't prepared me for any of this. It was a total blitzkrieg of the senses. I wondered if my surprise showed. Remembering old newsreels I'd seen of American soldiers rolling through newly liberated French villages, gathering bouquets and kisses from fresh young maidens in skirts and puffy white blouses, I tried to imagine the benign expression I ought to be wearing and then tried to imitate what I imagined. It was hard work. The constant assault on my nose kept causing my face to wrinkle like a prune. As the jeep inched through the crowded marketplace at Dien Ban, turning off Highway 1 and onto Highway 28, I smiled and nodded at the alien faces, waving stiffly from the elbow.

"What are you doing?" asked Saunders. He startled me.

"Oh! Well, you know, uh, just...waving," I replied.

"Who do you think you are? Douglas MacArthur?" Then Saunders broke into a broad grin and clapped me on the back with the flat of his hand in a gesture of good will. "Better pay attention, kid. We get sniped at along this road all the time. Half the people you're waving to are probably VC. Couple of weeks ago, some gook tossed a grenade into a truck right here in this marketplace. Messed up a few guys real good."

Corporal Jimmy Saunders was twenty years old. His red hair, high forehead and round, red face made him appear both heavier and more impatient than he was. The intelligence assistant for 1st Battalion, 1st Marines, he'd been in Vietnam ten months, since March 1966, and was due to rotate back to the States in less than ninety days. I was his replacement. "I certainly am glad to see you," was the first thing he'd said when he'd picked me up. "Redondo Beach, here I come!" he'd added, gripping the wheel like a racecar driver and cackling madly to himself.

The twenty-mile drive from the airfield at Danang to the Battalion compound four miles northwest of Hoi An took nearly two hours. At one point, we had to get off the highway and wait our turn to cross a narrow pontoon bridge laid beside the twisted wreckage of the steel highway bridge. "VC blew that again last week," said Saunders, offhandedly tossing his thumb toward the ruined structure as though he were pointing out a local landmark of minor historical importance. "I don't know why they bother to fix it. Gooks just blow it up again every time they do."

"That's it," Saunders finally said, pointing down the road, "That's Battalion." At first I thought he meant the small cluster of huts just ahead, and I was about to ask him if he was joking or what. Then I noticed, just beyond the hamlet, a sloping sand berm and multiple coils of barbed concertina wire that marked the perimeter of the battalion compound. Nothing was visible on the other side of the berm but the tops of a cluster of antennas. As we got closer, we turned onto a rutted track that led from the highway through the wire to the front gate of the compound. An armed sentry in a small wooden sentry box waved us through.

"I hope you like sand," Saunders laughed. "It's a seven-mile hike to the ocean, but we got one hell of a nice beach." There was sand everywhere, bleached white and steaming hot even though the monsoon season was only just ending and the dry season had hardly begun. Nothing grew inside the command post compound, which contained the battalion's headquarters and support company. Rows of large, green, canvas-covered strongback tents filled much of the area inside the berm, and the rest contained a bewildering assortment of military hardware.

Saunders slammed the jeep into four-wheel drive, took off across the deep loose sand, and pulled up in front of one of the tents in the first row. "Home, sweet home," he said. "Grab your seabag and let's get you settled. Then we'll go meet the boss." I picked up my seabag and followed him into the hooch — any living facility from a strongback tent to a Vietnamese house was called a hooch. Like every

22

other strongback tent in the compound, it wasn't really a tent at all, but rather a one-room plywood house with a canvas roof. It had a plywood frame, raised plywood floor, walk-in screen door at either end, and screen-covered windows with hinged plywood covers that could be raised outward to form plywood awnings. The whole structure was draped with a large general purpose tent that formed the roof.

Two naked lightbulbs hung suspended by single wires from the roof beams, and twelve cots lined the walls, six to a side with an aisle down the center. No one was home, but the trappings of regular habitation were everywhere: mess kits, bandoleers and other gear hung from pegs in the walls, and most of the cots had wooden artillery ammunition boxes beneath them which were used as footlockers.

"We share the hooch with the scouts," said Saunders. "We got nine scouts attached to S-2. They're out on a patrol now, but you'll get to meet 'em tonight. Probably end up doing a lot of scout stuff yourself. Technically, you're an intelligence assistant, not a scout, but that doesn't mean much. Anyway, it beats sitting around the COC all the time. That's yours," he said, indicating a vacant cot, "We'll get you a footlocker later; we gotta get to supply before 1600."

At supply, a bored sergeant loaded me up with an M-14, ammunition magazines, magazine pouches, cartridge belt, canteens, mess kit, shelter half, blanket, helmet, flak jacket, jungle boots, haversack, suspender straps, bayonet, and various other goodies. "No jungle utilities," he said, "You'll have to scrounge some."

"I got a pair you can have," Saunders volunteered, "You'll need 'em. Those Stateside utilities'll give you crotch-rot before you've humped a mile. We better drop this stuff in the hooch and go find the Lieutenant. He probably thinks I hit a mine or something. It's been known to happen. Happens quite a lot, actually."

"So I've heard."

The command, operations and communications center was a huge, heavily sandbagged bunker just inside the berm at the front of the compound. The heart of the entire battalion, as well as of the battalion command post, it contained the S-3 operations section, the S-2 intelligence section, and all of the communications gear that linked the command post to the battalion's four rifle companies, and to regimental headquarters. The antennas I'd seen from the road were sticking up out of the sandbagged roof of the COC.

Lieutenant Roberts, the battalion S-2 officer, was sitting at a field desk in a corner of the bunker set aside as the intelligence shop. He put down the map he was studying when we came in.

"This is Ehrhart, sir."

"Lieutenant Roberts," he said, standing up and extending his hand. "Welcome aboard." He was much older than me, perhaps twenty-three or twenty-four. I shook hands and handed him my service record book. "At ease," he said, "Sit down." He took the SRB and began to flip through it, commenting out loud:

"Air intelligence, huh? What the fuck are you doing here?"

"I wanted to get over as fast as I could, sir; got a girl waiting back home. I didn't much care if I went infantry or air, and they said I could go right away if I went infantry."

"Get some and get back, huh? What else we got here? Rifle sharpshooter. PFC out of boot camp. First in class from intelligence school. First in class from language school. You speak Vietnamese?"

"Well, not exactly, sir. It was one of those four-week quicky schools. There were some Vietnamese up at the airfield today; I couldn't understand a word they were saying. I don't know, sir; maybe I learned enough to pick it up after I've been here awhile."

"Don't worry about it. Nobody ever learns anything at those schools. We got Viets assigned to us that speak English. Your record looks pretty good, Ehrhart. You got a few months before Saunders goes home. Stick with him; he knows what he's doing. Pay attention and you'll do okay. Did he get his gear yet?" the Lieutenant asked Saunders.

"Most of it. They're out of jungle utilities again. Fuckin' supply. Those assholes up at Danang must be makin' a fucking fortune on the black market. Every damn Air Force clerk's got a pair of camouflaged jungle utilities, and we can't even get regular ones."

"Life in the war zone. What time is it? 1630? You're on watch tonight, aren't you?"

"Yessir; twelve to four."

"Okay, check Ehrhart in with admin and medical and then knock off. When you go on tonight, take Ehrhart with you. Might as well break him in — oh, never mind; let 'im sleep tonight. We'll start him off fresh tomorrow. Glad you're here, Ehrhart, we can use you."

Unfortunately, I wasn't exactly fresh the next morning. The battalion command post compound contained three heavy artillery batteries, one each of 155s, 105s, and eight-inch guns, and they fired all night long. They were exceedingly loud, shaking the hooch with each salvo and punching rude flashing holes in the darkness, the projectiles tearing through the stars with a rattling sound like rippling large sheets of steel. Each time they fired, I would start up violently, convinced that we were under attack. And then I would lie there, listening to the shells fading down the long corridor of the night. Just about the time I'd settle down enough to doze off again: Boom! Wide awake.

"You'll get used to that," Saunders said the next morning. "You won't even notice it after awhile. You just need time for your ears to learn the difference between outgoing and incoming." We were sitting in the intelligence shop trying to get me familiarized with a bewildering array of material when a radioman handed Saunders a message. "Alpha Company's sending in a batch of detainees from the Horseshoe," he said, crumpling the yellow slip of paper, "Let's go get 'em."

Detainees, I'd learned in intelligence school, were civilian Vietnamese. They were not prisoners, but were only temporarily detained for questioning about Vietcong activity. The coastal plain where we were located was heavily populated, and there was a lot of VC activity, mostly mines and snipers — the farmer by day, fighter by night guerrilla stuff. The care and questioning of detainees was the responsibility of the S-2 section.

So we shuffled off through the heat and the bleached sand toward the amtrac park, arriving at the same time as the amphibious tractors. There were two of them coming in through the back gate of the compound: large, rectangular armored boxes on treads, each with ten to fifteen raggedy-looking Vietnamese sitting on the flat top eight feet above the ground. They were mostly old men and women, with a few younger women and some small children. All of them were bound hand and foot with wire. As the tractors pulled up, the Marines on top began pitching and kicking people over the sides onto the sand in a quick succession of thuds, groans, sharp screams, snapping of breaking bones, and soft crying.

"My God, Jimmy, what the hell are those guys doing?" I grabbed Saunders' left arm with both hands. "They aren't even prisoners. They're just civilians! We're responsible for those people! Aren't you going to do something?!"

Saunders said nothing. The last bodies tumbled off the amtracs onto the others. Sowell looked at me, then at my hands on his arm, then back at me. He gave a slow shake of his head. I let go of his arm. "You'll understand soon enough," he said — this almost without breath, and with no perceptible emotion. "Untie their feet."

I undid the wire on the feet of an old man nearest to me. His nose was bleeding. Then I went for the wrists, but Saunders clapped me gently on the side and motioned for me to stop. "Just the feet," he said, again in that flat, hollow voice. As we marched our little band to

25

the barbed-wire prisoners' compound, Saunders warned me that I'd better keep my mouth shut tight and my eyes wide open until I'd been around awhile.

"Those tractor boys hit mines out there in the sand every day — great big fucking mines. And they get shot at a lot. A driver was killed by a sniper the day before yesterday. These people know where those mines are and who's planting 'em and who's doing the sniping. Treat 'em nice within sight of the tractor park, and those guys'll rearrange your head and ass for you, and walk away grinning."

Chapter 5

The war went on from there, or at least that's what I gathered. I didn't get to see much of it for the first few weeks; I was much too busy trying to learn my small part in it, a part that revolved around that dark musty corner of the COC set aside as the S-2 intelligence shop. There were no windows. I had to put the war together like a jigsaw puzzle from the bits and pieces of information that poured into the COC through the radios and land-lines and message center, creating a picture of the war in the daily intelligence summary for the consumption of everyone from the regimental commander to the President.

The intelligence section, S-2, consisted of four men: Lieutenant Roberts, Gunnery Sergeant Judson — the tall, thin, gaunt intelligence chief whom I seldom saw because he was suffering from alcoholism, and who would soon be sent back to the States on a medical discharge — and the two assistants, Saunders and myself.

Gunny Judson did nothing except put in a token appearance for a few minutes every morning. And I quickly learned that Roberts' primary function was to sign documents and reports prepared by Saunders and me, punctuating every signature with the exclamation: "When I get home, I'm going to have my wife suck my cock until it explodes! And then I'm going to have her do it again." Like Saunders, Lieutenant Roberts was due to rotate home in a few months. Most of his time in-country had been spent as a platoon commander, and later, company commander. He'd done a good job, and spending the last few months as the S-2 officer was a kind of reward.

That left me and Saunders to do most of the work. This consisted of the daily intelligence summary, or I-Sum, a kind of daily diary of the battalion's activities prepared every morning from the reams of field reports, agent reports, weather surveys and other material that had accumulated during the previous twenty-four hours, the nightly plotting of artillery targets for harrassment and interdiction fire, the preparation of intelligence estimates and terrain studies on an as-needed basis, the handling of prisoners and captured material sent in from the field, and an assortment of miscellaneous duties loosely classified under the heading of intelligence.

In addition, I pulled my share of night watch in the COC for four hours several nights a week, making coffee for the duty officer, playing cards with the man on radio watch, and answering the field telephone when anyone bothered to call. When I didn't have bunker watch, I pulled guard duty on the berm, two hours on and two off all night long, or was assigned to one of the listening posts, the series of three-man patrols just beyond the perimeter wire that were supposed to serve as an early warning system in the event of an attack on the battalion compound.

It was all very routine, and I began to get the hang of it pretty quickly. I kept wondering when I'd get a crack at the real war. About the only time I even got outside the command post at all was when Saunders and I would make one of our periodic runs to the Vietnamese National Police headquarters in Dien Ban or Hieu Nhon. The National Police were the local civil authorities, and we regularly checked in with them to see what kind of scoop they could give us in our search for the wily Vietcong. Our battalion's tactical area of responsibility covered all of Hieu Nhon district and a good chunk of Dien Ban, Vietnamese districts being roughly the political and geographical equivalent of counties back in the States. Our four rifle companies were scattered around the countryside from the South China Sea inland ten to twelve miles, with the battalion compound more or less in the center of the box formed by the rifle companies.

Whenever Saunders and I made one of our runs, Sowell at the wheel of our American Motors Mity-Mite and me riding shotgun, I'd wonder in a flurry of excitement and tension if this would be the real thing at last. From the constant chatter on the radios in the COC, the incidents I recorded daily in the I-Sum, and the talk of the guys who'd been around awhile, I knew that the Vietcong could turn up anywhere among the rice fields and hamlets and hedgerows and sand barrens that covered the coastal plain — an invisible enemy perpetually watching and waiting behind the unreadable faces of the peasants in the paddies and markets and conical straw hats. As we'd pull through the front gate of the compound, I'd always chamber a round, and as the jeep turned onto the highway, I'd click off the safety.

The day I finally started receiving mail from home, Saunders and I made a run to Dien Ban. I'd just gotten about a dozen letters from Jenny that morning, whom I hadn't heard from since I'd left the States weeks earlier, and I was feeling fat and happy. As we drove up the dusty highway, I was thinking about her and about the lovely secretaries at Dien Ban in their pink and blue *ao dais* who giggled like schoolgirls whenever I appeared and clearly thought I was a pretty handsome young fellow, and we were just north of the bridge near Binh Xuan cruising along at thirty-five or forty when suddenly my stomach took a dive as I realized that there was movement in the corner of my eye just beyond the paddy dike not twenty meters to the right, and reacting instantly, I turned and leveled my M-14 and put ten or fifteen rounds into the general direction of the Vietcong sniper before I realized that I'd just shot up our right front tire.

"Jesus fucking goddamned shitbag jeep!" Saunders let out at the top of his lungs just about the time I opened fire. I was very embarrassed, but he didn't seem to notice, nor did he seem to care that I'd fired upon the Firestone. His face was as red as his hair. "Goddamn fucking jeep, my fucking ass!" he screamed, pulling the jeep to a halt with the front end tilting down toward the right front because the wheel had snapped off at the axle and gone bounding into the rice where I had instantly killed it.

"So what do we do now?" I asked nervously when Saunders had finally stopped kicking the Mity-Mite and calmed down.

"Wait," he said, lighting a cigarette.

"Wait?"

"Yes, wait. Unless you'd like to walk back to the CP. Somebody'll come along eventually. I hope." I felt like a naked man as we stood on the open road, bare fields on either side laced with paddy dikes, treelines within sniping range beyond them, and a kid on a water buffalo in the middle of one of the fields suspiciously pretending to ignore us. I tried to huddle up to the jeep without Saunders noticing, using the stricken vehicle as cover.

"That's the third goddamned wheel I've lost in two months," Saunders went on, lifting his M-14 from the jeep and chambering a round. "Fuckin' Marine Corps. You see those nice jeeps the army MACV guys cruise around in? *Their* wheels never fall off. The Army buys them jeeps that work. But the Green Mother spend money for good equipment?" Saunders was beginning to go bright red again. "Fuck, no! Some asshole congressman's liable to start bitching that the Corps's wasting the taxpayers' money, and the army can do anything we can anyway, so why not get rid of us? Can't have that! Balanced budget year after year, year after year. Did you know that, Ehrhart? Did you know the Green Mother's never overspent its budget in its entire existence?! Fuckin' ARVN got better equipment than we do. Eat the apple and fuck the Corps. Holy Jesus!"

I lit a cigarette, keeping a keen eye on the kid and his water buffalo. By and by, one of those incredible Vietnamese buses came into view, weaving all over the highway like a drunk and listing heavily. "Keep an eye on these gooks," Saunders warned as the bus got closer, "They like to throw grenades at suckers like us." But the bus went right on by, humanity clinging to the runningboards, as though Saunders and I didn't exist. "I hope they hit a mine," Saunders muttered.

Three hours later, we got back to the battalion, courtesy of a tow from a passing truck. It was getting dark. The mess hall was already closed. "Greasy chow gives me the runs, anyway," said Saunders, "Let's see if we can scrounge some C-rats." I followed Saunders back to our hooch.

When we walked in the door, the scouts were there. Just in from three days with Bravo Company, they were sprawled out on their cots in crusty disarray, boots off and boots on and flak jackets scattered around the floor. Nobody was talking. "Anybody got any C-rations left?" Saunders asked. "Me and Ehrhart missed chow. Lost another wheel today up near Dien Ban. Can you believe those fucking Mity-Mites? Hey, what's up?"

"Three days and not a goddamned thing," Corporal Calloway responded after a long pause. "So we're humpin' back in and wham! Right into an ambush. Right there by that 51st ARVN compound. Think those fuckers did a goddamned thing to help us? They never left their compound. Started firing a .50-caliber machinegun at us, for chrissake! Moon and Watson bought it. Sergeant Wilson got hit, too, but not bad; he's over at the aid station gettin' patched up. Never even saw the gooks that jumped us. Fuck, man; I'd like to call an airstrike on that fuckin' ARVN compound."

30

Chapter 6

county Sair

One afternoon several days later, Saunders and I were covering a bunch of maps with plastic for Alpha Company to use on a County Fair the next day. The County Fair was a special counterinsurgency operation designed to build good will among the civilian population by distributing food and medical aid while rooting out Vietcong guerrillas and political cadre and gathering intelligence.

"Ehrhart," said Lieutenant Roberts, walking over to us and sitting down, "How'd you like to try out your Vietnamese?"

"Well, uh, yessir, I guess so. What's up?"

"Saunders here has been telling me you're pretty well on top of things in here already. I think it's time we give you a little field work. The scouts are going out with Alpha Company tomorrow, and they're a couple of men down. Why don't you go with 'em?"

"Oh, yessir, that would be fine." That was understating it. I'd been in Vietnam more than a month, and still hadn't been on a field operation. The high points of the war so far were mail call and weekly chapel. "I sure wouldn't mind getting out of *here* for a day!" I nearly shouted.

"Okay. Be down at the tractor park with the rest of the scouts at 0400. Sergeant Taggart and Sergeant Trinh will be along to do the interrogating. Stick with the scouts until things are pretty well secured, then find Taggart and Trinh. You got any duty tonight?"

"Yessir, I'm on the berm."

"Call the sergeant of the guard and tell him Ehrhart's going out tomorrow early," the Lieutenant said to Saunders. "Oh, and Saunders, three national policemen are going along tomorrow, too. They should be here this evening. Get 'em equipped and bed 'em down for the night — and make sure they're up in the morning."

"Yessir. Sir, we give those guys brand new equipment every time they go out with us. What the hell do they do with all that stuff, eat it?"

"You know damned well what they do with it. But orders are orders. They're our brothers in arms. I can't help it. Just do it — and keep counting days."

Saunders and the Lieutenant both grinned as if they were sharing a private joke. "What do they do with it?" I asked Saunders when the Lieutenant had gone.

"They sell it on the black market," said Saunders. "How do you think the VC get those American rifles like the ones Bravo Company captured last week? There's a good living to be made on this war."

The next morning long before dawn, we all piled on top of two amtracs and headed out: me and the other seven scouts, Staff Sergeant Taggart from the Regimental Interrogation and Translation Team, Staff Sergeant Trinh, a Vietnamese soldier attached to our battalion who spoke fluent English, the three national policemen all decked out from head to toe in full field gear, the civil affairs officer and his assistant, a team of corpsmen from the battalion aid station, and several officers and men from battalion operations and communications.

Though the amtracs had big ramp-type doors that opened into cavernous cargo holds, we all rode on the flat tops of the lumbering vehicles. If you happened to be inside when a tractor hit a mine, you'd get blown around like a human pinball. On top, you had a good chance of getting blown clear of the wreckage. So we rode on top. My stomach was doing a little dance-step as I sat up there in the darkness, but I tried very hard to appear as sleepy and bored as the rest of the scouts.

The village we were sweeping that day was out near the Horseshoe, a large horseshoe-shaped lake six or seven miles northeast of the battalion compound. A village in Vietnam was similar to a rural township in the States. What Americans might call a village — a small cluster of houses, anywhere from six to a few dozen — was called a hamlet, though as often as not, the Americans called them "villes." A number of hamlets, together with the surrounding rice fields which separated them, constituted a village. This often encompassed a sizeable chunk of land and many hundreds of people. (A number of villages made up a district, and a number of districts made up a province.)

It was still dark when the two tractors ground to a halt, but I could see armed men milling around, and the outlines of thatch-roofed hooches in the near distance. Two platoons from Alpha Company had already moved into position along the far side of the village to serve as the blocking force should any Vietcong try to escape ahead of the advancing sweep force. The third platoon, together with the scouts, would sweep through the village, searching every house in every hamlet and rounding up man, woman and child in the process. We waited now only for first light.

"Ehrhart, you stick with me," said Sergeant Wilson, the chief scout. He still had a bandage on the side of his neck that extended down under the collar of his shirt, a souvenir from the ambush a few days earlier. Like most of the scouts, Wilson had been in a rifle company when he'd first come to Vietnam. Older than the rest of us, perhaps thirty-three or thirty-four, he was a career Marine. He'd been made chief scout, some time before my arrival, after the previous chief scout had stepped on a mine out near Phuoc Trac bridge.

On his own initiative, Wilson had learned to speak conversational Vietnamese quite well, but he did his best not to make a big thing of it. "I let the brass know I speak Viet, next thing you know they'll stick me on one of those interrogation teams back in the rear. I'd rather be out here where I can keep you boys out of trouble. Somebody's gotta look after you; Uncle Sam's sure not doin' it."

As the gray false dawn gave way to a glowing pink fringe on the edge of a cloudless sky, we fanned out in a single line abreast along a front of several hundred meters and started forward through the rice fields. "Keep your interval and watch your step," Wilson cautioned me, "Especially crossing dikes and hedgerows. This whole village is regularly mined." I knew that already from the incident reports sent in from the field day after day — the battalion sustained about seventy-five mining and sniping incidents each month, better than half of them resulting in casualties — but Sergeant Wilson's reminder, coupled with the realization that I might shortly become one of those "incidents," caused the fluttering knot in my stomach to clamp down into a tight fist.

Chickens squawked and flapped on the hard-packed ground between hooches as we approached the first hamlet. Most of the villagers came out of their hooches before we even got there, as though they knew we were coming, but one hooch nearby remained closed and shuttered. A couple of Marines approached and banged on the door with their rifle butts. Without waiting for a response, one of them kicked the door in, jumping back quickly as though expecting it to explode. An old man and a very young girl emerged. Both were immediately knocked to the ground by the two grunts.

"Whaddaya doin' in there, hiding?!" one of the grunts screamed as he kicked the old man heavily in the ribs. "You goddamned gook motherfucker!" He began to kick the old man toward the other villagers who were rapidly forming into a large herd behind the sweeping force, prodded along by a few guards.

"A little rough, aren't they?" I commented to Sergeant Wilson. My stomach was turning, but I kept my voice as even as I could.

"Look at these people, Ehrhart," he said. I looked at the rag-tag band. Some of them looked sleepy, or bored, or frightened; most of them were expressionless. "See any young men about your age? Where do you think they are? Some of them are ARVN — but a lot of them are Vietcong. And these people are their mothers and sisters and wives and children."

Just about then, someone hollered, "Fire in the hole!" and a loud explosion erupted 150 meters to the left of us, causing me to flinch involuntarily and leaving splintered trees and white smoke in the middle of a hedgerow. It was obviously a mine someone had managed to discover without stepping on it. "Fire in the hole" is the signal for a controlled explosion.

Without interrupting the flow of his words, Sergeant Wilson went right on talking. "That mine they found. Maybe the next one will take somebody's leg off. Maybe yours. Ever wonder why none of these villagers step on mines? Look, I know how you feel. Sometimes I wonder if we're doing anybody any good at all. But you haven't been around here very long. A lot of these guys have been dealing with this shit day in and day out for a long time. You do what you have to. With any luck at all, you might get to go home in one piece." He patted me on the shoulder almost gently. "Come on; I'll teach you how to check out a hooch," and he entered the one nearest to us.

I followed him. There was no one inside, but we found two large bags of rice in an underground hole large enough to hold five or six people. "Lunch for the VC," said Sergeant Wilson, shouldering one bag and gesturing for me to take the other one. "Let's dump this stuff on the tractors." As we passed Calloway, Wilson pointed to the hooch we'd just left. "There's a bunker in there," he said, "Blow it." A few minutes later, the bunker, along with the house on top of it, disappeared in a smokey roar, debris shooting a hundred meters into the air like a fountain, raining down again slowly in a tinkle of tiny pieces.

34

The whole process was repeated over and over again for several hours, hooches periodically disappearing in great fireballs, occasional gunfire, the herd of Vietnamese swelling to many hundreds as we moved slowly from one hamlet to the next. The temperature must have been somewhere up around 90 or 95. Finally, the blocking force came into view, standing like a line of sentries at the edge of a rice field, and I could see a large barbed-wire enclosure set up on a sandy patch of dry ground off to the right. Three general purpose tents, two with their sides rolled up, stood inside the wire. As we approached the enclosure, Marines herded the Vietnamese into it. There was no place to sit but the ground, and there was no shade except for the tents.

Under one of the open tents, cooks had begun heating up half a dozen huge tubs of rice which would be fed to the Vietnamese. Under the second open tent, several medical corpsmen soon began treating people for cuts and bruises, giving shots of penicillin and other simple medications. The three national policemen immediately began picking through the throng of people, shouting at some, cuffing others, now and then hauling one out by the scruff of the neck and dragging him or her off to the one tent with its sides still down, so that you couldn't see inside.

That's where I found Taggart and Trinh. Taggart was a small man, no taller than me, with a heavy moustache. He was standing over an old man who was squatting down on his haunches so that his rear end was almost touching the ground. Taggart had an M-16, the new rifle not yet issued to most Marines, and he held the sharp three-pronged flash suppressor against the flesh on the top of the old man's foot just behind the toes. He kept twisting the rifle in a rotating fashion, causing the flash suppressor to cut into the old man's foot. The foot was bleeding. Trinh stood off to one side translating for Taggart.

"Who dug the bunker?!" Taggart was shouting as I walked in. The old man mumbled something I couldn't understand. He was crying. I couldn't understand a word he or any of the other Vietnamese said.

"He says he dug it," said Trinh. "At night the artillery explodes in his village. He says he dug it for his family to hide in when the artillery comes."

"You're lying!" Taggart shouted into the man's face, twisting the rifle harder. The man shook his head frantically, not understanding the words, but clearly comprehending the gesture and tone of voice. One of the national policemen punched the old man on the side of the face.

"Do the VC hide in the bunker?!" Taggart shouted. "How many VC are in this village?! Were the VC here last night?! Where is your son?!"

The interrogation continued in this fashion for several minutes. Trinh looked at me from time to time with deep burning eyes set in an expressionless face. Trinh and I had talked together a few times, but I didn't know him very well. I wasn't sure what he was trying to convey, but his eyes, coupled with the incomprehensible pleas of the old man, made me feel lightheaded. Maybe it was the heat in the closed-up tent. I turned and walked out into the bright sunlight.

The cooks were serving the rice now, dolloping out gluey dippersful into tin pans. Sergeant Wilson called to me from a small barbed-wire enclosure set in one corner of the larger one. It contained about fifteen or twenty Vietnamese, some of them bleeding from their feet and noses, and all of them bound.

"These are the ones the national police want to keep," he said, "There'll be a few more before we leave. Make sure you get them on the tractors when we go back in this afternoon. When we get back to the CP, you'll have to go over to motor pool and arrange for a truck to take 'em to Hieu Nhon."

As we were standing there, the civil affairs assistant, an enlisted man who spoke a smattering of Vietnamese, approached us. "Sergeant Wilson, that gook over there's yammering about some chickens or something," he said, pointing to an old woman with black teeth who was talking excitedly and waving her arms in the face of the civil affairs officer. "We can't figure out what she wants."

"What's the trouble, sir?"

"I don't know, Wilson," said Lieutenant Johnson, the civil affairs officer who was responsible for the battalion's dealings with the civilian population. "Can you understand her?"

"She says we killed three of her chickens this morning," said Sergeant Wilson, after a brief dialogue with the woman. "A guy shot 'em. She doesn't know why. She wants to be paid."

"*I* can't pay her!" the Lieutenant shot back with a pained expression. "If I pay *her*, I'll have to pay the whole village! Tell her I'm sorry, there's nothing I can do. Tell her she's lucky she still has her house. It's not my fault. I'm sorry. Tell her that."

By 1400, the County Fair was over. Everyone was turned loose, except the ones we were taking with us. We had about enough rice to cover the bottom of one of the amtracs, but we'd gotten no weapons or military hardware, and no confirmed Vietcong. We'd discovered

36

several mines, though, and we'd taken no casualties. The tents were packed up, Alpha Company pulled out, and we loaded onto the amtracs for the ride back to battalion. But instead of heading southwest, the two tractors headed east.

"Where are we going?!" I shouted in Calloway's ear, trying to be heard above the tremendous roar of the amtrac's engine.

"Can't go back the same way!" Calloway shouted back. "Vc know the route we took! Liable to be waiting!"

Soon we broke through a treeline and suddenly found ourselves on a broad white beach. The South China Sea rolled in all the way from the eastern horizon until it broke over and over again on the beach. It was the first time I'd seen it, and the green water was dazzling. I wanted to go for a swim.

The tractors raced south along the water's edge for a mile or so, then turned west and struck out across the vast sand flats that lay between the ocean and the battalion compound. Scruffy trees, hedgerows, and an occasional shallow pool of stagnant water dotted the flats, along with an abandoned hooch here and there, but mostly it was all sand: hard and flat in some places, deep and loose in others, and criss-crossed with thousands of tracks from the treads of tanks and amphibious tractors. Much of the land had once been irrigated and farmed, but it was all abandoned now.

"Hey, home is the hunter!" Lieutenant Roberts beamed as I walked into the COC a few hours later. "How'd it go today?"

"Okay, I guess, sir. It beat hanging around here. I don't think we made many friends, though. Boy, sure wasn't like the county fairs I used to go to back home! I got those three national policemen outside, sir, and a bunch of detainees they want to take with 'em. I'm gonna run 'em down to Hieu Nhon."

"Saunders, why don't you take 'em down?" said the Lieutenant. "Ehrhart's had a long day already — and you've got guard duty tonight since you were off last night, Ehrhart. Sorry."

"That's okay, sir. I sort of expected it. War is hell. Can I get some sleep, sir, or would you like me to make out my report this afternoon?"

"First thing in the morning will be good enough, so long as you can do it in time for the I-Sum. Oh, and when you write it up, just stick to facts and figures. Regiment and Division won't want to hear that we're not making friends. Did you get all the scoop from the corpsmen on how many people were treated, and all that good stuff?"

"Yessir. It's all here: 392 people provided with medical

assistance; 1180 meals served; 850 pounds of rice confiscated; 17 enemy bunkers destroyed; 85 people questioned about vc activity; 33 suspects detained and turned over to the national police."

"Okay. Good."

"Stop by the post office before you hit the rack, Ehrhart," Saunders added. "You've got some mail — and the whole battalion got a present today from the Avis Rent-a-Car Company. It's not chocolate chip cookies, either."

I had two letters from Jenny and one from Sadie Thompson waiting for me in the post office hooch. "What's this present we got from Avis?" I asked the mail clerk as he handed me the letters.

"This," he said, lifting a large box off the floor and plunking it down on the counter. "Have some."

Inside, there must have been about 2,000 little round metal buttons. They were colored a mottled green and black, just like camouflaged jungle utilities, and in black letters each button announced: "We try harder."

Chapter 7

Reporting for duty with the sergeant of the guard several hours later, I discovered that I'd been assigned not to the berm, but to one of the listening posts instead. That was fine with me. Perimeter guard consisted of sitting in an open bunker up on the berm with one other man from 2000 to 0800, the two of you alternating two hours on and two off all night long, a tough schedule that meant very little sleep and hell to pay trying to stay awake the next day.

The listening posts, on the other hand, went out for just four hours at varying intervals throughout the night, three men to a post, and you did your four hours straight, and done. Back to bed. Sleep was always at a premium. Tonight I had a 2200 to 0200 listening post with Corporal Roddenbery from the operations section and a guy from supply named Maloney.

"Hey, hot damn!" said Roddenbery after we'd received our assignments, "I'll take an LP over berm duty any day."

"Me, too," I answered. "I wasn't exactly looking forward to staying awake all night. I've been up since 0400 stomping around in the boondocks. Now I can get a little sleep before we go out."

"How about a hand of rummy first?" asked Roddenbery. He and I had been playing a lot of cards together in the few weeks since he'd been assigned to the S-3. He'd been a grunt with one of the rifle companies, but had gotten shot in the leg, and when he came back from the hospital, he'd been transferred to operations. Along with two other junior enlisted men, Frank Scanlon and Ivan Pelinski, he was a kind of S-3 equivalent to Saunders and me. Since we worked in the COC together, and lived in adjacent hooches, we were getting to know each other pretty well.

"Why not?" I answered. "But only one game. I'm really beat from that County Fair today. County Fair — what a name! You shoulda seen it, Rod. Just crazy. You wouldn't believe it."

Oh, yes, I would. You forgettin' I been there? Listen, this whole fucking war is crazy. You start thinkin' about it, you'll end up crazy, too. Ours not to reason why. Let's play some cards."

At 2200, we mustered with the sergeant of the guard in front of the COC. Roddenbery volunteered to carry the radio, a PRC-10 with a short-range tape antenna worn like a backpack. "You know how the LPs work, right? No new guys tonight?" said the sergeant to the outgoing listening posts. "You all got your coordinates? Radio check every hour. Green flare coming back in. Everybody got red and green popups? Okay, report back here when you're back in."

"I always wanted to be on the radio," said Roddenbery, jostling the radio into a comfortable place on his back while I checked our coordinates on the map. We'd been assigned a position on the other side of the hamlet at the northwest corner of the battalion compound, about 400 to 500 meters beyond the perimeter wire. We slipped through the wire at the front gate and set out north on Highway 28, then northeast through the center of the hamlet. It was always eerie at night. The hamlet, which bubbled with activity during the day, was completely closed up and silent. Night belonged to the Vietcong, and every cough and groan from the sleeping people in the shuttered hooches sent a ripple of electricity up and down our spine. Our boots on the gravel road sounded like static on a public address system.

We moved through the silence single-file, keeping about ten meters between each man to minimize casualties in the event of an ambush or mine. Coming out of the hamlet on the north side, we turned east again along a treeline at the edge of a rice field until we reached the place that approximated the grid coordinates we'd been given as our position for the night. We took up a position in a clump of bushes beside a paddy dike that afforded good visibility in all directions.

It was never really silent in Vietnam. Night after night, all the way to the four horizons, 360 degrees around, there was color and sound all night long: the flash and boom of artillery from the three batteries at battalion, and the flashes from dozens of batteries elsewhere, sometimes close enough to hear the boom, sometimes not; the impact of their rounds, often so far away that there was no noise but only a white pulsing at the fringe of the sky like heat lightning; parachute flares, dropped from droning C-130s, whose spent casings whistled down to earth and often landed so close you could hear the thump, and whose brilliance lit up the darkness like floodlights; lighter, smaller illumination rounds fired from mortars, the dull plot of the rounds leaving their tubes, the light pop overhead as the rounds ignited; the red and green signal flares of incoming patrols approaching company perimeters miles away; tiny pencil flares that laced momentary arcs of color delicate as cobwebs; the fast orange zip of tracer bullets, and less often, the green lines of tracers manufactured in China or Czechoslovakia, accompanied by the tat-tat of small arms fire; and always the thump and whine of choppers and jets prowling the skies with their rotating beacons and winking wing lights.

But Saunders had been right: it hadn't taken me very long to learn to distinguish which sounds were okay and which were not. It was only a new sound, or a different sound, that sent a distress signal from the ear to the brain. The sounds you heard night after night rapidly became something to ignore, like a commuter train that passes every half hour, meshing so completely into the background that out on a listening post like this one, or asleep in your hooch, the sounds made no impression. Something subconscious heard the sounds, and discarded them. On guard duty, or out on listening post, the light and sound of the Vietnam night became a kind of mindless entertainment, like watching a fireworks display. What you remembered was color, and near-total silence.

The first hour went by. "Annunciate radio check," came crackling faintly over the radio.

"Annunciate, Annunciate," Roddenbery responded, "This is Lima Papa One. All secure. Over."

"Roger, all secure."

You could hear the other listening posts checking in one at a time. All secure all around. The silence descended again, and I went back to the tedious strain of peering out over the ricefields into the darkness, trying not to let my eyes settle in any one spot for more than a moment. Eyes behave differently at night than they do in the daytime; it has something to do with the rods and cones in the eyeballs. On my very first night on guard duty, near midnight, I'd spotted half a dozen crouching figures on the ground right at the edge of the wire not thirty meters in front of me. My heart had stopped cold, and I'd nearly screamed. I'd even awakened my partner and insisted he go get the sergeant of the guard, who took one look and said, "There's nothing out there; settle down, private."

But after he'd gone, I looked again, and they were still there: six Vietcong trying to cut the wire, sneak over the berm, slit my throat, and blow up the COC with satchel charges. It was a terrible night, full of waking nightmares and violent death, and I didn't sleep at all. In the gray light of dawn, however, my Vietcong melted into the posts holding the concertina wire in place. I had just learned Rule One about night vision: don't stare. Never let your eyes stop moving. Whatever those rods and cones do, direct vision drops sharply at night while peripheral vision increases. If you begin to stare, if you try to focus, you can turn a fencepost into a tank. The trick is to find the outlines, literally look askance, letting your brain collect a composite impression from what your eyes record in their flickering movement.

The second hour went by. "Annunciate radio check."

"Annunciate, Annunciate; Lima Papa One. All secure. Over."

"Roger, all secure."

"Annunciate, Annunciate; Lima Papa Two. All secure. Over."

"Roger, all secure."

"Annunciate, Annunciate; Lima Papa Three. All secure. Over."

"All secure, roger and out."

"Get some sleep," Roddenbery whispered. "Me and Maloney are okay."

I couldn't really sleep, but it was a welcome relief to rest my eyes from the strain of peering and peering at nothing. I sort of dozed, moving in and out of sleep like seaweed awash on a beach. The worst part about listening post was that you couldn't smoke. A burning cigarette can be seen upwards of half a mile at night, especially on a dark night like this. Give your position away like a neon sign. But without the smoke, the insects attacked like vultures. Though I'd rubbed my hands and neck and face and the inside of my helmet with insecticide before we went out, the mosquitoes now gnawed away at my exposed flesh like Bowery bums at a Salvation Army Thanksgiving dinner. I could hear the soft swish of Roddenbery and Maloney rhythmically swatting. you weren't supposed to bat at them — too much noise and movement — but we were relatively safe here, so close to the command post, and the mosquitoes were ferocious. You could almost believe the tall tales about mosquitoes dragging their victims screaming into the night, to be eaten later at leisure, perhaps with a bottle of wine.

"Annunciate radio check."

"Annunciate, Annunciate; Lima Papa One. All secure, over."

"Roger, all secure." The other posts checked in, all secure.

"One of you guys, knock off," I whispered.

"I'm fine," said Roddenbery, "Still wide awake. See you in dreamland, Maloney."

One more hour to go. One of the letters I'd gotten from Jenny that afternoon had said that she was going to the senior prom with Niles Mancini. I didn't know the name, but I didn't mind. Or tried not to. "Must be hard on her," I told myself as I swatted mosquitoes and peered out over the rice, "Senior year, everybody cutting up and letting loose, and her all by herself." I thought of my last few months in high school — one long, rolling party from weekend to weekend, made extra-fine by the constant companionship of the blond-haired, blue-eyed wonder I'd met at a dance in March of that year, a little over a year ago. "She should have a good time while she can. No point in both of us having no fun."

Mom had written that Jenny and her mother had stopped by the house a few weeks earlier. Jenny had gotten a haircut and she looked real nice, Mom had said. I liked knowing that they were staying in touch. It made me feel a little closer to all of them. I wondered what Jenny looked like with her new hairdo. Would she be sending me a photograph? Maloney moaned in his sleep. Roddenbery nudged him hard. "Sshh," he whispered hoarsely. "Wake up; it's almost time to go in."

"Annunciate radio check."

"Annunciate, Annunciate; this is Lima Papa One. All secure. We're coming in. Over."

"Roger, all secure, One. Come on in."

Roddenbery lifted the radio pack to his back, the headset still crackling as the other listening posts checked in. I stood up stiffly, my seat wet from the damp ground and the night chill protesting in my joints, and moved out "tail-end charlie" behind Roddenbery and Maloney. As always, instead of retracing our route out, we went back a different way, passing along the back of the hamlet toward the road. You could hear the Vietnamese turning in their sleep. There was a baby crying somewhere.

And then the night erupted.

Roddenbery lit up in a quick flash of light like a silhouette, leaping off the ground helter-skelter and crumpling into darkness. If he screamed, it was lost in the blast of the explosion. My heart stopped dead, then took off full throttle, and my stomach filled with acid. I hit the deck and came up ready to fire, but the silence that followed the explosion was deeper than ever, and all I could hear through the ringing in my ears was someone crying, "I'm hit, I'm hit."

I crawled over to Maloney. "Jesus, I'm hit, I'm hit, oh God, it hurts!" he cried.

"You're okay, you're okay," I kept whispering, "You'll be okay. Hang loose; I'll be right back." I crawled over to Roddenbery. One leg was gone from the knee down; the other was gone from the ankle. His crotch was split open. The radio, miraculously, was still working. There was frantic chatter coming from the headset. I broke in:

"Annunciate, Annunciate; this is Lima Papa One. We're in trouble; Get somebody out here quick. We got casualties, over."

"Lima Papa One, Annunciate. What's happening? Repeat. What's happening?"

"Hit a mine, I think. I don't know. We're not taking any fire. I got one Kilo India Alpha, one Whiskey India Alpha. Hurry the hell up, will you? And put up some illumination."

"That's a roger on the illum, One. Sit tight. Where are you now?"

"Along the first paddy dike on the north edge of the ville, about 150 meters east of the highway."

"Roger, One, we're on our way. Look for a red pencil. Fire your red pop-up when you see it. Over."

"Roger, Annunciate, red pencil, red pop-up, over."

I crawled back over to Maloney, who was groaning loudly. It's okay, buddy. Lemme see." He was clutching the top of his right thigh. I ripped away the cloth. A chunk of his thigh had been torn out, and he was bleeding heavily. I took out my bandage and wrapped it around his leg as tightly as I could. "It's okay, buddy, it's just the muscle, it doesn't look too bad."

"Oh, Jesus, it hurts!" he kept saying over and over again.

"You're gonna be okay, Maloney. Got help coming right now; they'll bring a corpsman. They'll be here soon. Here, bite on this," and I took the wrapper from the bandage and stuck it between his teeth. I could hear mortars firing in the compound, and shortly half a dozen parachute flares burst overhead, lighting up the whole area.

Jesus fucking Christ! There were three Vietcong running down the road toward me, maybe 200 meters away, trying to make the cover of the paddy dike. Jesus shit! I threw myself down prone and opened fire. One of the running figures snapped up straight and dropped over backwards. The other two dove headlong into the irrigation ditch on my side of the road. I kept firing as I crawled back over to the radio.

44

The vc started firing back. I could hear the sharp thwack of bullets striking into the dirt around me.

"What is it?! What's going on?!" Maloney shouted.

"Shut up! Can you reach your rifle? There's vc along the highway. Annunciate, Annunciate; this is Papa One. I'm taking fire. Repeat. I'm taking fire! Three Victor Charlie at least, right along the highway north of me."

"Gimme coordinates, One; I'll get cover fire."

"Coordinates, fuck! I don't even know where my map is, for chrissake! Where the hell's the relief?!"

"This is Annunciate Zulu, Papa One," someone broke in. It sounded like Dodd, one of the scouts. "We're on the highway right in front of the ville. We got muzzle flashes up ahead on the east side of the highway."

"That's Charlie, Zulu. I can't see you yet. I'm behind the hooches. I don't think they see you either yet; they're still firing at me. Hurry it up, will you?"

"That's a roger." Small arms fire opened up on my left, and I could see tracers following the highway toward the vc. The vc fire shifted toward the approaching patrol, then stopped altogether.

"I can see you now, Zulu. Hold your flare, and get off the road. You're an easy target." Illumination rounds were still popping overhead, the burning magnesium hissing loudly, the flares drifting slowly toward earth beneath their tiny parachutes, casting an eerie patchwork of moving light and shadows. Figures moved through the moving shadows of the hooches. I held my finger on the trigger.

"Hold your fire, Ehrhart; it's us." Half a dozen figures, seven, eight, nine, loomed out of the shadows of the hooches nearby. It was Sergeant Wilson and the rest of the scouts, and two corpsmen. Four of the scouts doubled back toward where the vc had been.

"Over there," I said to one of the corpsmen, pointing toward Maloney, who was quiet now. "Roddenbery's dead. Jesus Christ, am I glad to see you."

"Welcome to the war, Ehrhart," said Wilson. "See what I mean about taking care of you guys?"

"What are you guys doing out here?"

"We heard the explosion. We were already in the coc by the time you called in for help. We weren't doin' anything important, anyway."

"What happened out there?" asked Lieutenant Roberts, who was waiting in the coc when we got back. He was dressed in nothing but his scivvy-drawers, flak jacket and helmet; his boots were unlaced.

"I'm not sure, sir. I think Roddenbery stepped on a mine. His legs and crotch were blown to hell. I spotted three VC up on the road when the illum started popping, but I don't think it was coordinated, sir. They were a good 200 meters away and they didn't start firing till I did. I think they heard the mine go off, and came running to see if they could pick the bones. The illum caught 'em off guard, I think. I might have gotten one of them."

"You did," said Calloway. "We found a lot of blood on the road, and heavy drag marks. The other two must have taken the body with 'em. Damn! How the hell do they do it?! The whole goddamned road was lit up like Broadway. Just once, I'd like to find a dead goddamned gook with a goddamned weapon in his hands."

One of the corpsmen came into the COC. "The other guy just died," he said. "He had a lump of steel in his belly the size of a golf ball."

"Oh, Jesus! I didn't see it. I didn't see it. I wrapped the leg; he had a big chunk out of his leg. I don't know, I was taking fire, and trying to operate the radio; I didn't have time...."

"You did okay, Ehrhart," said Lieutenant Roberts, cutting me off. "It happens. It's not your fault. You got one of them, at least. Don't worry about it. Go get some sleep."

"Yessir. Thank you, sir." I walked out of the bunker, took a few steps, felt a rush of dizziness, and leaned back against the sandbagged wall of the COC to steady myself. I leaned over and threw up, retching like my insides were going to come up. The next thing I knew, Wilson and Calloway were standing over me.

"You okay, Ehrhart?" asked Wilson.

"Yeh, yeh, it's just — I'm sorry, you guys, it's just — Jesus...."

"Hey, you're not the first guy to get sick after a little excitement. Doesn't matter what you do afterwards," said the Sergeant, pulling me to my feet. "You handled yourself okay out there. Did I ever tell you about the time down on Go Noi Island?" And the three of us walked off through the darkness toward the hooches.

Chapter 8

I think that night was a kind of Ordeal by Fire for me in the eyes of Lieutenant Roberts and Sergeant Wilson, though neither of them said as much, because afterwards I began patrolling with the scouts fairly often. I still couldn't go on any of the patrols when they'd be out for two or three days at a time; I had my duties in the S-2 shop that required daily attention, and with Saunders counting down his final weeks, I had pretty much taken over. But the afternoon strolls through the countryside were a welcome relief from the monotony of the routine around the battalion command post.

The patrols were mostly unremarkable. On a couple of occasions, we took sniper fire, and then Sergeant Wilson would call in an airstrike, and the screaming A-4s and F-8s would rip up a treeline with 500-pound snake-eye bombs or fry a hooch in an awesome orange fireball of napalm. Corporal Dodd stepped into a punji pit one afternoon, skewering his foot on the sharpened bamboo stakes the Vietcong used when they couldn't get any dud American artillery rounds to rig up as mines, and had to be taken out on a medevac chopper, and a few days later we got a corporal named John Walters to replace him.

But mostly we'd just walk and walk through the rising heat of the approaching Vietnam dry season, seeing nothing but the Vietnamese farmers behind their lumbering sleepy water buffalo, or the women trotting along beneath great baskets of produce on their way to market. They ignored us for the most part, the deep untouchable silence of their almond eyes causing my stomach to tighten.

The only remarkable thing about those patrols was Sergeant Trinh, the ARVN soldier attached to our battalion, who often patrolled with the scouts. I learned that he was not Sergeant Taggart's regular partner on the interrogation team, but was only pressed into service in that capacity when the need arose. I also learned that he had an uncanny ability to detect mines. Walking point—lead man on patrol—time and time again he saved us from the flying jagged steel that left men dead and crippled with no enemy in sight, spotting waiting trip-wires as if he could smell them. Perhaps he could.

Aside from those patrols, though, life went on as usual: daily I-Sums, nightly artillery lists, guard duty, listening posts, chow, sleep, and more of the same. Sometimes I'd go out to the front gate when things were slow in the afternoon and play with the children who always gathered there looking for candy, C-rations and cigarettes. My Vietnamese wasn't getting any better, but we'd make faces at each other and play handgames and laugh. I never knew where they came from; they would simply appear every morning and remain until nearly sunset, begging for hand-outs from the vehicles passing in and out of the command post compound.

A few weeks after Roddenbery was killed, his replacement was killed by a sniper near the relocation camp on the road between Hoi An and Hieu Nhon. The refugee camp consisted of several hundred one-room tin shacks with no doors, and rags over the windows for curtains, all jammed in one next to the other in tight rows on bare hardpacked earth and surrounded by barbed wire and chainlink fencing. It reeked of squalor. I had to pass it every time I made the run to Hieu Nhon. After Roddenbery's replacement was killed, I always gave the Mity-Mite a good shot of gas when the relocation camp came into sight, hoping like hell the jeep wouldn't throw a wheel.

The replacement for Roddenbery's replacement was a PFC named Randy Haller, a school-trained operations assistant from Berkeley. The day he arrived, toward the end of March, he set up a battery-powered portable record player in his hooch, and since his hooch was right next to mine, I couldn't help hearing it. The music was awful: a jumble of screeching electric guitars and what sounded like someone in his death-throes.

"The Doors," said Haller in reponse to my inquiry. "It's a group called The Doors." I had never heard of them.

"They're terrible." He put on another record. It was even worse.

"Unagoddadavida," he beamed, or something like that. "The Iron Butterfly." I had never heard of them, either.

48

"You got any Beatles, or Rolling Stones, or Supremes?"

"Where you been, man, in a war or something? This stuff is what's happening back in The World!"

I'd only been gone a few months. I'd read my *Time* magazine every week. Was it possible that I could have lost touch so quickly? As I stood there in the hooch, the lines of a Buffalo Springfield song I'd heard on the radio back at Camp Pendleton flashed through my head: "Something's happening here; what it is ain't exactly clear...." I decided I didn't like PFC Haller or his music.

"Don't go stepping on any toes around here till you know what's going on," I warned. "You might step on something that bites."

March turned into April. Early that month, Gunny Judson was finally sent back to the States. In the previous few weeks, he hadn't bothered even to make his token daily appearance in the S-2 shop. I didn't miss him much; he'd been a kind of nonperson anyway, a whiskey-powered skeleton. On paper, the S-2 was now short an intelligence chief, but that only reflected what had been the reality since before I'd arrived.

About the time Judson left, I found out that I'd made the cut for lance corporal. It meant an extra twenty-one dollars a month, and that meant a little more for my savings account. Except for incidentals like haircuts and cokes at the "gook shop"—a kind of all-purpose mom-and-pop store run by some Vietnamese—there wasn't much to spend your money on. It wasn't like you ever got a night on the town or anything like that. So I was saving almost everything I earned, including the extra sixty-five dollars a month combat pay, building a little nest egg for the future, for marrying Jenny and going to college.

Also in April, we were issued M-16s. Up until then, the basic rifle of the Marine Corps had been the M-14, a souped-up M-1 modified from clip-fed to magazine-fed. The M-14 was a remarkably dependable weapon. You could leave it out in the rain all night, bury it in the sand, drive over it with a truck, dig it up, and it would still fire. But it was a cumbersome weapon, long and heavy, and it could only fire semiautomatically.

The M-16, developed by the Colt Company—the folks that made the gun that tamed the West—was much shorter than the M-14, with a plastic stock that made it much lighter, and it was both semiautomatic and fully automatic. It packed as hard a punch as the M-14, had about equal range and accuracy, used smaller and lighter ammunition, and kicked less.

The day we fired for familiarization, I was amazed at how light the M-16 was, and how little it kicked. The weight, especially, was important. As the heat increased noticeably from day to day, every pound you had to carry mattered.

Of course, we still had to use the old M-14 magazine pouches, which were too large for the smaller M-16 magazine and too small for two M-16 magazines, but that was par for the course with the Corps. M-16 magazine pouches, which hooked onto your cartridge belt and carried five magazines, were in the same category as the sturdy jeeps used by the U.S. Army. Eventually, I managed to trade my mosquito net to Pelinski for two M-16 magazine pouches he'd gotten from a soldier at the MACV compound in Hoi An for a Vietcong flag he'd had made by one of the barbers in the gook shop. It was a good deal; the mosquito net didn't work, anyway. Every time you climbed under it, a horde of raging mosquitoes climbed in with you and spent the night feasting on your face.

The battalion also made military history in April, becoming the first American field unit to be hit by rockets. We'd been mortared a few times since I'd been there, but this was something entirely new: Russian-made, self-propelled 130-millimeter rockets.

None of us had ever heard rockets before, and everybody in my hooch was sound asleep at the time, but the instant that strange whooshing sound broke the usual nonsilence of the Vietnam night, there was a mad scramble of bodies piling out the door of the hooch and diving headlong for the nearest of the deep, open, sandbag-lined bunkers dug between the hooches for just such emergencies, everybody landing in the hole at once in a cursing, laughing, confused tangle of arms, legs, elbows, wrenched knees, bent backs, jammed fingers and bloody noses.

You could see the rockets coming in two waves, the first wave already at the apex of their trajectory and beginning to drop back to earth, the second still rising out of the southern horizon. They made a very loud noise, like water gushing from a high-pressure firehose, and each rocket left a thin orange trail of fire and sparks like an aerial torpedo. We all watched for a few seconds, our heads sticking up above the top line of sandbags like targets in a shooting gallery, until we determined that the rockets were right on target and had to plaster ourselves to the bottom of the bunker as the earth around us erupted in columns of smoke, noise, sand, shattered wood, shredded canvas, steel slivers and fire.

Our hooch wasn't hit, and nobody in our bunker got wounded, but in the rush to get out of the hooch, I had gotten tangled up in my mosquito net, lost my balance, tripped over another cot, and hit my shoulder hard against the door frame. The next day, when Pelinski said he was looking for a mosquito net, I gladly traded him mine for the two M-16 magazine pouches.

April was full of surprises. One day the wire went out that a USO show was coming to battalion. Hot damn! I knew it wouldn't be Bob Hope — he only went to war at Christmas — but there were sure to be a few ripe American beauties! I wondered if they'd be wearing miniskirts.

I'd never seen a miniskirt on a real American girl, or on any girl for that matter; miniskirts were another new phenomenon that had seemed to blossom during my absence from The World. But a full-page airline ad in a recent *Time* magazine had fired my imagination to the boiling point. It was a photograph of a woman from the waist down: just a pair of the trimmest, shapeliest legs I'd ever seen, rising gracefully up past the knees, and still up and up until they disappeared beneath the hem of a blue skirt that couldn't have been six inches below that lady's snatch. Oh, God! I'd torn the page out, covered it with laminating plastic, and hung it over my cot. I used to stare and stare at it, imagining Jenny from the waist up and me gently slipping my hand right up under that skirt. I'd even come one time, just lying there in the middle of the afternoon, staring. The intensity and surprise of the orgasm had nearly frightened me out of my wits.

And now I was going to get to see a woman like that for real, in 3-D, right up close. Sweet agony! Me and Frank Scanlon got right up in the front row, and everybody was hollering and whistling and stomping and clapping, and out walked Mrs. Miller.

Mrs. Miller?! Remember Mrs. Miller? She was a plump matronly middle-aged housewife who, back in sixty-five or sixty-six, had made a gimmicky, 45 rpm AM radio hit single spoof of a Petula Clark song. And here she was, right in front of us, big as a barn and just as shapely. She crooned her way through her famous song, her voice like an empty coal train passing through Shamokin on its way to Wilkes-Barre on a rainy night in March, then she went into a stand-up comic routine. Me and Scanlon left long before it was over. I spent the rest of the afternoon writing a monumental letter to Jenny, crammed to the margins with every endearment I could command. God, how I missed her!

Chapter 9

Corporal Saunders went home at the end of the month. He gave me a lot of good stuff before he left: a few more pairs of jungle utilities, a pair of jungle boots that still had a little wear left in them, a comfortable Army-issue ass-pack to replace the binding, confining haversack that was regular Marine Corps issue, and a beautiful pair of padded suspender straps for my cartridge belt, again Army issue. He'd accumulated the Army gear in the same manner as I'd acquired the M-16 magazine pouches.

"I'll miss you, Jimmy," I told him the day he left, and I meant it. "Thanks for everything."

Take care of yourself, Bill. If you're ever in Redondo Beach, look me up. I'll be in the phone book under PFC: Proud Fucking Civilian!" We stood there looking at each other for a few moments, not knowing what else to say, then he jumped into the jeep that would take him to the Freedom Bird waiting in Danang, and took off out the front gate of the compound. I stood on the high berm for a long time, staring after the jeep until it finally disappeared far up the road, and then staring at nothing.

"Hey, Ehrhart!"

"Sir!" I turned around to see Lieutenant Roberts standing down by the entrance to the COC.

"You gonna stand up there all morning?" he shouted up. "Come on down here and stop moping like you just lost your dog. I've got some good news for you."

I looked back up the highway in the direction Saunders had disappeared, then jump-trotted down the slope of the berm through the loose sand. "What's up, sir?"

"The cavalry's on the way."

"What?!"

"Regiment's got a brand new school-trained intelligence assistant just in from Stateside. They've assigned him to us."

"But Saunders just left."

"Maybe because we don't have a chief; I don't know. Ever hear the one about the gift horse? Regiment just called down and said they'll be sending him along when the driver comes back from dropping Saunders at Danang. Name's Rowe; he's a PFC."

I was out by the front gate playing with the kids when the jeep returned. There were two passengers. I jumped into the jeep when it pulled up and rode back inside the compound. "Which one of you guys is Rowe?"

"I am," said the smaller of the two. He was about my size, with black hair and a face even younger than mine. At least I thought so. The big guy, a lance corporal named Griffith, said he was the new Secret & Confidential Message clerk.

"Pull over to that hooch," I told the driver, pointing to mine. "Then take Griffith around to the S&C hooch. You know which one it is? Ask for Corporal Basinski, Griffith; he's your man. Come on, Rowe," I said, stepping out of the Mity-Mite. Then I remembered a joke Saunders had told me the day I'd arrived. "Say, I hope you guys like sand," I said. "It's a seven-mile hike to the ocean, but we got one hell of a nice beach!" Nobody laughed.

"How long you been here?" Rowe asked as he tossed his gear down on Saunders' old cot.

"Almost three months."

"Man, I wish I had that under my belt."

"You will," I said, feeling a surge of paternal warmth. "It goes pretty quickly, mostly. Sometimes, I feel like I just got here, but it's been ninety days already. Guy who had that bunk just rotated this morning. Did the whole thirteen months without a scratch. Where you from?"

"Davenport, Iowa. How about you?"

"Little town in Pennsylvania called Perkasie. Near Philadelphia. Enlisted right out of high school; been in almost a year now."

"Me, too, except I waited until the end of the summer to go in. My parents wouldn't sign for me, so I had to wait till I turned eighteen.

What a summer, though; the condemned man's last meal. I did some *serious* foolin' around!" Rowe grinned, the glories of the previous summer almost visible in his eyes.

"Lieutenant Roberts says you're school-trained. Where'd you go?"

"The amphibious school at Little Creek."

"Oh, yeh? So did I. How'd you like that Navy chow?"

"You gotta give 'em that much; they sure know how to eat. How's the chow around here?"

"You know the jeep you rode in on today? The axle grease was yesterday's lunch. But don't worry; you can have it for breakfast tomorrow. Tell your mom to start sending you Care packages — but no chocolate chip cookies; Christ, don't let her send you any chocolate chip cookies. I'll mail her a bomb if she does."

"What?" Rowe looked puzzled.

"Stick around. The Daughters of the American Revolution have taken it upon themselves to win the war by fattening us all up with chocolate chip cookies. Never mind, you'll see." Rowe began to unpack his seabag. "You can stow stuff in those ammo boxes," I said, indicating the wooden artillery shellboxes under the cot. "Saunders left 'em for you. He's the guy that just left. I'll bet he's airborne already, wingin' his way back to The World. Geez!"

"Yeh? I wonder what kind of welcome he's in for," said Rowe. "It's crazy back there, man. The last day I was in L.A., the weekend before we left Pendleton, I got caught right in the middle of one of those demonstrations. Bunch of crazy hippies hollering and carrying on. Hassled the hell out of me. I wasn't even in uniform. They just started raggin' me about my short hair. 'Peace now! Peace now!' Shit. They oughta ship 'em all to Russia."

"I've been readin' about that stuff. I don't understand it. We're over here getting our asses shot off defending them, and what do we get for it? Goddamned traitors. I ever run into any of 'em when I get back, it'll be kick-ass-and-take-name time. Fuckin' parasites. Hey, are girls really walking around in public in skirts like that?" I asked, pointing to my plastic-coated miniskirted airline stewardess.

"Hell, yes. Drives you absolutely crazy. Jesus! You just walk around with your hands itching all the time. Tongue hangin' out. Beavers everywhere. Tits bouncing around — they don't wear bras anymore, you know? It's beautiful, I'll tell you — but if my wife ever tries to go out in public like that, I'll lock her up."

"You married, huh?"

54

"Yeh. Just got married at Christmas." Rowe reached into his wallet and pulled out a picture of a young girl with shoulder-length dark hair and a wide smile. It was one of those yearbook portraits. "Ellen," he beamed.

"Pretty," I said.

"She's a swell kid, too. Only girl I ever dated. We're gonna have a baby in July."

"July?!" I blurted out before I realized the rudeness of my observation.

"Well, you know how it is," said Rowe, beginning to blush. "We were gonna get married, anyway, when I got back from Vietnam. So we just got a little impatient. I don't mind, really—except I won't get to see the kid until he's nearly a year old. Who belongs to those?" he asked, pointing to the pair of black nylon stockings draped one on either side of the airline ad.

"My girlfriend. She sent 'em to me a few weeks ago. Smell 'em." Rowe got up and stuck one of the heavily perfumed stockings under his nose.

"Mmm-mm. Good enough to eat."

"Damn right!" I laughed, rapidly stuffing half of one of the stockings into my mouth. "Umm, yum, mumph," I growled through the mouthful. "That lady makes me tick," I said. "My guiding star. Just get me back to The World, and I'm home free." I reached into my own wallet and drew out a picture of Jenny. Rowe whistled through his teeth.

"She's something," he said. "A real cutie."

"You can say that again. Hey, come on. We gotta get you checked in, then go meet the Lieutenant. He probably thinks you hit a mine or something on the way down."

As we walked toward the COC in the late afternoon heat, the Vietnamese from the gook shop were all standing up near the front gate—three men and five women. Three armed Marines stood around them.

"What's that all about?" Rowe asked.

"They work in the gook shop. We don't have a PX or anything like that, but we got a gook shop where you can get a haircut, buy souvenirs and stuff. They do laundry, too; that's what's in those big bags. They take stuff home overnight and bring it back in the morning. Stuff comes back smelling like paddy water and buffalo shit, but I guess it's better than nothing."

"What's this here, honey?" we could hear one of the guards

saying. He had his hand up the front of a young woman's pajama top. He laughed as she flinched and drew away.

"Cheap way to get a feel," said Rowe. "What's he gotta do that for?"

"He's searching her. Well, anyway, he's supposed to be searching her. All the gooks at the shop get searched on the way in and going back out again at night. They could be carrying grenades, who knows what?"

"What do we let 'em in here for if we can't trust 'em?"

"I wouldn't trust Nguyen Cao Ky if he showed up here," I said.

"Who's that?"

"The premier of South Vietnam. Listen, that's just the way it is. There's Vietnamese around here, and there's VC. And most of the time, you don't know which is which until it's too late. You want one of those ladies to lob a stick of dynamite under your cot?"

"It is that bad?"

"It's worse," I replied. "Two weeks ago, Saunders and I were driving through Hoi An, right through the middle of town, and a goddamned kid maybe eight or nine years old runs up and tries to flip a grenade into the jeep. A grenade! I had to blow 'im away. A little kid. It was really bad, you know. My kid brother's only twelve. And you know — the grenade went off and killed a couple of gooks — so you know what? Some guy shows up here the next day and wants the civil affairs officer to pay him compensation for his dead wife. I couldn't believe it! The goddamned kid tries to kill us, and they want money. Like I don't feel bad enough already, you know?"

"What's this?" Rowe asked the next morning, pointing to the piece of paper tacked to the wall above my field desk in the COC.

"Read it," I said. On the paper were pasted an article from the daily military newspaper, *Stars 'n' Stripes*, and four entries clipped from our battalion's I-Sums. All five items were dated within a few days of each other and arranged in chronological order with the newspaper story first. It detailed how a platoon from Bravo Company had captured a cache of Vietcong supplies during a firefight in which three VC were killed; the take included several bolt-action rifles, a few cases of Chinese-made grenades, some explosives, ammunition and rice. The article concluded with a quote from some general up at Division that we'd set the VC war effort back in our battalion's area by at least four months. The excerpts from the I-Sums included: amtrac loaded with grunts from the Horseshoe hits fifty-pound box mine, five dead, eleven wounded; Delta Company patrol ambushed near Phuoc Trac bridge in broad daylight, two dead, six wounded; bridge on Highway 28, 500 meters north of battalion command post, blown up by VC sappers; Charlie Company platoon commander wounded by sniper. At the bottom of the page, I'd typed in: "If you can't trust your local general, who can you trust?"

"Are you kidding me?" asked Rowe when he'd finished reading.

"There it is," I said, "in black and white. Lyndon Johnson says we're winning the war because Lyndon Johnson's generals tell him we're winning the war. *You* figure it out."

"That goddamned piece of paper is seditious, Ehrhart," said Lieutenant Roberts, entering the S-2 shop in the middle of our conversation.

"Oh, good morning, sir. I can't help it, sir; it's the funniest thing I've ever seen in my life. You could order me to take it down, sir."

"I can't. It's the funniest goddamned thing I've ever seen in my life."

"I don't think it's funny at all," said Rowe.

"You just got here," said the Lieutenant.

Chapter 10

That night I pulled guard duty with Griffith, the new S&C man. It was a welcome relief. Three nights before, I'd had to stand a shift with Haller from S-3. I just couldn't get along with Haller. He was a wiseguy, too damned cocky. Nights on berm were long enough without having to spend them next to someone you didn't like.

It was still light out when we took our posts. I'd been assigned, as usual, to the bunker just to the right of the COC. The guard bunkers were just open pits dug around the top of the berm, squared off on the inside with sandbagged walls, about chest deep and four feet by eight feet. They had duckboard flooring, and the side facing into the compound had a walk-in opening.

"They didn't waste any time getting you up on the berm," I said to Griffith. S&C stands for Secret and Classified. The S&C section was responsible for all of the battalion's classified documents. It wasn't really a section like Operations or Intelligence; just one enlisted man — two for the brief period until Basinski rotated out — who lived alone in a hooch with eight or nine safes. "I guess we'll be seeing a lot of each other," I said, which was true because Intelligence used a lot of classified materials. "Where you from?"

"Roseburg, Oregon," he answered. "At least that's where I ended up. I grew up in northern California, but I married a girl from Roseburg while I was in college. She's from Roseburg. When I dropped out of school, we went back there."

"You been to college, huh?"

"Sort of. I finished one semester by the skin of my teeth. I didn't have my heart in it, I guess. I don't know why. Looked like I was going to flunk out, so I quit in the middle of the second term. Jan and I — that's my wife — Jan and I went back to Roseburg and I got a job in a lumber mill, but when I left school, my draft board lifted my student deferment and reclassified me 1A. They were going to draft me anyway, so I enlisted. I sure as hell didn't want to be in the Army. What about you?"

"What about me?"

"Come on! Where you from?"

"Little town called Perkasie. It's near Philadelphia, about thirty-five miles north. Kind of a hick town, I guess, lot of farms around and stuff like that, but it's close to New York and Philly. We used to go up to New York when I was in high school — they'll serve anybody in the bars on the lower east side — get all loaded up. And the Jersey beaches are close, too. I like the beach. You like the beach? Go body-surfing, you know. Pick out a middleaged fat man standing in the surf and head right for 'im — bam! Glub, glub. 'Geez, I'm sorry, mister!' I saw the China Sea one day last month, no, two months ago," I said, pointing east in the direction of the ocean. "But we were on an operation. I wouldn't mind going back sometime when I could go swimming. It was really pretty. I guess this whole country would be pretty if it wasn't for the war."

"I guess so. Maybe after we win the war, Lady Bird Johnson can organize a 'Beautify Vietnam' campaign. Make billboards and barbed wire illegal. You aren't married, are you?"

"No."

"I didn't think so," Griffith laughed. "You look too young."

"Oh, right, you must be Old Man River. What are you, twenty, twenty-one?"

"Twenty. I was nineteen when Jan and I got married."

"Well, I'll be nineteen when I get married. Got a girl back home just waitin'. We're going to get married as soon as I get back."

"How long you got to go?"

"Ten months." Ten months. It sounded like a long time. I'd been used to speaking in terms of how long I'd been there, not how long I had to go. Three months sounded like a respectable amount of time; I'd had the sense that time was passing pretty rapidly. But suddenly those three months seemed to trail away behind me like the fading echo of a freight train's whistle in the dead of night, and the ten months ahead were almost incomprehensible. The sun was down behind the mountains to the west, and a red glow hung above the mountains, reflecting in the water of the river that flowed just beyond the highway in front of us and in the scattered paddy fields beyond that. Deep blue arched in the sky overhead, and behind us the eastern horizon was rimmed with black. "Yessir, I've got three months in-country already," I said, but it didn't sound the way it had when I'd said the same thing to Rowe the day before.

"How long you in for?" asked Griffith.

"Three years. My recruiter said if I went in for just two, they'd make me a grunt and that would be that. Two years isn't enough to train you as anything but a rifleman. So I took the extra year and got Intelligence. I'll have a year in next month."

"My recruiter told me the same thing. You'd think they didn't want any grunts. Why'd you enlist in the first place?"

"Seemed like the thing to do at the time," I laughed. "I figured they'd get me sooner or later. I coulda gone to college, you know. Got accepted at a couple of schools; I was all set to go to UCLA — spent a summer in southern California two years ago, just me and a buddy, got jobs in an aluminum sliding door factory, went to Tijuana, learned how to surf; what a summer! I was gonna go back there for school. But then I got to thinkin'. I didn't know what I wanted to study. And it didn't make sense going to college and then getting drafted when I graduated, just when I'd be ready to start a career. This way, I've got a few years to figure out what I want to be, and I won't have to spend four years worrying about the draft. And I'll be able to get GI Bill money for school — my family isn't exactly loaded. It all just seemed to make sense, especially with all this stuff in Vietnam. I guess it sort of means something to me — you know, that old lump in the throat when you hear the Star-Spangled Banner. This ain't much of a war, but as they say, it's the only one we got."

"You seen much shit?" asked Griffith.

"Oh, a little," I tried to sound nonchalant, like a veteran. I told him about the County Fair, and about Dodd stepping into the punji pit, and about the kid in Hoi An. "Got into it real good one night on an LP. Right over there." I pointed over the tops of the hooches in the hamlet just beyond the wire to our right. "Point man stepped on a mine, then we got hit by the VC. I was the only one to get out alive." I paused to let the full impact of the statement register on the new guy.

"Right over there?!"

"About 500 meters out. Just on the other side of those hooches. Hey, buddy, you look out there in the daytime, all those folks in their straw hats and pajamas trotting around with their market baskets and stuff, planting rice, looks real nice and peaceful. Don't let 'em fool you. This is Indian Country. You ain't safe anywhere."

"We been hit here?"

"The CP? We've been mortared a few times, and we took some Russian rockets a while back—big damn jobs, whoosh! Boom! But they haven't hit us head-on yet. They don't do that around here. Not enough of them, I guess. I almost wish they would. Mostly they just plant mines, snipe at you, ambush patrols when they know they've got you outnumbered. And then they disappear. Just fuckin' vanish. Turn into vampire bats or something. It's weird. Drives you nuts. How many guys we got over here? Three hundred thousand? Something like that. Jets, tanks, choppers. Like trying to find a needle in a haystack with a shotgun. I keep reading about some damn light at the end of the tunnel, but we're right squat in the middle of the tunnel and I don't see a fucking thing. Aw, I don't know. Whaddo I know? The papers say we're knockin'em off ten to one. I guess we're just supposed to sit around till the VC run out of warm bodies."

"That's encouraging," Griffith laughed. "You're just what I need to brighten up my day," and he started singing: "You are the sunshine of my life...."

"Aw, listen, I don't know. I keep trying to put the face on it, but the more I think about it, the crazier the whole fuckin' thing gets. I don't even think these people like us, you know, and we're supposed to be—oh, fuck it. Stick around awhile. I can't explain it. Just this feeling I get sometimes."

It was completely dark now, and the night had taken on its usual blanket of color and silent nonsilence. Theoretically, one man was supposed to be asleep by now: one on, one off, all night long. But neither of you ever slept for the first two hours at least. It just worked that way; it always took awhile to settle down. That's why it was nice to have somebody comfortable to shoot the breeze with. Later on, when you were tired enough to sleep through the off-shift, it didn't matter.

"Cover the berm for me—what's your first name?"

"Gerry."

"Mine's Bill. Cover the berm for me, Gerry, I want a smoke." I dropped down into a squat behind the wall and lit a cigarette.

"Those guys ARVN out there?" asked Gerry, pointing in the direction of the Popular Forces compound at the south end of the nearby hamlet.

"PFs. Popular Forces. It's a kind of militia. Everyone that manages to evade the ARVN draft or can't pass the physical gets put in the PFs. Got guys with one leg, two heads. Sort of like the Boy Scouts. They aren't worth a fuck, but neither are the ARVN, so I guess it doesn't matter. Keep an eye on 'em, though. They're probably all VC. Like to come through the wire some night and slit our throats. Don't laugh. It happened to one of Delta Company's Combined Action Platoons."

"I never heard of PFs. I heard the ARVN aren't so good, though. One of my DIs was an advisor back in sixty-five."

"Not so good, huh? They're pathetic. Can't fight. Won't fight. Spend more time shooting at us than they do at the VC. You watch, I'll lay bets before the sun comes up, they open up with that big fifty down the road a ways—they got a company CP a couple of miles south of here—tomorrow morning, there'll be a pissed-off platoon commander in the COC hollering about another Marine patrol shot up by the ARVN. Happens all the time. Wait till you try to go to the national police headquarters some Saturday afternoon. Nobody home. They take weekends off: Saturday noon to Monday 0800. National police, ARVN—everybody but us and the VC. It's their own goddamned country, and they work it like a nine-to-five job. Just crazy, man."

"One war's as crazy as the next, I suppose," said Gerry.

"Yeh, well, maybe so, but I never read about a war like this in history class." Gerry flinched sharply as the big guns across the compound opened up. "Outgoing," I said.

"Loud suckers, ain't they?"

"You'll get used to it. It's the incoming you gotta worry about. You tired enough to sleep yet?"

"Not really."

"Well, I am. You mind? Wake me up about midnight." I curled up in a ball in one corner of the bunker and lit another cigarette. It would be about 10 a.m. back in The World. "Jenny must be sitting in class right now," I thought. I tried to imagine the sound of her voice. It wouldn't come. I couldn't fix it in my mind. Damn! I could see her face, but there was no voice. I tried to hear the sound of my mother's voice. Another blank. A deep involuntary shudder ripped through my stomach. Off to the south, abruptly, came the sudden slow heavy boomp-boomp-boomp-boomp of a .50-caliber machinegun punching periods into the night. "Wha'did I tell ya, Gerry?" I said without looking up. "That's the ARVN fifty."

"Hey, wake up, it's nearly midnight." Gerry was gently nudging me. "Wake up. What the hell is that?"

62

I rubbed the sleep out of my eyes and stood up. Gerry was pointing toward the east. "What?" I asked.

"That red streak," he said. It was gone, but I could see the lights of an airplane circling in the sky far out over the dunes, maybe six or seven miles, out near the ocean. I was awake now.

"Keep watching," I said. The lights continued to circle over the same spot. The aircraft was too far away to hear the engines. Suddenly a brilliant red streak silently began to descend toward the earth until it connected the flashing lights to the ground below with a solid bar of color. Many seconds later, as the flashing lights and red bar continued to move like a spotlight sweeping the sky from a fixed point on the ground, a sound like the dull buzz of a dentist's slow-speed drill came floating lazily through the humid night air. Sound and visual image appeared to be synchronized for awhile. Then the red streak slowly fell away from the circling lights and disappeared into the earth, leaving the thick sound humming alone in a black vacuum. Finally, long after the lights had stopped circling and begun to move off in a straight line toward the south, the sound abruptly stopped.

"That's Puff the Magic Dragon," I said. "The gunship."

"What's that?"

"Air Force C-47 with Vulcan cannons." I explained that the old transport plane, a military version of the DC-3, had been converted into a flying battleship by mounting three Vulcan cannons along one side of the fusilage. The Vulcan worked like a Gatling gun; it had six barrels that rotated as the gun was fired, so that each barrel fired only once every six shots. Each of the three cannons could fire 6,000 bullets per minute. Since the guns were in fixed mounts, they could only be aimed by tilting the entire aircraft toward the ground and circling around and around over the target.

"That's 18,000 rounds a minute, my man," I said, "300 bullets per second. Chops up anything and everything like mincemeat: fields, forests, mangroves, water buffalo, hooches, people. Everything. Take a patch of redwood forest and turn it into matchsticks before you can hitch up the horses. I've seen places where Puff's left his calling card. Unbelievable. Looks like a freshly plowed field ready for planting. I saw a body once, got chopped up by Puff. You wouldn't have known it had ever been a human being. Just a pile of pulp stuck to little pieces of cement and straw that used to be the guy's hooch — or her hooch, absolutely no way to tell the difference. It was so gross, it wasn't even sickening. It was just there, like litter or something."

"Jesus fucking Christ," Gerry whistled. "Puff the Magic Dragon?"

"That's what they call it."

Well down on the southeastern horizon now, the lights began circling again. Then the red streak, like a bar of hot steel just off the rolling mill, stabbed deliberately into the earth.

"What are they shooting at?" asked Gerry.

"God knows. Whatever's there."

We were both silent for a little while, just watching. Then Gerry began to sing the Peter, Paul and Mary song very softly. "Puff the Magic Dragon lived by the sea..."

Chapter 11

Rowe was turning out to be okay. He was a little slow to pick up on things around the S-2 shop, but he was a real hard worker and so genuinely apologetic that it was hard to get impatient with him. He would even come in an hour early in the morning, just to be sure he got the I-Sum done on time. Sometimes, he'd have to start all over again two or three times, but eventually he'd get it right. "Look at that, Bill," he'd beam. "Not a single mistake." Often, there'd be one or two things missing even then, but I'd send him down to the mess hall to get a canteen of coffee, and make the last corrections while he was gone.

Rowe had an easy-going manner that made it impossible to dislike him in spite of the fact that he was a wicked rummy player who seldom lost. "Shit, boy," Walters would shout in his Texas accent. "If I hadn't dealt that hand myself, I'd swear you stacked the deck. You got a mirror hidden somewhere?" And Walters would proceed to root through the gear at hand in an exaggerated manner, looking for the suspect mirror.

"You just have to remember which cards have been discarded, Wally. Wanna try again?"

"Deal, sucker!" Wally would snarl. "And remember I'm watchin' real close. Where I come from, we shoot card sharks." He'd twirl an imaginary six-gun, and snap off a few rounds with one eye closed.

Wally and Calloway teased Rowe mercilessly about his shotgun wedding and, as they called it, his premature baby. "What did ya think the rubber was for?" Calloway would roar. "Keeping your cigars dry?"

"He put it on his middle finger," Wally would add, "to keep from gettin' stink-finger. But she sat on the wrong finger."

"Hey, take it easy on him," I said to Calloway one day, pulling him quietly aside. I couldn't help being embarrassed for Rowe.

"Oh, hell, Ehrhart," said Calloway, loud enough for the whole hooch to hear. "It's okay. It's an inside joke. My daughter was born five months after I got married. We just couldn't keep the little bugger in there any longer." He began to gesture wildly, as though trying to stuff laundry into an overstuffed sack. I turned bright red, and Rowe started giggling, and then the whole hooch collapsed in a spasm of hysterical laughter.

"You guys are sick," I said, still laughing. "Come on, Bobby," I added, turning to Rowe. "Let's get out of here before it rubs off. We got work to do."

Rowe and I walked into the COC. Lieutenant Roberts was in the S-2 shop. "Afternoon, sir," I said. Rowe and I looked at each other and burst out laughing again.

"You guys sound like a couple of magpies," said the Lieutenant. "What's so funny?"

"It's Calloway, sir," said Rowe.

"He's crazy," I added.

"Everybody's crazy around here."

"Oh, no sir, not us," I said. "We're perfectly sane. That's how come we can tell Calloway's crazy."

"You guys?! You're the worst of the lot. Heckle and Jeckle. Don't they look like a couple of talking magpies, Griffith?" Gerry had just walked into the bunker.

"Absolutely, sir. They trying to deny it? Look under their shirts — black feathers."

"So you're on your own now," Lieutenant Roberts continued, still talking to Gerry.

"Yessir. Basinski went home this morning. You're getting pretty short yourself, aren't you, sir?"

"Two weeks. First of June. I'm afraid you'll have to win the war without me, boys."

"Oh, don't worry, sir, we'll take care of the war; you take care of your wife."

"I'm not worried — but I think my wife is!"

"Hey, I gotta run, you guys," said Gerry, talking to me and

66

Rowe. "I just stopped up to see if you wanna play some cards tonight. Either of you got duty?"

"Ehrhart can't make it," said Lieutenant Roberts. "He's going out with the scouts tonight."

"Sir?" I said.

"You want to go? They're going out on an ambush. Be back in the morning."

"Yessir! Where do I sign?"

"How come Bill always gets to go?" asked Rowe. "No disrespect intended, sir, but I wouldn't mind getting out of here once in awhile."

"Don't be in such a hurry to get yourself killed, Rowe," said Lieutenant Roberts. "You've only been here two weeks. You'll get your chance."

"Cards it is," said Rowe, shrugging his shoulders. "What time?"

"Whenever you're free," said Gerry. "When're the showers working tonight?"

"1800 to 1900," said the Lieutenant.

"I haven't had a shower in a week," said Gerry. "I can never get that damned schedule right. Come over after the showers close, Bobby."

"I don't even take showers anymore," I said. "I've given up trying to catch up with that schedule. Every time I think I've got it figured out, they go and change it."

"What's the point of takin' a shower when you just have to put on the same clothes you've been wearing for a month?" Rowe added.

"Hey, Griffith!" someone called from the other end of the COC. It was Lieutenant Burns from Operations. He walked down our way. "Got some bad news for you. Corporal Basinski's dead."

After a long few moments, Lieutenant Roberts asked, "What happened?"

"Apparently their jeep got ambushed north of Dien Ban. Regiment just called down. The driver bought it, too. Guy named Doyle. You know him?"

"Yessir," I said. "Corporal in Admin. Tall skinny guy."

"Well, anyway, I'm sorry," said Burns. "Basinski was on his way home, wasn't he?"

"Yeh," said Gerry. "Yessir. He was going home."

As we moved out through the wire around the Alpha Company command post, someone on the perimeter whispered, "Good hunting." None of the scouts responded. It was very dark. Far over to the west, a line of half a dozen large parachute flares, the kind dropped by the

C-130s, burned above the horizon like fiery stars, but they were much too far away to illuminate our little corner of the war. The butterflies in my stomach, sluggishly fluttering through the last few hours, were now wide awake.

I'd been around long enough to become almost accustomed to the perpetual anticipation of action, which was like the feeling I used to get as a kid in age-group swimming, standing on the starting block crouched down in a racing dive waiting for the starter's pistol to fire. Most of the time, nothing ever happened on patrol—or anywhere else, for that matter. The hair-trigger tension simply existed, constant and unconscious, like the sound of an automobile engine on a long drive.

Tonight, however, the razor was particularly sharp. For one thing, though I'd been on numerous listening posts and a number of patrols with the scouts, this was only my second night scout patrol. In addition, Staff Sergeant Trinh, our human booby-trap detector, had been detained at Hieu Nhon and wasn't with us. The butterflies teased and danced on the edge of the razor.

We set out directly west at a brisk pace, moving silently across the sand, among the rice fields and along the edges of treelines, avoiding the hamlets we encountered. The patrol route was a long one; we would be up all night. Late in the afternoon, we'd ridden an amtrac out to the Alpha Company command post near the Horseshoe, where we'd eaten supper out of cans and rested until well after dark. Now we would patrol west by southwest for several hours, then set up in ambush for the rest of the night near a hamlet around which there'd been an unusually heavy number of minings and snipings in the past few weeks. At daybreak, we'd return to the battalion command post on foot.

The news of Frank Basinski's death had shaken me badly. He'd been a nice guy, pleasant and helpful when I'd first arrived, with none of the condescending air that many of the "old salts" tended to assume with the new guys. Though I hadn't known him very well, he'd been a friend of Saunders', and my duties had brought me into contact with him nearly every day. In the previous two weeks, he'd sat in on a couple of card games with Griffith and me.

Only a few days before, he'd leaned back in his chair in the middle of a game—we'd been talking about the war and whether or not we were winning—and he'd said, "You know, if anybody had ever taken the trouble to try to understand Vietnam and the Vietnamese, we might have had a chance to win this war. But you just can't send a bunch of untrained kids like us charging into somebody else's country like gangbusters and expect to accomplish much. Not in this kind of war; not with this guerrilla stuff."

I'd protested that we were neither kids nor untrained, to which he'd responded, "You're not even old enough to drink legally in your own hometown, Bill, and I don't mean the kind of training *we've* had. We're just gunslingers. Anyway, I guess it doesn't matter now. Those guys in the Pentagon and the White House have all the answers in their silly little computers, and there's not much point in trying to reason with 'em, even if you ever got the chance. Reason isn't a requirement for national leadership, and in the case of senior military commanders, it's an absolute handicap."

Neither Gerry nor I said a word. I could see in Gerry's eyes the same uneasiness and puzzlement I was feeling. There was a seriousness in Frank's dry, steady tone of voice that I hadn't before encountered in Vietnam, a resignation devoid of humor, and I had no idea what to do with it.

"Oh, well," he finally said. "It won't be my problem much longer. Who's turn is it?"

And now Basinski was dead.

Already I'd seen enough guys die to know that you could get it anywhere anytime. The long pauses between deaths, the days and weeks where nothing ever happened but the crippling heat and the daily boredom of I-Sums and detainees and guard duty and bunker watch, had already taken on the dull hissing sound of a burning fuse. But it seemed somehow grotesquely unfair that Frank should have survived thirteen months only to die almost within shouting distance of home, as though God had played carrot-on-a-stick with Frank's dreams.

"Christ!" I thought, shaking my head back to the long night's patrol in front of me. We'd been out nearly an hour now. Increasingly, treelines, bushes, cultivated fields and hamlets began to encroach on the dry wasteland of the dunes. I was second-to-last man in line. Lance Corporal Roland Morgan was just in front of me; Calloway was tail-end charlie. Up ahead of Morgan, I could barely make out the thin column of forms gliding through the darkness. With no body armor — left behind in favor of less weight and greater mobility — and only the minimum of equipment, the patrol stalked as soundlessly as Americans ever can in a foreign place. It was well after 2300.

The rustling ripple of heavy artillery shells cutting the air rose quickly to the south. With no signal, the whole column halted. Five or six 155s erupted about a mile away, their echo trailing away slowly over the countryside. H&I fire—harrassment and interdiction; the random fire sent out all night long just to keep the Vietcong jumping. Most nights, I plotted many of the targets, piecing together a list from the jumble of confused and unreliable reports received every evening from the national police at Dien Ban and Hieu Nhon. I hoped Sergeant Wilson had remembered to report our patrol route to the COC. Again with no signal, we moved on.

We were well in among the hamlets and rice fields now. We walked through the flooded fields themselves to avoid the narrow paddy dikes that were easy places to lay mines and tripwires. New rice shoots parted gently as I slogged through the water, the thick mud of the bottom making movement awkward and silence impossible. I thought of the leeches wriggling down into my boots, and shuddered, but there was nothing to be done about it but burn them off in the morning. The column turned southwest and entered a grove of trees, closing the interval between each man a little to keep visual contact. Suddenly Morgan motioned me off the trail and disappeared into the underbrush.

There was no one in front of him, and I quickly realized that everyone else had stepped off the trail, too. Motioning to Calloway, I dropped down into the bushes. I had no idea what was going on, but the blood started pumping in my temples and my hands began to sweat against the plastic of my rifle stock. I saw something moving on the trail up ahead. The head of the column was reversing direction....

"Jesus Christ!" I almost shouted. That wasn't a scout! I pulled my rifle in tight against my side. Walking right down the trail was a gook. Two. Three. Four of them! I stopped breathing. Jesus Christ. They were going to pass within a few feet of me. My stomach clamped down into a hard, knotted fist. Without moving a muscle, I tried to pull my arms and legs into me, tucking my whole body up under my helmet. Don't move. Don't move. Jesus Christ. They were right in front of me. I could have reached out and poked them with my rifle. I was certain they would hear my stomach tumbling, or the blood thundering in my head, but they walked on by without seeming to notice, loping along with easy strides, rifles slung over shoulders or dangling loosely in one hand.

They were past me now. I caught Calloway out of the corner of my eye, across the trail from me, rising and taking aim at the receding figures. Without even thinking, I rose up, leveled my rifle, and we both opened up at the same time, full automatic, trying to knock down all four figures before they could react and take cover. The sudden bark and snap of my rifle was a surge of furious relief, the Vietcong went down like dominoes, and then Calloway and I were running and standing over the bodies in the charged silence and the other scouts were coming up, and I was breathing heavily and reeling with a mighty rush of elation, my nostrils flaring.

"Got 'em all," said Calloway to Sergeant Wilson, who was checking to make sure all four were dead.

"Nice work, gentlemen," said Wilson. "I was hoping you'd have sense enough to hit 'em as soon as they got past. We couldn't fire on 'em. They came out of nowhere, and then we couldn't see where you guys were back here."

"There's your dead goddamned VC with a goddamned rifle, Calloway," I said, prodding one of the bodies with my boot.

"It's about goddamned time," he said. "I was beginning to think all them mines and snipers and dead Marines were a figment of my imagination."

"Morgan, Newcome, Seagrave, Willis," called Sergeant Wilson, "post the corners. Some of their buddies might wanna know what all the excitement's about. Wally, get on the horn and let battalion know what's goin' down. You got our coordinates? Get 'em to put up some illumination, and find out what they want us to do. The rest of you, spread out and sit tight."

Calloway and I squatted down by the side of the trail. I was still shaking with adrenalin, my stomach alternately tightening and turning. "Jesus, that felt good!" Calloway whispered. "I get so fuckin' tired of chasing phantoms and comin' up with squat. I'm keepin' one of them rifles for a souvenir, man. That's the first damn weapon I've gotten in ten fuckin' months. You get one, too, if you want; it's your kill."

An illumination round popped overhead, then three more, hissing lightly and casting an eerie pattern of moving shadows down through the trees. The four bodies lay sprawled out in the trail, twisted and askew like ragdolls.

"They want us to leave 'em here and come in," said Sergeant Wilson, coming over to Calloway. "Follow our original patrol route, but skip the ambush. We lucked out here; no point in trying our luck twice tonight."

"Why don't we set up here for the rest of the night?" asked Calloway. "Maybe a few of their pals'll get curious. National police might be able to ID these gooks in the morning. We take off now, ain't gonna be no bodies here in the morning."

71

"I know," said Wilson with a shrug. "Ours not to reason why. Ehrhart, come on, let's search 'em." Aside from the four rifles, some ammunition and rice, the guerrillas had been carrying nothing but a few papers. I stuffed most of it into the big thigh pockets of my trousers. As I was gathering up the rifles, Private Davis, one of the newer scouts, came over to one of the bodies, drew a knife and bent down.

"Get away from that man, Davis," Sergeant Wilson growled, suddenly bristling.

"Aw, Sarge, I was just gonna take an ear...."

"Get away! Now."

Early the next morning, Sergeant Wilson and I went up to the COC to check in. We'd gotten back to battalion about 0330, so we'd had time to get a little sleep. Lieutenant Roberts was already in the S-2 shop. So was Rowe, bent over a typewriter, banging away at the I-Sum.

"Heard you had a good night," said the Lieutenant.

"Yessir," said Sergeant Wilson. "Four confirmed. All with weapons. Lieutenant, send Davis back to his outfit. I don't want 'im in scouts."

"What's the problem?"

"He's a headhunter. He tried to take ears last night."

"Come on, Wilson, you know how things are in some of the rifle companies. Give the kid a chance to break in. He's got a damned good record."

"The people that gave him his good record are probably no better than he is, sir. Look, I can't help what goes on in other outfits, but I won't have it in my scouts. This whole fuckin' thing's bad enough without butchery. Davis had his chance."

"Wilson, I know —"

"Sir, with all due respect, are they my scouts or aren't they?"

"Okay," said the Lieutenant after a brief pause. "I'll send him down, but I don't know how soon we can get a replacement."

"Why don't you make Ehrhart a permanent scout? He's damned good out there. Has all the right instincts, and he's smart." I straightened up.

"That's exactly why we need him in here. He runs the whole damned section single-handed. I can't let him go." I drooped down again. "Don't look so disappointed, Ehrhart," Roberts laughed. "You've got it both ways now. Leave well enough alone. I'll have to get somebody else, Wilson. I'll see what I can do."

"You guys get those rifles last night?" asked Rowe, pointing to the four weapons I'd brought in with me.

"Yep," I said. Bobby's mouth hung open with envy. There were two Russian K-44 bolt-action rifles with swing-bayonets, though one of the bayonets was broken off half way down the shaft, a bolt-action French MAS-36 dating from the French-Indochinese war, and an American M-1 carbine. I picked up the MAS-36. The hideaway bayonet was missing; the rotted leather shoulder strap was patched together with thin strips of bamboo and tied to the stock with wire.

"Look at the barrel on this thing," I said, extracting the bolt and holding the chamber up to the light. The rifling was almost completely gone, and the barrel was heavily pitted. "You couldn't hit a Cadillac at twenty paces with this piece. I wouldn't even try to fire it — blow up right in your face. How the hell do they fight with this kind of equipment?"

"It's called having the courage of your convictions, I think," said Sergeant Wilson.

"Or blind stupidity," added Lieutenant Roberts. "Get anything else?"

I emptied the sack I'd put the loose things into. There were several dozen loose rounds of ammunition, a ten-round magazine for the carbine, several small packets of rice wrapped up in some kind of leaf, and some papers written in Vietnamese.

"Hey, look at this," I said, lifting two very small photographs out from among the papers. "I didn't even notice these before." One of the photographs showed seven women, three kneeling and four standing behind them, all holding rifles. The other photo was a close-up of one of the women in the back row of the first photo. She was holding a Russian-made AK-47 automatic rifle at the ready, and had a look of fixed determination on her face.

"How'd you like a date with one of those ladies?" said Roberts.

"A whole squad of VC women," Rowe whistled. "There's not a one looks as old as my wife."

"Probably won't live to be as old as your wife, either," said Sergeant Wilson.

I thought back to the night before, to the four dead men lying in the trail. I took the picture of the girl with the AK-47, and tucked it into the edge of the frame around the color portrait of Jenny sitting on my desk. "I wonder which one of those guys was her boyfriend," I said.

Chapter 12

One morning a week later, Rowe and I entered the COC to discover pandemonium. A Marine battalion in Tam Ky, a district twenty miles south of us, had made heavy contact with a force of North Vietnamese Army regulars early that morning, Lieutenant Roberts explained. The engagement was still underway, and our battalion had been ordered to send reinforcements immediately, before the NVA could slip away.

"They're sending one platoon from each company," said the Lieutenant, "plus a command group. Scouts'll provide security for the CO. You guys have got to get map and field packets together. Get on it, boys; we need as many as you can make before they leave. Choppers are on the way in now."

"NVA?!" I said. It was the first time any of the units in our vicinity had run into regulars, though we'd been getting scattered rumors of NVA in the mountains to the west of us for months. "Can I go, sir?" I asked. "The scouts are still a man down. Sergeant Wilson'll want the extra man for sure."

"Not you," said Roberts. "We got no idea how long they're going to be gone. We need you here. You know I'm going home in a few days. The new S-2'll need somebody around here to break 'im in." The Lieutenant paused, then looked at Rowe. "You wanna go?"

"Shit, yes!" Rowe shouted. "I mean, yes, sir. It's about time I get some action!"

"Okay, get saddled up — tell Wilson to get up here right away."

74

"You lucky stiff, Bobby," I whined, giving Rowe a fake punch to the stomach as he went by. "Hey, Bobby," I added, "keep your ass down, will you?"

"No sweat," said Rowe as he disappeared out the door.

I turned to the Lieutenant. "That's what I get for reminding the Lieutenant of the manpower shortage, huh, sir?"

"Gimme a break, Ehrhart," Roberts laughed. "At least give Rowe a break. He's been cooped up in here since he got here. You know damn well you get stir-crazy around here, and it doesn't take long."

"Yeh, I know. Sorry, sir."

"Come on, I'll help you with the map kits."

My day was brightened several hours later by the arrival of the mail, which Gerry took the liberty of delivering to me in the S-2 shop. "I was picking mine up anyway," he said, flopping down a pile of letters and a package from my parents. I immediately separated out the three letters from Jenny and began to check the postmarks to see which one to open first.

"Hey, fuck those letters, turkey!" said Gerry. "What's in the Care package?"

"Ah, ha! The dutiful postman unwittingly reveals the secret behind the first class service."

"You betcher sweet ass, pal. You got a mother that can bake, and my mother didn't raise a fool."

"The hell she didn't. What're you doin' in that silly green clown suit?" But I put the letters aside and began to open the package. "What if it's chocolate chip cookies?"

"I fuckin' well know better. Your mother wouldn't do that to you. Hurry up, will ya? I ain't got all day."

Gerry was right. Inside the package were a loaf of banana bread, a date bar, a bag of red licorice, a wind-up plastic duck in a baseball uniform, a rubber spider, a plastic speedboat, and several packages of presweetened kool-aid. Each pack of kool-aid made one quart, which is exactly what your canteen held, and effectively masked the bitter taste of the halizone water purification tablets we had to use in our drinking water.

"What good is this?" Gerry asked plaintively, holding up the baseball duck. "You can't eat it. Duck Dimaggio!"

"Aw, my mom — " I started to say. I could feel myself blushing, my face getting hot and sweaty. "How the hell should I know? She probably thought it was cute."

Gerry and I were stuffing banana bread into our faces as fast as we could while having a dogfight between the spider and the speedboat when Al Talbot, the mail clerk, came into the COC carrying a large box. "Chocolate chip cookies!" he hollered like a peanut vendor at a ballgame. "Fresh — well, kinda fresh — homebaked chocolate chip cookies! Get 'em while they last."

"I don't believe it," I said. "I don't fuckin' believe it! Where'd they come from this time, Talbot? Backscratch, Arkansas?"

"Some high school cooking class in Grand Forks, North Dakota."

"Check the postmark. You sure they didn't come from Hanoi?"

"Oh, no," said Gerry. "No way. I can see it all now. Here's the Daughters of the American Revolution, and the Wives of Plumbers Local 104, and the American Legion Women's Auxiliary, and they're all sitting around playing bridge. And suddenly some fat old fart says, 'Gee, we ought to do something for our gallant boys in Vietnam. Show 'em our support.' And a wrinkled up mushroom says, 'Splendid! Let's send them some homebaked treats. Now let's see, what does every patriotic red-blooded American boy like?' And everybody in the room drops their cards and hollers, 'Hey!!! Chocolate chip cookies!'"

And so, the chocolate chip cookies came to Vietnam. At first, it was just small parcels of them with little cards inside that read: "We love you, fellas. Keep up the good work, and come home safely and soon. Aardvark, Minnesota, Volunteer Fire Company Number 1, Women's Auxiliary." But then the parcels began to get bigger and bigger. The mail jeeps couldn't carry them anymore. Trucks had to be used, and they rolled into the battalion command post every day, until Highway 28 backed up all the way to Dien Ban. Then they began arriving by parachute, huge pallets of chocolate chip cookies falling from the sky. Four-engined C-130 Hercules cargo planes, filled with nothing but chocolate chip cookies, blotted out the sun. Mighty ships plied the storm-tossed seas. We were buried alive in chocolate chip cookies. We ate them by the ton until we couldn't eat any more. We filled sandbags with them. We stuffed our air mattresses with them, tossing and turning at night to the sound of crumbling cookies. We gave them away by the thousands to the kiddies at the front gate, until *they* didn't want any more. We tried to send them to the guys in the field, but they sent them back again with grenades hidden in them. We fired them out of cannons at the Vietcong, but they loaded them into mortars and fired them back with notes saying, "We got enough, already. Eat 'em yourselves. Chop, chop."

We wrote letters to Robert McNamara and McGeorge Bundy.

We sent telegrams to the President: "Please, Mr. President. Make them stop. Stop." Still the cookies came. We tried to renounce our citizenship, explaining that we were really illegal aliens from Mexico. They wouldn't believe us. "You're not Mexican," said the notes in the boxes of cookies. "Keep up the good work." We fell to our knees and wept and prayed, but the cookies kept on coming and coming—the Kamikazi Chocolate Chip Cookies. We buried them in the ground, and blew them up with dynamite, and filled our knapsacks with them. We crushed them beneath the heels of our boots, and under the treads of massive tanks and amtracs. Nothing worked. As fast as we could grind them under, the YWCA Girls Glee Club Booster Mothers sent us more.

"You want any or not?" asked Talbot.

"Al," I said, "take those chocolate chip cookies and blow 'em out your ass."

"Hey, don't blame me. I'm just the King's messenger."

"Get lost, creep," Gerry roared, menancingly rising to his feet and brandishing the rubber spider.

"Good banana bread, huh, Gerry? Want some date bar?"

Lieutenant Roberts left for the States on the first of June. Lieutenant Kaiser, formerly Bravo Company commander, was pulled from the field to replace him. Kaiser had three months left to go in Vietnam. He was a big man, well over six feet tall, with an air of boyishness, though nothing about him looked boyish. He must have been twenty-five or twenty-six years old.

His first words were: "Don't worry, Ehrhart, I'm not going to screw you all up around here. Lieutenant Roberts says you're pretty good at what you do. You just keep doin' what you're doin' the way you've always done it, and I'll catch on eventually. After ten months in the boondocks, believe me, I wish for nothing but peace, domestic tranquility, and the rapid departure of my soul from this enchanting land— preferably with my limbs still attached." I liked him immediately.

I was far less pleased by the simultaneous and unexpected arrival of Gunnery Sergeant Johnson, the new S-2 chief. We'd been so long without a chief—had never had one, really, since I'd been there— that I'd almost begun to believe that I would forever be the acting intelligence chief of 1st Battalion, 1st Marines, an arrangement providing me a degree of independence with which I'd become quite comfortable. Fresh from the States and ready to win the war singlehandedly, Johnson would undoubtedly have a million ideas on how an S-2 shop ought to be organized and maintained, none of them corresponding to anything I was doing, and all of them utterly useless.

77

Sure enough, my worst suspicions were born out within fifteen minutes of Johnson's arrival. An enormous man, obviously strong in spite of the ample layer of fat wrapped around his torso, he careened around the S-2 shop poking into every folder, file, box and carton he could get his hands on, declaring in a voice that matched his physique that nothing was as it should be. His upper lip sweat profusely.

"This stuff can wait till tomorrow, Gunny," Lieutenant Kaiser finally said. "Why don't you just get settled in today? Come on, I'll show you around. I've still got some checking in to do myself. Might even be able to find a couple of cold beers."

Johnson hardly broke stride until Kaiser got to the part about the cold beers, and then he came up short. "You got cold beer?" he said, his voice drooling. He wiped his upper lip with a green handkerchief. "Lead the way, sir."

"Ehrhart," said Lieutenant Kaiser, "I'll be in my hooch if anything comes up. Otherwise, I'll see you in the morning."

"Aye, aye, sir," I said with little enthusiasm. After the two of them left, I slumped down in a chair to wallow in my misery, roundly cursing all of the unseen unknown powers that had delivered the overstuffed Gunnery Sergeant into my life. "Jesus shit!" I thought. "This asshole's gonna be a real ball-buster."

"Hey, my boy!" I looked up. It was Lieutenant Kaiser. "You look like death warmed over. Don't worry about Gunny Johnson, okay? He's all smoke and steam, but he'll cool off fast enough. You haven't been here so long to forget how that works, have you? Just do what he says for now, and don't argue. I'll take care of the rest, okay? You're my main man, Ehrhart. You didn't think I'd let ya down, did you?"

"Yessir! No, sir!" I said. "Thank you, sir!"

"Better not keep the Gunny waiting. He's liable to come back and discover our conspiracy." Kaiser smiled. "Say, you get done this afternoon, drop by my hooch. Maybe find a cold beer waiting for you."

Gerry and I were sitting in my hooch playing rummy and sharing the beer Lieutenant Kaiser had given me when the scouts walked in.

"Hey! You guys are back!" I shouted. "How'd it go? Everybody okay?"

"Pretty damn heavy down there," said Morgan, shaking his head. "Them NVA are the real McCoy. Rowe got hit." My stomach wrenched.

"Is he dead?"

"Naw," Wally cut in. "He got a ricochet up here." Wally stuck his finger on his neck just above the collar bone, pointing straight down. "Mighta punctured his lung, the corpsman wasn't sure; but it missed his heart. He'll make it."

"He was conscious the whole time," Morgan added. "He was even bitchin' about bein' evacuated. Wanted to find the gook that tagged him. He'll probably be back in a month. Where'd you get the beer? You got any more?"

"We got any mail?" Newcome hollered.

"In that sack there," I said, pointing to the large canvas mail sack in one corner of the hooch. "You can have the rest of this," I said to Morgan, holding up the remains of the beer. "It's all I got. The new S-2 gave it to me. Lieutenant Roberts went back to The World. Got a guy named Kaiser. Used to be Bravo CO."

Hey, fuckin' -A!" said Wally. "He used to be my CO. He's a good dude."

"We got a new chief, too. Gunnery Sergeant Johnson. Stateside wonder. Just got in this afternoon. Got all the answers. Fuckin' lifer! Could turn out to be a real pain in the ass."

"Grenade under his pillow'd slow him down," Newcome observed.

"I don't believe it!" said Calloway. He was sitting on his cot at the other end of the hooch. "I don't believe this shit." We all turned to look. Calloway was stark white, the color beneath his tanned face completely gone. He was staring at a letter.

"What'sa matter, Cal?" asked Wally.

"My wife's divorcing me. My best friend knocked 'er up. She wants to marry 'im." Nobody knew what to say. In the awkward silence that followed, Calloway crumpled up the letter, let it drop listlessly at his feet, reached up to the cartridge belt hanging from a nail above his cot, pulled out his .45, chambered a round, put the barrel to his temple, and pulled the trigger before any of us understood what we were seeing.

Three days later, Lieutenant Kaiser, Gunny Johnson and I were sitting in the S-2 shop when a corpsman from the battalion aid station came in and told us that Rowe had died the night before on a hospital ship in Danang harbor.

"Oh, Jesus!" I blurted out. My eyes filled with tears. I turned my head away from the others. It took a dozen deep breaths to regain my composure. "It just doesn't let up, does it, sir?"

"You got duty tonight?" asked Kaiser.

"No, sir."

"Why don't you go find Griffith? Play cards or something. See you in the morning."

"Yessir; thanks." Then I noticed the sheet of paper on the wall above my desk — the one with the *Stars 'n' Stripes* article and the excerpts from the I-Sums pasted to it. I got up and stood in front of it. "Me and Lieutenant Roberts used to think this thing was the funniest damned thing we'd ever seen," I said. "Bobby never could see the humor in it." I ripped it off the wall and tossed it into the trash basket. "I guess he was right."

Chapter 13

"I wonder where they finds dogs like that," Gerry mused.

"Beats me," I said. "They probably swim over behind the troop ships, barking like seals all the way." We were walking back from the mess hall. About once a month, the Red Cross "Donut Dollies" would show up to serve lunch, and today had been our lucky day. The Donut Dollies were nonmilitary women volunteers who'd come to Vietnam God knows why—patriotism, find a husband, I had to idea, though I suppose their immediate purpose was to raise our morale: a good hot meal served by smiling American girls, cheer you right up or something—but nothing could improve the food and the Donut Dollies were invariably homely enough to warp sheet-steel, though it was possible their hearts were pure.

"How do I manage to get suckered in every time?" Gerry said. "I wasn't even hungry."

"Because you keep hoping Joey Heatherton'll be there, blowing kisses as she scoops dehydrated mashed potatoes into your messkit."

"It was your idea to eat."

"So? You got the miracle market cornered or something? Joey Heatherton really might be there someday—blowing *me* kisses."

"Listen. No more Donut Dollies, okay? Next time the Dollies are in town, we eat C-rats, agreed? God is dead; I read about it in *Time* a couple of years ago—big red headline on black. Joey Heatherton's in Saigon getting her picture taken for the six o'clock news, and the only thing she's blowing is General Westmoreland's weiner."

"You know who came here? Mrs Miller," I said. Gerry gave me a blank look. "You know, Mrs. Miller. Big fat lady that sings — if you can call it that. That was our USO show. Jesus Christ! I couldn't fuckin' believe it. All those newsreels of USO shows — stage packed with beautiful girls, practically nothin' on. And there's always millions of troopies packed around the stage. How come we don't get nothin' like that?"

"Those guys are all Hollywood extras. You know where they film all those things? Burbank. No kidding. Directed by Governor Reagan. Okay, take two! Whoop it up, boys! Lights! Action!"

"Hey, Private Ehrhart!" I turned around to see Father Ligon, the battalion chaplain, approaching. "How are you, son?"

"Oh, hi, Father. Pretty good, sir. I'm not a private anymore. Made lance corporal in April."

"Well, congratulations, son. Glad to hear it. Has it been that long since I've seen you? I guess it has. I haven't seen you in chapel lately. Is anything the matter?"

"Oh, no, sir. I, uh, just, you know, sir, I been pretty busy. Got a war on here, you know."

"Yes, yes. I guess we do at that. Who's your friend?" I introduced Gerry. "Nice to meet you," said Father Ligon. "How's your girlfriend, Ehrhart?"

"Oh, she's just fine, sir. Graduates from high school next week. She'll be going to nursing school in September. St. Francis Hospital in Trenton, New Jersey. It's a Catholic school."

"Fine. Fine. Well, I've gotta run, boys. I just wanted to know how you were, Ehrhart. I miss seeing you. Maybe you can make it this week."

"Yessir, I'll do my best."

"You go to church?" Gerry asked when the priest had gotten out of earshot.

"Fuck you."

"No, I just wondered. You don't seem like the type."

"What do I got, horns or something?"

"Hey, come on. I just wondered."

"I used to go. Damn near every week for awhile. I'm not Catholic, but Jenny is. I guess it made me feel a little closer to her — but after awhile, I don't know, I started feeling really weird. Sittin' there, you know, love your fellow man, do unto others — in the middle of all this? Somebody's got his wires crossed somewhere. You know what I mean?"

"You ever talk to Father Whats'is Name about it?"

"Father Ligon? Are you kidding me? I know what *he'd* say.

82

'It's okay, son' — calls everybody 'son,' d'ja notice that? 'It's your Christian duty. God's on our side, so just keep up the good work and don't worry about a thing.' Dig this: Father Christopher Ligon, Society of Jesus, major, United States Marine Corps. Think about *that* for awhile."

"I don't think about anything around here. No future in it."

"What makes you think you got a future?"

"Hey, what's eatin' you? You been poppin' off at me all day. I do something wrong or what?"

"Aw, I'm sorry, Gerry. It ain't you. Bobby's dead. He died last night up at Danang."

"I thought he was going to — "

"So did I, but he didn't. He had a punctured lung. They couldn't stop the bleeding. He drowned in his own fuckin' blood."

"Jesus," said Gerry.

"Je-sus, all right. Jesus shit." We walked the rest of the way to Gerry's hooch in silence.

"Hey, Gerry," I said when we got inside.

"Yeh?"

"Listen. Something ever happens to me — you know, I buy the farm or something, will you look out for Jenny? Go see 'er once in awhile or something, make sure she's doin' okay?"

"Oh, sure, *I'll* take care of her."

"No, I mean it. I'm serious. She's so damn young. I don't know how she'd take it."

"Don't worry. I'll make sure she's okay. Hey, come on; you start thinkin' too much, you'll get yourself a one-way ticket for sure. Nothin's gonna happen to ya. Trust me!"

"If you can't trust your local Gerry, who can you trust?"

"What?"

"Oh, nothin'. You had to be there. I don't know, Gerry. Sometimes it feels like I'm gonna die of old age here. I been here forever, man. Fuckin' *forever*. And I still got nine months to go. Nine months! That's twice as long as I been here already. Jesus, sometimes I wonder if she even remembers who I am."

"Jenny? Christ, she must remember something. You get three or four letters every mail call. Jan doesn't write *that* often, and we're married, for chrissake. You think too much. How'd you meet her, anyway?"

"At a dance. I went to a dance at her high school — we didn't go to the same school — picked her out all the way across the dance floor. Just like in the movies. Our eyes met, and wham! She was beautiful. Shy little blue-eyed doll. I danced with her once and I was hooked. You know, I used to go out with three or four girls, sometimes, on one weekend. I had 'em lined up all over the county. Bangin' their heads against the wall trying to figure out how to get to me. No dice. Nobody hooks the kid, ladies. Then Jenny comes along, and all that shit comes to a screechin' halt, just like that. I knew she was the one right away."

"Hook, line and sinker, huh? Well, that's the way it happens. I married Jan two months after I met her."

"You like bein' married?"

"Yeh, it's okay. Jan's a hell of a girl."

"Must be nice gettin' laid regular."

"Yeh," said Gerry, laughing and groaning at the same time. "Don't remind me. I got three months longer than you have."

"You know somethin'? I haven't slept with Jenny yet. Haven't even touched her. Oh, we get into some pretty heavy breathing — dry humps the hell out of me; Jesus, you wouldn't believe it. Sits on my lap with her skirt up to her waist and rubs that thing around till I come in my pants — but I haven't even touched her bare tit."

"Will you shut up? You're driving me crazy."

"How do you think her priest feels. We go to the drive-in on Saturday night, fog up the windows, don't even know what movie we saw. Sunday morning, off she goes to confession. Jesus, the guy must go nuts listening to stories like that every Sunday morning."

"Don't worry about the priest, pal. What do you think all those nuns are for. He's gettin' his. What are *you* waitin' for?"

"Well, I can't do much about it now, asshole. Anyway, Jenny's only seventeen — sixteen when I met her. I got the rest of my life to screw her. I can wait."

"You better hope you got the rest of your life, chump," Gerry laughed. "I'm sorry, Bill. I was just kidding." There was a long pause. "Hey, you know, I expect you to do the same thing for Jan if anything ever happens to me."

"Yeh, sure."

"Promise?"

"Promise. Shit, this sucks, man! You see what the Israelis did to the A-rabs?"

"Yeh, I heard about it yesterday."

"That's the way to fight a fuckin' war, man. Kick ass, take names, and go home for supper. Six fuckin' days! Whole fuckin' thing's over. Damn."

84

"So maybe the gooks are smarter than the A-rabs."

"Maybe we're dumber than the Israelis."

"What's the difference?"

"You know what I tell Jenny? I tell her we're winning."

"What else can you say? I tell Jan the same thing."

"No, I don't even tell her what I'm doing. I don't tell anybody. Christ!" I snorted, "my letters must be boring as hell. 'Yesterday I went to Dien Ban. Today I go to Hieu Nhon. Tomorrow I've got bunker watch. I love you so bad I can taste it. I'll be home soon.' It must get monotonous after awhile, but what else can I say? You know?"

"Do her letters bore you?"

"Hell, no! I read every one of them a hundred times."

"Well, there you are."

"Yeh, but she tells me what she's really been doin'. She ain't been out — like, well, doin' stuff like I been doin'."

"Give yourself a break, will ya? You think too much."

The next morning, half-awake, I stumbled out of my hooch about 0730, set out across the sand toward the COC, and practically stepped on a snake. It startled me. I hadn't seen any snakes in Vietnam, and I certainly wasn't expecting to see this one. It had been sunning itself on the sand, which was already warming up in spite of the early hour, and my shadow had interrupted its nap. It was staring up at me with its eyes unblinking and its tongue testing the air. I walked around it at first, then paused, and walked back.

I looked at the snake for a moment. Then I unslung my rifle from my shoulder and began to beat on its head with the rifle butt, thrusting the rifle straight down like a pile-driver. Because of the deep loose sand, my blows only drove its head harmlessly into the sand. Between the blows, it tried to run, but I pinned it again and again, its three-foot body whipping and thrashing helplessly. "This is getting us nowhere," I thought. I pinned the snake firmly behind the head, took out my bayonet, and severed the head from the body.

"I killed a snake this morning, sir," I told Lieutenant Kaiser when he came in. "Right out in front of my hooch."

"No kidding. How big was he."

"About three feet."

"Any weapons?"

"Two fangs."

"Okay. VC. Put it on the I-Sum," the Lieutenant laughed.

"You aren't serious, sir."

"Why not? They report dead water-bo, don't they? Why can't

we claim our snake? Hell of a lot more dangerous than a water buffalo."

"You mind if I take the scouts out today, sir?" asked Sergeant Wilson, entering the bunker with Gunny Johnson. "They're getting a little restless. That Calloway business—I just don't want 'em sittin' around thinkin'."

"I'll buy that," said Lieutenant Kaiser. "Christ. Right there in front of everybody. He was a good trooper, too, wasn't he?"

"The best, sir," said Wilson. "They don't get you one way, they get you another."

"Where do you want to go today?" asked the Lieutenant, reaching for a map.

"Oh, I thought we'd take a little stroll up through here, sir," said Wilson, indicating the route on the map. "Just a cake walk. Be out about four hours." I gave the Sergeant my best pleading look, opening my eyes wide and bobbing my chin. "Can I take Ehrhart along?"

"You wanna go, boy?"

"Pope Catholic, sir?"

"Well, get caught up on everything before you go. And you'll have to get the H&I list in before 1800, don't forget. You got bunker watch tonight, don't you?"

"Yessir, two-oh to midnight. I can have the I-Sum done in fifteen minutes, and we'll be back—when, Sergeant Wilson?"

"Fifteen hundred. No later."

"Plenty of time, sir, no sweat."

It was a routine patrol, like most patrols, the tension so low-key you were hardly aware of it, but it got me out of the bunker for awhile and away from the tedium of the battalion compound. The heat rose out of the earth with the same dull intensity that made each motionless day a mirror image of the ones on either side of it. It was easily 120 degrees.

"Cake walk, Sergeant Wilson?" I said. "Bake me a cake that won't melt in this stuff. You'd have to make it out of concrete."

"Wait till the monsoons hit, Ehrhart. You'll wish you'd never heard of rain. You'll be delirious for a slice of sunshine."

We were about three miles north of battalion, moving slowly through the rice fields between two small hamlets on the back side of the loop formed by the circular patrol route. We'd been out nearly three hours. Aside from a few water buffalo standing around asleep on their feet, we hadn't seen much of anything. Everyone but us obviously had sense enough not to be out in heat like this.

And then I saw the figure in black pajamas running along a paddy dike about 300 meters ahead and to the left. "Got one!" I hollered. "Ten o'clock. He's mine."

The muttered warning to halt—regulations: "Dung lai!" Drop to one knee. Safety off. Sight in. Squeeze. *Crack!* The figure in black went flying like a piece of paper in a gust of wind.

"Get some!" Morgan shouted.

"Nice shot," said Newcome.

When we reached the body, it was sprawled in one of those impossibly awkward postures only people who die violently while in motion are capable of assuming. I nudged the corpse face-up with my boot. It was a woman of indeterminate age, perhaps fifty-five to sixty.

"Stupid gook," said Wally. "What'd she run for?" Vietnamese from the nearby hamlets were beginning to gather in clusters nearby, afraid to approach the old woman while we were still there, some of them keening softly as Wally radioed in to battalion:

"Annunciate, Annunciate; Annunciate Two Sierra."

"Annunciate; go ahead Two."

"We got one Victor Charlie Kilo India Alpha; Bravo Tango two-niner-two three-six-zero; negative weapons."

"That's a roger, Two. Do you require assistance?"

"Negative assist, Annunciate. Everything's cool here. We're proceeding in. Over." One of the guys dropped a playing card by the body, an ace of spades, and then we moved on through the silent steel heat. It took us another hour to reach battalion.

"I killed a snake today, Gerry," I said. I was on bunker watch, and Gerry had stopped by to keep me company for awhile. The assistant operations officer was sitting in a corner reading. The radioman was writing a letter.

"When? On that patrol this afternoon?"

"No, this morning. Right by my hooch. It was just lying there curled up in the sand. I beat it up for awhile, and then I cut its head off."

Gerry continued shuffling a deck of cards. "Snakes give me the creeps," he said.

"They give most people the creeps. But not me. I ain't afraid of 'em. Never was. You know, when I was a kid—nine, ten years old—me and my pals used to spend all summer paddling around this creek in Perkasie. We had this old boat we found one time, leaked like a sieve. One guy'd push the damn thing along with a big pole like a gondolier; 'nother guy'd sit in the bow and steer with a short plank; third guy'd sit in the middle and bail like hell. We used to catch snakes in that creek with our bare hands. Dive right in the water after 'em. Take 'em home and keep 'em for pets. Funny. I don't know why I killed that snake today. Wasn't botherin' anybody. Certainly wasn't bothering me."

Chapter 14

I picked up Rowe's replacement at Regiment one day toward the middle of June, dropping off a couple of guys who were going back to The World on the way up. I did a double-take when I saw him; if he hadn't been wearing the insignia of a Marine lance corporal, I'd have sworn he was ARVN. Moreover, his first words — delivered in a heavy Asian accent — were unintelligible.

"Amagasu," he said. "Kenokura Amagasu." Or something like that.

"What the fuck is going on?" I thought. "Huh?" I said.

"That's my name. I'm Japanese. Nobody ever gets my name right anyway. Just call me Kenny."

"Oh. Okay," I said. "Well, let's go." We got into the jeep and started back to Battalion.

"Don't you want to know what I'm doing in the U.S. Marines? Everybody else always does."

"Uh, well, yeh, I guess so."

"I came to study in the U.S. a year and a half ago, and decided I wanted to stay. If you've been in the American military, you only have to wait three years to be naturalized instead of five. So here I am. Volunteered. I'll be eligible for citizenship when I get out."

"Seems to me it's worth the extra two years to avoid this bull-shit."

"Well, I guess I'll find out, won't I?" Amagasu grinned. His eyes wrinkled up into sharp slits behind his glasses, and his round face and wide toothy grin made him look just like one of those sadistic guards in *Bridge over the River Kwai*, except that he exuded an infectious warmth and good humor that confounded all my Hollywood notions of the Japanese. I didn't know what to make of him.

"So how come you want to be an American so bad?" I asked.

"Have you ever been to Japan?"

"Nope."

"Nothing like the States. Somebody like me can't get anywhere unless I want to be a company man. There's a lot more opportunities in America. Wow. College is so different. Everything. I can make something for myself on my own. There's a lot more freedom."

"You got family in the States?"

"Nope. They're all back in Japan; father, mother and one sister."

"Look out!" I shouted, swerving sharply to avoid hitting an old man who had stepped out of a crowd right in front of the jeep. I slowed down and shook my fist at the old man, trying to drive and stand up at the same time. "You dumb gook motherfucker!" I hollered. "Next time, I'll run you over, you son-of-a-bitch! You okay?" I asked Amagasu. "Jesus, these people are stupid. You think they'd know by now to look. Never do. Just ditty-bop along like they ain't got a care in the world. Get hit all the time, then they come lookin' for com-pen-sa-tion. I'll tell you what; we picked a hell of a place to make our stand. Jesus. You better hang on to that thing, too," I said, nodding my head toward the M-16 lying between us. "You fired one of these yet?"

"We used them at Pulgas a little."

"You know how it works then? You better chamber one and keep your eyes peeled. May look peaceful enough around here, but this is Indian Country."

"What's Indian Country?" asked Amagasu, giving me a blank look.

"Indian Country—like the Wild and Wooly West? Oh, never mind. Just look sharp. There's Cong all over the place. That old geezer coulda flipped a grenade at us. Some little kid tried to do that to me couple of months ago. Uncle Charlie says, 'Here, give this present to GI Joe.' Kablooie! Deep six. Anything you don't like the looks of, blow it away. You won't get a second chance."

Amagasu turned the M-16 over in his hands like he was inspecting a cut of beef. "I heard these things aren't so good," he said.

"I don't know. I haven't had any trouble with mine, but I've heard some bad stories. Something wrong with the chamber—too tight

90

or something. Spent brass gets stuck in there, extractor tears off the ass-end, throws another round in on top of it, and everything comes to a screechin' halt. Wally said Rowe's sixteen jammed — you'll meet Wally. Radioman for the scouts. Rowe is the guy you're replacing. Bought the farm on an operation against the NVA a few weeks ago. Wally said Rowe's sixteen jammed up on him; he was tryin' to bang the casing out with a cleaning rod when he got it. Just like the fuckin' Corps to give us a piece of shit. If the Army wasn't usin' 'em too, I'd swear it was a conspiracy to exterminate the Marines. Maybe the government's tryin' to get rid of all of us. Give the gravediggers at Arlington somethin' to do. They oughta bury the Colt Company's board of directors. Hey, look at that, man. Ain't that beautiful?"

We were driving past a large temple that looked like something out of a travel poster. A three-story central building with red tile roofing and blue and red tile mosaics laid into the walls was flanked by two tall square-sided towers. All three structures had two tiers of sloping tile roofing gracefully pointed at the corners. Four pillars supported a low portico over the entrance to the main building, and the doors to the temple and towers were painted blue with red trim.

"They got stuff like that in Japan, don't they? Are you Buddhist?"

"Shinto."

"What's the difference?"

Amagasu laughed. "Everything. Are Catholics and Jews the same? Shinto is the main religion in Japan. Used to be the state religion; the emperor was worshipped as the Deity on earth — but we lost World War Two, and here I am in the U.S. Marines." Amagasu laughed again.

"I thought Japanese were Buddhist. I never heard of Shinto. We studied it a little in high school — Buddhism, I mean. There's a Confucian shrine in the center of Hoi An." I adopted my best Asian accent: "Kunfooshus say: He who piss in bed have wet dream." Amagasu looked at me out of the side of his face. "That's supposed to be a joke," I said.

"Oh," said Amagasu.

"Listen, I gotta stop at the national police headquarters in Dien Ban. It'll only take a minute. You might as well know where it is; we gotta stop there about once a week or so. Supposed to gather intelligence from 'em," I said, emphasizing 'gather intelligence.' "It's a bunch of bullshit — they haven't given us one fuckin' piece of useful information in the four months I been here, but the secretaries are cute. Hey, you see that thing?" I pointed to what looked like a miniature temple on top of a three-foot pole by the side of the road. "You know what they are?"

"What are they?" Amagasu asked.

"I don't know. I thought you might know; you're—no, you're not Buddhist. Sorry. They got 'em all over the place. I've seen people putting incense sticks in the windows and stuff. Must be something with their religion. Maybe they're Buddhist birdhouses. I keep meaning to ask Trinh."

"Who's Trinh?"

"Staff Sergeant Trinh, the ARVN interpreter assigned to Battalion. Speaks English, French and Chinese. Got a nose for tripwires like you wouldn't believe. Saigon'd win the war hands down with an army full of Trinhs. Good man. There's another one of those birdhouses. Watch this." I swerved the jeep to the right and caught the supporting pole with the right front bumper, sending the miniature temple flying into the field. "We used to do that with mailboxes when I was in high school." I broke into a wildly off-key rendition of the Rolling Stones: "I can't get no! No, no, no!"

"You're crazy," Amagasu laughed.

"Have to be around here. Only way to stay sane. Yahoo!"

The minute we walked into the police station at Dien Ban, the three young secretaries in their flowing *ao dais* stopped working, congregated around one of the desks in the far corner of the office, and began a furious muffled conversation punctuated with giggles and sidelong glances.

"Chow ong Truong," I said, greeting the policeman who rose at our entrance.

"Chow ong," said Truong, taking my hand in both of his, smiling and nodding repeatedly. I was about to introduce Amagasu when Truong turned to him and began speaking rapidly in Vietnamese. Amagasu went red and turned to me with a look of helpless bewilderment on his face. I burst out laughing.

"No, no Truong, he's not Vietnamese. Non Viet." It was Truong's turn to go red, and most of the rest of the visit was occupied by Truong's embarrassed attempts to apologize in broken English. As we got back in the jeep to leave, I burst out laughing again. "He thought you were a gook!" I roared. "Oh, it's gonna be fun havin' you around."

Amagasu was burning; you could tell he was laboring hard for words. "That stupid asshole!" he finally blurted out. "I took enough of

92

that shit in boot camp. I'll be goddamned if some *gook's* going to call me a gook."

"You better ask Trinh how to say 'Fuck you' in Vietnamese. It's gonna be a long thirteen months."

We were within sight of the battalion command post when a couple of F-8s roared by low overhead and began to dive at a cluster of hooches about a mile on the other side of the river in front of the compound. Each of the jets made repeated passes, leaving billowing clouds of black smoke in their wake. We could see flames from secondary fires almost immediately.

"They're smokin' somebody over there," I said. "That's pretty close to the CP. Wonder what's up."

"What's all that?" Amagasu asked, pointing down the road. I'd been so busy watching the airstrike that I hadn't noticed the commotion in front of us. What looked like the rear end of a truck was sticking up out of the road, and there were several vehicles beyond it. Marines were milling around all over. "Shit!" I said. "Charlie blew the bridge again." We pulled up and stopped. "Gimme that rifle, Kenny."

"What am I supposed to use?"

"Here," I said, handing him a grenade. "Don't drop it all in one place." We got out of the jeep and walked over toward the crowd. The truck that had looked like it was sticking up out of the road was actually lying with its nose in the water and its rear wheels still on the roadway. It was a twisted smoking wreck. The bridge over the creek had been blown out from under it. The wounded—there had been seven, I soon discovered—had already been taken to the aid station. Another ambulance was waiting for the bodies of the dead to be pieced back together and collected. Nobody was sure how many Marines had been killed; some of the bodies had been completely dismembered, and they were still trying to collect enough pieces to count them. "Yo, Lieutenant," I hollered, spotting Lieutenant Kaiser and Gunny Johnson standing on the far side of what was left of the bridge. "Come on, Kenny." I turned around and Amagasu was puking in a ditch. "Sit down," I said, gently pushing Amagasu down.

"Holy fuck," he muttered.

"Don't worry about it. Wait here; I'll be back in a few minutes. Here, take this," I said, handing back the rifle. Whoever had blown the bridge would probably be long gone by now, anyway. I waded into the creek toward the other side.

"Watch yourself, Ehrhart," Lieutenant Kaiser shouted. "There may be more surprises laying around."

"What the fuck happened?" I asked when I got to the other side.

"You can see for yourself," Gunny Johnson replied. "You know as much as we do. Happened about a half hour ago. These guys were going on R&R. Now they get to go home instead."

What's goin' on over there?" I asked, pointing toward the smoking ruins of the hamlet that the planes had worked over.

"Gate guard thought he saw a couple of gooks runnin' for the ville right after the explosion," said Johnson. "Christ, that musta been a big fuckin' charge; we could feel it in the COC."

"Fifty pounds, at least," said the Lieutenant. "Maybe a hundred. I spilled my coffee."

"Look at this, sir!" It was Sergeant Wilson. He was carrying some kind of pole as he walked out of the field on the west side of the road. "This is what they set it off with. Just enough juice to spark a detonator." When he got close, you could see that it was a whole long double row of flashlight batteries rigged together in series and taped between two long pieces of bamboo. There must have been fifty batteries — mostly green-colored ones like the ones we were issued, but with a few silver-colored civilian-style EverReady's, too — and there were two wires sticking out of either end of the contraption.

"Where'd you find this?" asked Kaiser.

"Out there," said Wilson, pointing out across the field. "Behind that paddy dike about two hundred meters out, where Morgan is standing. Wires leading right to the bridge. They just sat out there and waited for a nice fat target."

There were several clusters of Vietnamese from the hamlet between the bridge and the battalion compound standing off to one side — old men, women and children; the usual assortment of civilians. "Round 'em up, Wilson," said Lieutenant Kaiser, nodding his head wearily toward the Vietnamese. "Let's take 'em in and see what they know. You got the new man, Ehrhart?"

"Yessir. That's him sitting on the other side."

"Might as well put him right to work. Give Wilson a hand getting these gooks into the compound. Then find Taggart and Trinh and see what you can find out."

"Aye, aye, sir. You know something, sir? Those gooks probably watched me drive over the bridge this morning. Jesus. Discarded American flashlight batteries."

"Ingenious little fuckers, aren't they?" said Sergeant Wilson.

"I don't fuckin' believe it!" said Gunny Johnson.

"You damn well better, Gunny," said Wilson.

94

Chapter 15

"Do you believe this shit?" I said, tossing an open *Time* magazine onto the table in front of Gerry. Several pages of color photographs from the riots in Newark and Detroit stared up at us like some bizarre *Playboy* centerfold. There were pictures of burning buses and gutted ruined buildings, riot police battling black looters, and National Guardsmen in full combat gear perched on machinegun-carrying armored vehicles. "It looks like a goddamned war zone back there."

"Pretty depressing, ain't it?" Gerry replied, casually flipping through the pages of the magazine.

"Depressing? That's a fuckin' 50-caliber machinegun on that APC. That's America, man! That ain't a hundred miles from Perkasie. Jesus, what the hell do those people want? Look at that lady," I said, pointing to one of the photographs. "That's a fuckin' television set. Color, I'll bet! She can't even carry the damned thing."

"There weren't many Negroes in Perkasie, were there?" Gerry asked.

"Just a few families in East Rockhill; went to my high school."

"Ever wonder why not?"

"Well, no, I guess not. So what?"

"I been in the ghettos in Oakland. Had a parttime job there for a few months when I was in college. It's bleak, fella. Not much to look forward to from one day to the next. One lifetime to the next, for that matter. Martin Luther King gets the headlines, but he ain't hardly made a dent in it. Maybe they got a right to be pissed."

Nobody has a right to do that kind of shit," I said, banging my fist down on the magazine. "I didn't come to 'Nam to sit on the sidelines and watch my country get torn apart right under my nose."

"What do you think we're doing here, waltzing Matilda?"

"Oh, fuck, I don't know! Sometimes I can't believe any of this shit. Sometimes, I wake up at night feelin' like there's a big invisible thunderhead hanging over me, and the lightning's just waiting to strike. Just waiting and waiting. I wanna scream, but it's dark and there's nobody there to hear me. And it's *really* scary when I start feelin' like that in broad daylight. Like somebody's strangling me and I can't see who it is or get at him. Jesus, this sure as hell ain't what I expected."

"What did you expect?"

"Christ, I don't even know anymore. I just get up every morning and mark another day off. Like moving through a dream."

"You could always quit."

"Right. Sure. 'Colonel, I resign.' "

"Hey, I've heard of guys doin' that."

"Yeh, and they end up with twenty years at Portsmouth makin' little rocks out of big rocks. Fuck, no. Let the fuckin' hippies and peaceniks make the waves. I'm doin' my fuckin' time, and I don't plan to do any extra."

"Well, we're doin' our time, all right," Gerry laughed. "My father-in-law wrote me a letter last week. He *never* writes to me; I don't think he even *likes* me. Said he was proud his daughter's husband was servin' his country."

"I'd *like* to think I was servin' my fuckin' country."

"Wonder what got into the old man," Gerry mused. "Say, how's that new guy workin' out? What's his name?"

"Amagasu. Kenny. He's okay. Nice guy. You know, he's not even American and he signed up. Wants to be a citizen."

"I know," said Gerry. "I was talkin' to him the other day."

"Hasn't been to the mess hall yet. He's got a seabag full of Japanese food—seaweed, dried squid, all kinds of weird stuff. Cooks it in the hooch with heat tabs."

"Can't say I blame him for avoiding the grease-wagon. Probably wants to send his asshole home intact, even if he gets his head blown off. Not a bad choice, if you gotta pick one or the other."

"Yeh? You oughta try some of that hot cabbage stuff he's got. Blow your fuckin' asshole out like the Roto-rooter man. Mogerty—you know Mogerty? Corporal Newcome?"

96

"Yeh. Skinny guy with the weird laugh."

"Yeh. Kenny was cookin' some of that shit, and Mogerty asks him what it is. Kenny says, 'Here, try some; it's good.' Mogerty takes a big mouthful and starts chewin' it, and gets it half swallowed and his fuckin' eyeballs get real big, practically pop out of his face. Spits the stuff all over the hooch and starts hollerin' for water. God damn, it was funny. Mogerty's runnin' around emptying every canteen he can get his hands on. Kenny's just sittin' there chuckling. 'Hey, Bill, you wanna try some?' Big shit-eating grin on his face. 'Fuck you, Samurai Sam!' He laughs, starts packin' the stuff in like it was ice cream. Don't bother him at all. Jesus, the guy's got cast-iron guts or something."

"Speakin' of cast-iron guts," Gerry said, "Gunny Johnson was in here this afternoon pissin' and moanin' about a 'security check,' he calls it. Wants to know if I got enough incendiary plates, just in case we get overrun. Christ, it'd take a week to melt these safes," he said, sweeping his hand around at the nine cabinet-sized safes lining the walls of the hooch. "What am I supposed to do, hold 'em off at the pass till the fuckin' things melt? Fuck if I'm stickin' around. That guy's too goddamned gung ho for me. Stick the fuckin' things up his ass, if he wants to; I won't be here to stop him."

"Oh, he's not so bad once you get used to him. Says a lot more than he does. Lieutenant Kaiser's got a saddle on him."

"What are you gonna do when Kaiser goes back to The World?"

"I'll worry about that when the time comes. Got a couple of months yet. Maybe the Gunny'll step on a mine before then."

"I wish to hell I had another couple of months," said Gerry. All of a sudden, he looked over at me and said, "What the hell *are* we doing here, anyway?"

"Killin' Commies for Christ," I laughed. "Making the world safe for Democracy. Helpin' the stockholders at Dow Chemical pay off their mortgages. *Now* look who's thinkin' too much."

"No, I mean it."

"So do I. How the fuck should I know? I knew the answer, you think I'd be a fuckin' lance corporal? Why don't you ask the Colonel?"

"I did," Gerry said. "Yesterday."

"Go on."

"No, really, I did. I hadda take him some documents and stuff, and I was just standing there waiting for him to sign 'em, so I asked him."

"Christ, you got brass balls. You buckin' for private? What'd he say?"

"He said, 'Our jobs.' "

"What?! What the fuck kind of answer is that?"

"That's what he said. That's all. Real serious-like. 'Our jobs.' "

"Jesus. Hell of a way to make a living."

"Yeh."

"Say, you think we could get on unemployment?"

"Oh, sure, swell! A lifetime supply of Kool-aid and chocolate chip cookies!"

"Kool-aid!" We both roared. "Chocolate chip cookies??!"

"No! Please! Gimme my job back. Quick!"

"I'll do anything! Send me to the front!"

"Oh, I can't fuckin' wait till the first time somebody offers me a chocolate chip cookie back in The World," I said, when I'd finally stopped laughing. " 'It's so nice to have you home again. Would you like a nice fresh chocolate chip cookie? I just baked them.' 'Chocolate chip cookie? Did you say CHOCOLATE CHIP COOKIE?!' "

"I'll have an epileptic seizure."

"I'll go into a coma. Whang! Just like this" — and I stood up straight and stiff as a board, and keeled over face-first onto the floor.

"I'll tear the stuffing out of the furniture."

"I'll eat the cat — raw!"

"I'll eat the cat box."

"I'll strangle 'em with my bare hands."

"I'll bayonet everybody on the block, and plead self-defense."

"I'll fart as loud as I can. Barroom!" I shouted, pressing the heels of my hands to my mouth and exhaling sharply. There was a loud knock at the door.

"Come in," Gerry croaked. The sergeant of the guard opened the door to discover two helplessly disabled Marines lying on the floor doubled up and holding their sides like human cannonballs.

"What the hell's goin' on in here? You guys look like you're ready for a Section Eight. Knock it off, will ya? It's after black-out."

"Please don't arrest us, Sarge," Gerry pleaded. "We'll be good. Cross my heart." He made a big X over his chest.

"Jesus Christ," said Barron, rolling his eyes. "Ehrhart, if your mother didn't make the best banana bread in town, I'd put you both on report."

"What are they gonna do to us, Sergeant Barron," I asked, assuming a look of raw terror. "Send us to Vietnam?"

"Hold it down," said the Sergeant, visibly suppressing a smile as he turned around and walked out.

98

Chapter 16

(Vietnam and the Cookie monsters!)

"Aw, gimme a break, Lieutenant!" I pleaded.

"Give you a break?" Kaiser replied. "I'm trying to keep you alive, you ungrateful boy."

"But I'm goin' *nuts* around here, sir! You don't lemme do *nothin'* anymore. I ain't been anywhere in a month. I'm goin' outta my fuckin' mind!"

"You just drove down to Hieu Nhon this morning."

"Oh, shit, sir, that's not the same thing, and you know it." It was true. Since the middle of June, I hadn't been on a single scout patrol, no operations, no County Fairs, nothing. I went through the motions in the S-2 shop, stood guard and bunker watch, and played cards with Gerry. For real excitement, I'd walk out to the front gate in the afternoon when things were slower than slow and play with the kids, hiding bars of tropical chocolate in the cavernous pockets of my jungle utilities for them to find. The book of those days would have been page after page after page of nothing but heat and sand, arduous love letters grown boring even to me, and black rumbling thoughts that never quite coagulated into words.

"But Ehrhart, you're my boy. You're goin' to college someday. How do ya think I'd feel if I let you go to the field, and you went and got zapped on me? Huh? The trouble with you, my boy, you don't know what's good for you."

"If I knew what was good for me, sir, I wouldn't fuckin' be here in the first place."

"What the hell are you doin' here, anyway? You shoulda gone to college in the first place."

"It's a long story, sir. What can I say? It seemed like the thing to do at the time."

"Second thoughts?" the Lieutenant chided.

"Well, what do *you* think, sir? Make any sense to you? I don't know—and I *don't* wanna think about it. And all there is to *do* around here is think. Will ya just lemme out of here once before I go Section Eight? If I gotta listen to that fuckin' Haller's fuckin' *music* one more fuckin' night, I'm gonna kill somebody."

"No, you're not; you're gonna go to college. That crap last month was the cat's meow. If they'd have hit that column, you'da been the first to go. They'da been scrapin' you off that tank with sandpaper. I'd have had a fun time tryin' to explain *that* to your parents."

"That crap" the Lieutenant was referring to was the night I'd ridden from Battalion to one of Bravo Company's platoon positions while perched on the left front fender of the tank leading a relief column, giving directions to the driver. We'd gotten reports of a possible largescale Vietcong attack on the position, and the battalion commander had decided to send reinforcements. The problem was that, with the scouts out somewhere else, nobody knew how to find the place in the dark—except me. So I'd volunteered for seeing-eye dog, and off we'd gone into the night.

"Oh, hell, sir; nothin' happened," I protested.

"Well, it *could* have. The answer is no, no, and no. You're the assistant intelligence chief. You're not a grunt. You're not a scout. And as long as I'm around, you're not goin' out anymore. So forget it. By the way, I put you in for a commendation."

"What for, sir?"

"For taking that fool tank ride, you fool."

That shut me up for a minute. "Sir?" I finally said. "That's very nice of you. I, uh, thank you, sir."

"What's on your mind now, for chrissake?"

"Well, sir, the truth is, well, what can I do with a medal? I'd rather have another stripe." I ducked my head, anticipating the blow.

"Another stripe? You're gonna be filthy rich by the time you marry that girl," said Lieutenant Kaiser, pointing to Jenny's picture. "Okay," he laughed. "I'll see what I can do. Will you stop your goddamned complainin' then?"

"I might, sir."

"Might?! If you didn't run this place, I'd have you flogged."

100

Just then the field phone rang. It was the guard on the main gate. "One of those little kids that hang around here all the time," said the guard, "he keeps hollerin' 'Ong Bill! Ong Bill!' Won't go away."

"What does he want?" I asked.

"How the hell should I know? He won't say anything but 'Ong Bill.' You're the only Bill I know that comes around here. Will you come out and see what he wants? He's drivin' me nuts."

"Okay, I'll be right there." I hung up. "One of the kids wants to see me. He's all exicted about something. Can I go down for a minute, sir?"

"Yes. Go. Get out of here. Leave me alone for awhile."

When I got near the gate, there was Tranh, one of the regulars, hopping up and down and gesturing wildly at the guard. As soon as he saw me coming, he skirted around the guard box and ran up to me, grabbing my sleeve and shouting over and over again, "Beau coup VC come, giet papa-san. Bang! Bang!" He pointed first beyond the river across the road from us, then to the hamlet nestled near the wire by the northwest corner of Battalion's perimeter. He was very frightened.

But Tranh spoke only a few words of English, and the language school from which I'd graduated first in my class hadn't taught me enough Vietnamese to ask directions out of a paper bag. He chattered on and on, but I couldn't tell if the Vietcong had just killed his father, or were going to kill his father, or if papa-san meant any adult, or what. After a few moments, I indicated for Tranh to wait, putting my hand over his mouth and gently sitting him down in the sand, while I went to find someone who could understand him. Trinh and Wilson were both out with the scouts, so I had to settle for Staff Sergeant Taggart, who at least might be able to understand Tranh better than I could. As we walked toward the gate, I explained to Taggart what little I had gathered from Tranh.

As soon as we reached Tranh, Sergeant Taggart jumped all over him. I couldn't understand much of what he said, but I could tell from the tone of his voice that Taggart was threatening Tranh with all manner of physical and spiritual harm. Tranh tried to hide behind me, but Taggart grabbed him and started shaking him. "Hey, lighten up on him, Sergeant," I said, but Taggart ignored me. Since he outranked me, there was nothing I could do but stand there helplessly. Tranh wouldn't say a word. "You brought this man here," his eyes said to me. He was crying now. I looked away. Taggart kept it up awhile longer, then slapped the boy a couple of times, kicked him in the rear end, and sent him packing. Tranh never looked back.

"That fuckin' little dummy doesn't know shit," Taggart said as we walked back into the compound. "What the fuck you bother me with shit like this for?"

"That boy knows something, Sergeant Taggart," I said. "At least he thinks he does. We might have found out what it was if you hadn't given him the third degree. He's only six or seven, for chrissake."

"Don't tell me how to do my job, Lance Corporal."

"Oh, absolutely not, Staff Sergeant; wouldn't think of it."

"Don't get smart with me, either."

I didn't respond. I went back into the COC, silently hoping that Taggart would go step on a mine somewhere.

"What's up?" asked Lieutenant Kaiser.

"I don't know, sir. One of my little friends was all excited about beau coup VC coming to kill his father or something. I couldn't understand him, so I got Sergeant Taggart. Jesus, Taggart jumped right down the kid's throat. He wouldn't say a word to Taggart. I don't blame him, either. That man's bad news, sir. Got a Hitler complex or something. I wish you'd send him back to Regiment, or some damn place."

"That's up to Regiment," said the Lieutenant. "He's not under me; he's Regimental IT Team. You know that."

"Well, sir, whatever the boy wanted, we're not gonna find out about it today. I'll try to get him to talk with Wilson or Trinh tomorrow."

"You shouldn't be hangin' around with those little beggars anyway, Ehrhart," said Gunny Johnson, who had showed up while I was gone. "One of these days, they're gonna give you a popsicle with glass in it. Didn't a little shit try to give you a grenade once?"

"Oh, hell, Gunny, these kids are all right," I said. "They're out there every day. I get along with 'em fine. I been eatin' those popsicles for months, and nobody's tried to slip me a Mickey yet. That's just boot camp propaganda."

"Famous last words," said the Gunny.

"You got the H&I list for tonight?" asked the Lieutenant. "Where's Amagasu? He know how to do that yet?"

"Hell, there's nothin' to it, sir. A blind man could do it in a snowstorm. Kenny's over at motor pool changing the oil in the jeep. Jeep, shit, Mity-Mouse. Wonder when we're gonna lose another wheel. 'Bout due."

"Well, make sure Amagasu knows how to do it, will you? I don't think he understands the rating system yet."

102

"Rating system?" I laughed.

"Just do it, Ehrhart."

"Aye, aye, sir."

Plotting harrassment & interdiction fire was supposed to work like this: agents and informants fed reports of Vietcong activity to the national police and ARVN, who passed the reports along to American liaison personnel at Military Assistance Command–Vietnam (MACV) in Hoi An, who called them in to our battalion late every afternoon: "VC political cadre meeting, Ban Me Thuot village, grid coordinates BT394551, between 2300 and 0100 tonight"; or "Possible VC rocket attack in your area some time tonight; probable launch site AT877159." Things like that.

The reliability of the agent was designated by a letter, A through E; a good agent got an A, a mediocre agent a C, and so forth, with F assigned if the reliability of the agent could not be determined. Similarly, the reliability of the individual report was designated by a number from one to five in descending order of reliability, with a six assigned if the reliability of the report could not be estimated. Thus, an A/1 report was a highly probable report from a highly reliable agent.

The reports reached Battalion already evaluated; I never knew who did the evaluating, nor did I ever meet or see any of the agents. All I had to do was write the reports down, then go through them to find the ones with the good ratings, and determine how much artillery to drop on them, when and where. The final list had to be signed by Lieutenant Kaiser, then given to the operations officer on duty, who would transmit it to the artillery batteries.

There were several hitches, however. First of all, easily seventy-five percent of all reports always came in rated F/6: reliability of both the agent and the particular report indeterminate — which didn't help you very much. Most of the rest of the reports came in with ratings like C/6 or F/3, which wasn't much better. You almost *never* got an A/1, and getting even a B/2 was like hitting it big in Las Vegas. Add to *that* the certain knowledge that while some of the reports might actually come from real agents supporting the Saigon regime, many more of them undoubtedly came from Vietcong cadre and sympathizers, double agents, paid informants willing to make up anything for a buck, and people with grudges against their neighbors. Then add to *that* the fact that half the land area within range of our artillery was designated a Free Fire Zone — which meant that you could fire anything anywhere at anytime with no questions asked before or after —

and that even within the so-called restricted zones, Marines were getting killed and wounded day in and day out by the Vietcong.

When I'd first started plotting H&I, back in the Dark Ages, it seemed, I'd labored by the hour, pouring over the reports again and again, trying to determine some reasonable kind of list. But day after day and week after week and month after month of F/6s and F/3s and C/6s had proven the rating system to be as crazy as the rest of the war. I'd long since reduced the whole process to a pure simplicity.

"Kenny, forget about the rating system," I said later that evening. "It don't mean a goddamned thing. Dump on the B/2s with everything you got when you get one. Then put the rest of the stuff anywhere you want. Down here," I said, pointing on the map to the Free Fire Zone below Go Noi River, "you can keep 'em up all night."

"But there's civilians all over the place out there," said Kenny.

"Okay, bang your fuckin' head against the wall. Operations wants an H&I list every night. You don't like my system, you figure out a better one." I handed him the stack of reports; there were about thirty-five of them. He plotted them all on the H&I map, then sat there for awhile, alternately staring at the map and shuffling through the pile of reports.

"What am I supposed to do?" he finally asked. "They're all F/6."

"Hey, you're the one that doesn't wanna throw darts. Don't ask me."

Kenny sat there awhile longer. "Fuck," he said, throwing up his hands in exasperation.

"You got it, pal," I said. "Now I'll show you how to make life easy for yourself. Look, here's a C/3; fifty-fifty. Best one we got tonight." I checked the position of the report on the map. "Let's see. How about six rounds of 155 at 2300. Another six rounds at 0315. Fine. Okay. Here's an F/3. Next best. Give 'em twelve rounds of 105 at two minutes after midnight. Great." I looked at the map on which we kept a running monthly record of mining and sniping incidents. "Look here," I said, pointing to a cluster of dots, "lotta mines here lately. And this report here," I added, moving back to the H&I map, "is right smack in the middle of the cluster. Says Charlie's gonna have a meet tonight. Let's give 'em eighteen rounds of the big stuff in three batteries at forty-minute intervals beginning at 0130. You get the hang of it?"

"Yeh, I guess so," said Kenny hesitantly.

"Hey, Frank!" I hollered down to Corporal Scanlon, the

104

operations assistant on duty at the other end of the COC. "Got a minute?"

"What's up?" he asked, walking over to the S-2 shop.

"H&I. Got any druthers?" I asked, pointing to the map.

"Ain't that the ville that patrol from Delta got hit in last week?" he said, pointing to a hamlet out near Phuoc Trac Bridge.

"Just outside of it," I said.

"Why don'tcha drop a few on those bastards?"

"Right you are, Frank. How much you want?"

"Oh, take it easy on 'em. Make it a Battery one, oh-fives."

"Six rounds it is. 0425 sound about right? Now you pick one, Kenny."

"I don't know," Kenny said slowly.

"Sure you do. Chinese restaurant-style. One from column A, two from column B. Come on; I don't wanna be here all night."

"Well, how about here?" said Kenny, tentatively pointing to a dot on the map.

"You got it. Where's the report? VC political team. No time. What time you want? Wanna listen to 'em go out? Make it early."

"2100? 2115," Kenny said, this time with more conviction.

"Fine. How much?"

"Six rounds?"

"Great. Want the big stuff? 155s?"

"Sure."

"Great. Okay. Done. See? It's easy. I told ya you could do it." We continued on until we'd completed a list of about a dozen targets. "That's all there is to it, Kenny. Operations gets their list, and we don't lose any sleep."

"I do," said Kenny. "I'm on berm tonight."

"Well!" I beamed, "more's the better. You can check off the whole list as it goes out tonight. Give you something to do. Take this down to Lieutenant Kaiser's hooch so he can sign it, then bring it back and give it to Scanlon or the officer on duty. I'm goin' over to Gerry's. See you in the morning."

Many hours later, the sudden sharp hammering of small-arms fire and exploding grenades sent me flying out of the hooch before I was hardly awake. "Jesus fucking Christ, we're gettin' hit," I thought as I stumbled full tilt in the general direction of the fire. Still in my skivvies, I'd had time only to grab the essentials: rifle, cartridge belt, flak jacket, helmet and boots. All around me, in similar states of disarray, other Marines scrambled pell-mell toward the berm. Orange and green lines of tracer rounds zipped through the air over my head. The gunfire and explosions were coming from just beyond the berm to the right of the COC.

"They're goin' for the COC," I thought, my stomach sinking. "Shit! We're in for it." I ran toward the guard bunker just to the right of the COC and pitched myself into it headlong. Untangling myself, I came up between Amagasu and Ivan Pelinski, one of the other operations assistants.

"Keep your head down," Pelinski said hoarsely. "All hell's broke loose out there."

"I can tell that much. What the hell's goin' on?" Someone behind us kept hollering, "Hold your fire! Hold your fire!"

"The VC are knocking hell out of the PFs," said Pelinski.

"Well, fuck, man! They could be comin' through our wire by now. Where the hell's the Claymore detonator? Somebody get a finger on it, will ya?" I stuck my head up for a quick look. Small dark figures darted back and forth inside the Popular Forces compound just beyond our wire. The gunfire continued without let-up, but only random fire was directed toward our berm. Several grenades exploded in quick succession. I ducked down again.

"Charlie's inside their wire," I said.

"I think they were inside the wire before they opened up," said Amagasu.

"Fuckin' PFs, asleep at the wheel. Who was on when it started?"

"I was," said Amagasu

"You didn't see anything?"

"Not till it started. They must have come in through the ville."

The intensity of the fire began to diminish. Pelinski spun around quickly. "Who goes there?" he challenged.

"Sergeant of the guard. Any casualties here?"

"No; we're all okay," I said. He crawled into the bunker, stuck his head up and looked around. "We goin' out after 'em, Sergeant Barron?"

"No. Got orders to hold."

"What the fuck for? I could hit 'em with a grenade from here. Let's go get 'em, for chrissake."

"Colonel says no. This may only be a diversion."

"But they're right fuckin' *there*! At least let us fire on 'em."

"Just shut up, will you? Who is that? Ehrhart? I mighta known. Say, your mother send you any banana bread lately?"

"Oh, Jesus Christ."

"Look, I got my orders. Don't gimme a hard time. Just sit tight. I'll see you later."

Rapidly now, the gunfire trickled away to nothing. I stuck my head up again. There were several fires burning. I could see a couple of bodies lying helter-skelter, but there was no movement. "I don't fuckin' believe it," I said. "We spend months and months runnin' all over hell lookin' for the fuckin' gooks, never find a goddamned thing. So here they are just knockin' at the door, and we don't lift a finger. Just fuckin' crazy, man."

I looked at my watch: 0430. We just sat there. And sat there. And sat there. An hour went by. Two hours. It began to get light. The breaking dawn, turning grey to pink to fire red and pale blue, revealed the aftermath of bedlam. The PF compound was a charred smoking ruin. Every bunker had been blown up and caved in. I could see at least four bodies, all of them in the green dungarees of the PFs. "They got every last one of 'em, I'll bet," I said.

"And all of the weapons and equipment," Pelinski added.

"Stand down!" someone shouted; word went down all along the line. Marines up on the berm began trudging back toward the hooches, shuffling slowly along in ones and twos and threes, shoulders bent with fatigue.

"I'm gonna catch an hour's sleep, Kenny," I said. "Wake me up when you come off. I'll do the I-Sum; you sleep in. I'll tell the Lieutenant." As I came down off the berm, I saw Lieutenant Kaiser walking out of the COC. "Yo, Lieutenant!" I hollered.

"Nice legs, Ehrhart," Kaiser laughed. I'd forgotten I was still in my underwear.

"Come-as-you-are party, sir. You been in there all night?"

"Since the fun started, yeh."

"What the fuck, sir. Why didn't we go after 'em?"

"It looked too damned easy, Ehrhart. The Colonel thought it might be an ambush or a diversion."

"Yeh, well, maybe so, sir, but how we gonna write it up in the I-Sum? 'PF compound annihilated as entire Marine battalion looks on.' You know something, sir? I think that attack's what Tranh—that little boy—was tryin' to warn us about yesterday."

"I thought of that, too," said the Lieutenant. He reached out and patted me on the shoulder. "Don't worry about it, boy; it's too late now."

"It wasn't too late yesterday, sir."

"Well, it is now. And listen, Ehrhart, hold your tongue about this around Sergeant Taggart. You'll lose your temper, and he'll run you up before the Colonel — and I might not be able to bail you out. Lose that new stripe of yours before you even get it. In fact, you better watch your mouth all the way around; Taggart and the Gunny are gettin' pretty chummy. Just let it go, will you?"

"Yes, sir. But what do I say to Tranh?"

"Go put some clothes on."

Later that day, I went out to the front gate several times, but Tranh never showed up. None of the children did. As the days slowly wore on, it became obvious that the kids were never coming back again.

Chapter 17

Early on the morning of August first, just before dawn, eighteen massive amphibious tractors roared to life and began churning single-file through the back gate of the battalion compound. Aboard the tractors were two companies of Marines and a sizeable command group. Accompanied by two amphibious tanks, the amtracs filed out one behind the other across the long low sand dunes, thrusting northeast toward the Horseshoe.

A mile or so south of the lake, the whole column suddenly veered due east and rumbled out onto the beach, turning south and lumbering along the coastline. The people of Phuoc Trac village, up early and already preparing their fishing boats for another day on the South China Sea, stood watching in silence as the column passed. Some of them waved, as a child might wave to a passing train, but their faces were expressionless.

When the amtracs reached the mouth of the Go Noi River, the column halted and the Marines riding on the flat tops of the huge rectangular boxes disembarked. The tops of the tractors cranked open. The front ramps dropped. The Marines scrambled into the cavernous holds. The front ramps closed. Then, one by one, the amtracs nosed into the surf, the vast bulk of each tractor disappearing below the water like a green steel iceberg.

Only the flat now-open tops were visible, as the whole column turned west up the river like some jerky mechanical watersnake. Off the port side to the south lay the low shoreline of Barrier Island, a sandy beach with scrubby trees and bushes just behind it. Heavy machineguns mounted in sandbagged positions atop the amtracs began firing, chattering hoarsely at the south shore of the river. Then the stubby modified 105-millimeter howitzers several of the tractors carried joined in, softening up the landing area in preparation for the assault.

The Marines aboard the tractors joked nervously, peering cautiously over the sides at the beach. At last the tractors veered left and bore in on the landing area. Stomachs wrenched. Men made the sign of the cross, or closed their eyes and dropped their heads. Equipment rattled as Marines checked one last time to reassure themselves that ammunition magazines and grenades were secure and accessible. A terrible exhilaration swept the tractors as the tractors swept ashore.

A square of light, sand and trees appeared in front of me as the ramp dropped. "Hit the beach!" someone shouted. "Go! Go! Go!" As fast as you can run with seventy pounds of combat gear, I raced down the ramp in a burst of fear and adrenalin, across the short beach, and up into the trees, flopping myself down behind the first cover I reached. All around me, Marines shouted, "Gung ho!" "Get some!" "Geronimo!" Officers and beach marshals directed men into the tree-line.

But no one was shooting. There was nothing to shoot at. Absolutely nothing. The battle cries rapidly died off into an awkward silence. I waited awhile, then stood up and walked over to Gunny Johnson.

"What the fuck, Gunny?" I said.

"Beats me," he replied, shrugging his massive shoulders. "Got a cigarette? I musta lost mine or somethin'."

"Yeh, sure," I said, handing him a pack of Lucky Strikes. "They're toasted."

"What?"

"They're toasted," I repeated. "Look on the pack. See? 'It's Toasted.'"

"So what?"

"I just thought you might like to know that. They must put 'em in toasters, you know; two packs at a time." The Gunny and I both sat down on a log. It was blazing hot already, the sun dancing vast sheets of rippling fire across the surface of the river in front of us. I took off my helmet and wiped my forehead with my sleeve. Gunny Johnson's upper lip dripped like a leaky faucet. I wanted to reach over and wipe it. "Looks like another hike in the country," I said.

110

"You wanted to come along."

"Oh, I'm not complaining. Anything's better than sitting around the CP." It was true: *anything* was better than that. I'd been cooped up in the COC for more than six weeks, give or take a few runs to the national police, and the new corporal's stripe had had only limited effect in keeping me out of Lieutenant Kaiser's hair. When this operation had come up, I'd finally managed to badger him into letting me go.

"Okay, Ehrhart," he'd finally said, "but you don't do *anything* with the scouts. Strickly S-2: prisoners and detainees, captured material. No heroics, no tank rides, no John Wayne. You do what Gunny Johnson says — and nothing else, or I'll kick your ass from here to Hanoi and back."

We'd known for months that the Vietcong were using Barrier Island as a staging point for attacks against our positions to the north of the Go Noi River. A triangular island bounded by the South China Sea on the east, the main branch of the Go Noi on the north, and a narrow finger of the river on the long hypotenuse-like southwest side, Barrier Island was about fifteen miles long and four miles wide across the top, tapering down to a vee at the south end. It was not garrisoned by American or ARVN troops, and was only occasionally patrolled. Sparsely populated by farmers and fishermen, it was a free fire zone for artillery, but was otherwise unmolested on a day-to-day basis. It was, in short, an area the Vietcong could use with impunity. This operation, Operation Pike, would give Charlie something to think about.

"So where the fuck are they?" asked Roland Morgan, directing his question to no one in particular as he, Wally and Sergeant Wilson approached the Gunny and me.

"You kidding?" said Wilson, plopping himself down. "They're long gone." He pointed toward the south. "They were packin' their bags before we ever left the CP. All those amtracs cluster-fuckin' around the CP yesterday — Charlie knew *somethin'* was up. The minute they fired up those engines this morning, every VC between Danang and Tam Ky musta heard the racket. A few smoke signals, tom-tom drums, and goodbye Charlie."

"You don't think we fooled 'em with that little head-fake toward the Horseshoe?" Gunny Johnson deadpanned.

Sergeant Wilson snorted.

"Well, hell," Wally beamed in his Texas drawl, as if he'd just discovered gravity, "in that case, why don't we just pack it in and go home?"

"The Colonel comes home with nothin' in the bag," said Sergeant Wilson, "and he doesn't get to be a general."

"Saddle up!" someone shouted. "Let's move!"

"If the mountain won't come to Mohammed," said Sergeant Wilson, "then Mohammed'll just have to go find the vc."

"Huh?" said Morgan.

"Don't you read the Koran, Rolly?" Wilson laughed.

"What's that?" said Morgan.

"The Moslem holy book. Like our bible. Come on, let's go." Wilson shouted to the other scouts: "Mogerty, Hofstatter, get out front with Morgan and Walters. Rest of you take the rear. Maintain visual contact." The two rifle companies had already fanned out on line all the way across the island. The idea was to flush the Vietcong out like a tiger hunt, driving them toward units of the 51st ARVN Regiment that were supposed to be blocking along the river on our right flank. The whole ponderous procession slowly started south, the command group just behind the rifle companies.

"You know a lot of stuff, Sergeant Wilson," I said as we shuffled along. "How come you joined the Marines? You oughta be an officer."

"Officer?! No thanks," he replied. "Anyway, I couldn't be an officer if I wanted to; never finished the tenth grade. My family was dirt poor, Ehrhart. Pa was a sharecropper in Tennessee. Still is. Works a worthless piece of land that wouldn't grow rocks, and had to feed six kids off it. I'm the oldest. Yanked me outta school to help as soon as he could. Wasn't his fault; he was just tryin' to get by, but I figured I'd be stuck in those hills on that worthless chunk of land till I died. So I ran off and enlisted. I was eighteen. I've sent 'em more money over the years than I'd ever been able to get outta the ground there. Bought 'em a tractor — used to use a mule when I was a kid. Put my brother and sister through college on Marine Corps pay. He's got a good business now in Chattanooga; she's a teacher in Memphis. And two more of the boys are in college right now. I owe that to the Corps; it's a fair trade."

"You been in since you were eighteen?"

"Fifteen years."

"Jesus."

"It ain't a bad life."

"You don't act like a lifer."

Wilson laughed. "How does a lifer act?"

"Well, you know. Like Gunny Johnson. Cover your ass and make the troopies sweat — all that Mickey Mouse stuff. You're like, well, you're like one of us."

112

"I just try to do what makes sense to me. Mind my own business and do my job."

The temperature was well above a hundred. The heat pressed down from a cloudless sky and rose out of the ground in visible waves that distorted vision at less than 200 meters. Progress was slow. Now and then, sporadic gunfire would erupt in front of us, but it never lasted long. As the hours ticked by, we picked our way down the flat sandy island dotted with stunted trees and ragged bushes, occasionally passing an isolated hooch in the middle of bone-dry rice fields waiting for the heat to pass and the autumn planting to begin.

We picked up every male Vietnamese we encountered. None of them were armed, but they would be questioned later about Vietcong activity on the island. By late afternoon, I found myself in charge of a straggly group of six older men, their dirty pajamas hanging from bony bodies, their gray wispy chin-beards dangling long strands of thin hair in the hot breeze, their hands tied behind their backs. We were moving across an open sandy area when suddenly the crack of incoming sniper fire erupted.

I hit the deck immediately as bullets zipped around me, thwacking into the earth nearby. Though there were no visible targets, Marines began returning fire in the general direction of the incoming, the intensity quickly rising to a sharp firefight. Suddenly I realized that most of the detainees were still on their feet, confused and frightened by the gunfire. I knocked a couple of them down with my rifle—those I could reach without standing up—wielding it like a club, but four of them took off running toward a treeline off to my left.

"Dung lai! Dung lai!" I hollered several times, but they kept on running. Staff Sergeant Taggart and Staff Sergeant Trinh were shouting at them, too.

"Waste 'em!" Taggart shouted at me. "Shoot, goddamn it!" I picked out the one farthest away, sighted in and fired one round. The man went down like he'd been hit on the back of the head with a brick. The others stopped instantly. Then one of the others suddenly snapped up straight and twisted sharply to the ground, caught by someone in the crossfire. The other two dropped to their bellies.

In a few minutes the shooting stopped, trickling off like an engine sputtering out of gas. Marines all over the ground began to rise warily. I helped the two prisoners near me to their feet, then headed toward the other four. Two of them were dead. Taggart came over and began kicking the other two to their feet, shouting at them in Vietnamese. Trinh glared at Taggart, but said nothing.

"Let 'em be," said Sergeant Wilson, walking over to Taggart and grabbing his shoulder. Wilson and Taggart stared at each other for a moment.

"Fuckin' gooks tried to run," said Taggart. He walked over to the two bodies, reached into his pocket and dropped an ace of spades by each body, then turned and walked away.

We camped for the night where we were. Nearby was a dry rice field surrounded by a high dike that formed a natural defensive perimeter. The amtracs had not come ashore with us, having been on short-term loan from other Marine outfits, but the two tanks had stayed. Both drove into the field, taking up positions at the two southerly corners. Morgan and Newcome walked over to a nearby hooch and came back with a Vietnamese man, leaving a woman and several children standing in the doorway. "Put him with the others," said Gunny Johnson. "Ehrhart, tie their feet — I don't wanna have to go chasin' after 'em in the middle of the night."

I tied all five of the prisoners, then sat down and opened a can of beef stew. I hadn't eaten all day, but after two or three mouthfuls, I realized that I wasn't hungry at all. It was nearly dark. I threw the unfinished can over the paddy dike, laid my poncho out for a ground-cloth, and stretched out. It felt good to lie down, but I couldn't sleep.

One of the prisoners moaned loudly. Lying there in the sticky darkness, I thought of the day on frozen Lake Lenape when I was about nine years old and for no reason I could understand, Jerry Dougherty had begun punching me in the face over and over again, taunting me to fight, and I didn't know how and was far too frightened even to try to defend myself, and so I'd just stood there crying while the other boys stood around us laughing. And the time in the boys' room on the second floor of the junior high school when Lloyd Drescher started pushing me around and I'd been saved only by the timely appearance of my tough pal, Larry Carroll, and Larry and I went off to lunch with me telling him what I had been about to do to Lloyd and knowing it was all lies and still shaking so hard inside I could barely control my voice. And the time, only a year before I'd enlisted, when Jimmy Whitson had spit in my face at a party and said he was going to kill me for messing with "his girl," and I'd left by the back door at the first opportunity, and after that "his girl" had never treated me the same again.

"Ask a Marine," the recruiting posters had said; "Tell It to the Marines." I thought of the old man lying a few hundred meters away, his hands still tied behind his back, the small hole in the back of his head, and half of his face blown off. I thought of the woman in the rice field back in June, and the young girl with the AK-47 in the photograph. I thought of Sadie Thompson, my Quaker friend. My stomach teetered on the edge of sickness, and the long hot night seemed to stand still.

The next morning, we continued south. The temperature must have broken a hundred within an hour after sunrise. No one said very much. You just shuffled along, pushing one boot after the other in an endless game of Slinky toy, unconsciously husbanding what little energy was available. Around mid-morning, we came onto a small cluster of houses — or rather, what was left of them. The hooches had been blown to splinters, probably the night before. There was no one around but a middle-aged woman sitting amid the rubble in a dark pool of coagulated blood. She was holding a small child who had only one leg and half a head, and she had a tremendous gaping chest wound that had ripped open both of her breasts. Flies swarmed loudly around mother and child. The woman was in a kind of trance, keening softly and gently rocking her baby. She did not notice us at all.

"Holy Christ, what hit this place?" said Pelinski.

"Artillery," I said, trying to hold my voice steady, "or naval gunfire. The VC got nothing big enough to do this kind of damage." One of the corpsmen came over and looked at the woman, then gave her a shot of morphine.

"Nothin' else I can do for her," he said. "She'll be dead soon."

We left her sitting there and continued south after the VC. Periodically, someone would keel over from heat exhaustion, and we'd pick him up and put him on one of the tanks for awhile.

"You better not crap out, Ehrhart," Gunny Johnson laughed. Lieutenant Kaiser said no tank rides for you." I tried to think of a snappy reply, but it was too hot to think.

"Hey, look at this!" Corporal Scanlon shouted. He was off to one side of the trail, standing in front of a tree he'd just urinated on. Several of us hustled over. Staring down at us from the tree was General Nguyen Van Thieu — or rather, a picture of him. It was a campaign poster for the upcoming presidential elections in September.

I knew from high school that the Republic of Vietnam was a democracy, but that there hadn't been a presidential election since Ngo Dinh Diem had become president back in the mid-fifties, not long after North and South Vietnam had been created by the Geneva Convention of 1954 that had ended the French colonization of Indochina. Elections were to have been held, but Communist guerrilla activity

115

in the South had made it impossible to hold free elections since. I knew also that Diem had been overthrown and killed, shortly before the assassination of John Kennedy, by a group of South Vietnamese generals, precipitating eighteen months of coup and counter-coup culminating with the flamboyant and colorful Air Vice Marshal Nguyen Cao Ky, the present premier, at the helm.

But the war against the Vietcong was going well enough, according to the *Time* magazine I got every week, that a new election was finally going to be held—the first in twelve or thirteen years. General Thieu was one of the candidates. I had no idea who he was, but I could tell that *somebody* didn't like him: the smiling face on the poster sported a hastily penciled-in-moustache, jaunty goatee and blackened left eye.

"Wonder who did the artwork," said Scanlon.

"Probably the VC," said Pelinski.

"Somebody's got balls putting that thing up out here in Charlie's front yard," I said, "or a strange sense of humor."

"Think he'll win?" Scanlon mused.

"Yep," I said. "I read in the papers that Washington likes him."

"What about Ky?"

"They talked him into being vice president. Probably offered him a vacation villa on the French Riviera and stock options on General Motors."

"Anybody runnin' against 'em?"

"Some neutralist. Wants a nonpartisan coalition government."

"Good luck."

That day passed, and a good part of the next one, but we made no contact with armed Vietcong guerrillas. The detainees we dragged along with us—there were about twenty of them by now—kept telling Taggart and Trinh that the Vietcong had left a few days before, but they couldn't have been too far ahead of us because we kept taking periodic sniper fire. It was tedious and nervewracking. The ARVN blocking units had reported no one trying to flee across the river on our right flank, and we were nearly to the southern tip of the island.

"I wouldn't trust the fuckin' ARVN, anyway," said Wally.

We reached the end of the island about midafternoon of the third day. There we were on one bank of the river. There were the ARVN, waving to us from the other side of the river, hopping up and down beneath their oversized American-made helmets, looking like self-propelled mushrooms. The Vietcong were nowhere.

"Wha'd I fuckin' tell ya?" said Wally.

116

"Hey, Sergeant Wilson," I said, "the Colonel ain't gonna like this. He's still comin' home with nothin' in the bag."

"Shoulda done like I said in the first place," said Wally.

"C'est la guerre," said Wilson, shrugging his shoulders.

"What now?" I asked Gunny Johnson.

"Chopper's comin' in to pick up these gooks," he said, pointing to the cluster of detainees. "You ride north with 'em. Dump the gooks at Hieu Nhon; somebody'll be there to drive you back to the CP."

"What are you guys gonna do?"

"Goin' back up the river in boats. Ain't enough choppers to fly us all back."

"Where's the boats? I wanna go on a boat ride."

"They're comin' in on the chopper—those inflatable rubber kind with the little outboards—and you're goin' *out* on the chopper. You know what the Lieutenant said. The prisoners go out on the chopper, and you go with 'em."

"Hello, Lieutenant!" I said, walking into the COC.

"Ehrhart! Well, glad to see you made it back, boy—though I must say, it certainly has been pleasant around here without you buggin' me all the time. How was it?"

"Hike in the country, sir. Never saw nothin' the whole fuckin' time. Got shot at a little, but couldn't run 'em down. Jesus, I don't know how they do it; slippery as eels. The ARVN blocking force worked about as good as a thin slice of Swiss cheese. You watch, sir, tomorrow night we'll get hit with rockets off the island. I get any mail, Kenny?"

"Yeh," said Amagasu, "it's over in the hooch."

"Why don't you go get cleaned up, Ehrhart?" said Lieutenant Kaiser. "You need a shave—got a little peach fuzz on your chin there. Get some chow, too. And go tell Griffith you're back; he's been up here five times a day askin' about you. Guy's worse than me. Amagasu, you go eat, too, if you want."

"Yessir," we both said, and off we went. Back at the hooch, I started through the mailbag before I even took my boots off.

"What are we supposed to do with these?" Kenny asked.

"What is it?"

"Look." Kenny was holding several brand new still-in-the-wrapper decks of playing cards. He opened a pack. "They're all the same," he said, flipping through the deck to reveal 52 aces of spades.

"No shit! Where'd you get 'em?"

"Talbot gave me a whole pile of them. Some playing card company sent a whole big box of them yesterday. Talbot thought it was funny. I was too embarrassed to tell him, but I don't understand."

"It's the ace of spades, Kenny. The high card. The evil eye." Kenny looked perplexed. "I don't know why, but the ace of spades really spooks the Vietnamese. Maybe somethin' to do with their religion or something. Wanna have some fun? Next time you drive to Dien Ban or Hieu Nhon, ride through the market flashin' one of them aces. Folks start shuckin' and jivin' and rollin' their eyes. They don't like it at all. Guys get a kill, you know, they leave the ace of spades on the body. 'Course, you gotta bust up a good deck of cards to do that. Somebody back in the World musta heard about it. A whole damn case of 'em, you say? Fuckin' thoughtful of 'em. Ranks right up there with Avis."

"What?"

"You know the Avis Rent-a-Car Company? Look," I said, putting the mailbag aside and reaching into one of my ammo-box footlockers. I pulled out one of the camouflaged "We Try Harder" buttons and handed it to Amagasu. "Here, have a cigar."

"Are you shittin' me?"

"Seein's believin'. Got 'em in the mail back in March or early April. Couple of thousand of 'em," I said resuming my search through the mailbag.

"That's sick."

"That's American free enterprise, buddy. Sort of like chocolate chip cookies, you know? What do you think we're fightin' for around here, the emperor?"

"It's still sick."

"I was born into it. What's your excuse?" I reached the bottom of the mail sack, coming up with a letter from my parents and one from Sadie Thompson. "Shit! Shit, shit! No fuckin' mail from Jenny. Goddamn it. Let's eat. You got any of that funny stuff?"

"Sure."

"Don't try to slip me any of that hot cabbage. Hey, I gotta go tell Gerry I'm back. You got enough for him, too? I'll give you some money on payday."

"I've got plenty. Don't worry about it. My parents send it to me free."

"You miss your folks?"

"Sure, don't you?"

"Yeh, sure. Oh, yeh, I forgot, we're kinda in the same boat around here, ain't we?"

118

"Sayonara. Go get Gerry; I'll start cooking."

The COC was alive with crackling radios and tension when Kenny and I walked back in. "What's up?" I asked Lieutenant Kaiser.

"The boats got ambushed about an hour ago," he said, "comin' up along the west side of the island—where the ARVN blocking force was supposed to be."

"*Shit!*" I shouted, banging my fist on the table. "There was *nothin'* there, sir! Three fuckin' days! Just *once* I'd like to get the goddamned fuckin' gooks out in the open!"

"Take it easy, boy," said the Lieutenant, putting a hand on my shoulder. "No point in busting up the two-shop."

"Sorry, sir, it's just ... Jesus fuckin' -A Christ. How bad did they get hit? Where are they now?"

"We don't know. They're somewhere in here," he said, pointing on the map to a place about midway up the west side of the island. "The boats got separated. A couple of them capsized. They're spread out all over on either side of the river. They're getting air support now, and we're tryin' to get enough choppers to extract 'em. Nothing to do but wait." The Lieutenant paused for a moment, then continued, "Ehrhart, I'm glad you ain't with 'em. At least I don't have to worry about you."

"I, uh—thank you, sir. It feels weird, though, sir, bein' here. You know? I hope they get out okay."

"I know you do, boy," he said. "I do, too."

An hour later, just before dark, the whop-whop of helicopter blades drifted into the COC, and shortly thereafter, Gunny Johnson walked in. He had nothing on but a pair of damp jungle utilities.

"Went for a swim, huh, Gunny?" said the Lieutenant without smiling. "You okay?"

"Yessir, but you'll need a new chief scout. Ward got hit in the neck and the side. He was still alive when they put him on the medevac, but he won't be back. Taggart's dead. Trinh got hit in the arm, but not bad; he came out with us. Rest of the scouts are okay. Those two operations clerks bought it."

"Pelinski and Scanlon?" said Kenny.

"Yeh. Bunch of other guys, too. I don't know who they were. Grunts from the rifle companies. Jesus Christ, I never saw anything like it. They had us cold right in the middle of the river. Opened up from both banks with machineguns." The Gunny plunked himself down wearily in a chair. "Well Ehrhart," he said, "too bad you missed the boat ride."

Chapter 18

The next afternoon, Amagasu and I were sitting in the S-2 shop when a bunch of strangers walked into the COC through the door down at the operations end of the bunker. Most of them were wearing green utilities, but a few were in civilian clothing.

"Hey!" I said to Amagasu, "I know that man."

"Who?"

"Down there. The Negro. That's Floyd Patterson."

"Who's that?"

"Floyd Patterson. Former heavyweight boxing champion of the world. Only man ever to win the title, lose it, and win it back again. Wow! What's he doin' here?"

The Champion moved slowly through the COC, stopping to shake hands and chat with the guys on radio watch and in the message center. He still looked like an athlete: tight and sleek, the muscles beneath his loose-fitting civilian clothes rippling perceptibly.

"You're Floyd Patterson, aren't you?" I said when he reached us.

"That's right," he said, extending his hand. "Who are you?"

"Corporal William Ehrhart. This is Lance Corporal Amagasu."

"Where you from?" asked the Champion.

"Perkasie, Pennsylvania," I replied, "near Philadelphia." Amagasu briefly explained where he was from and how he'd ended up in the Marine Corps.

"Well, good for you," the Champion said to Amagasu. "That's what America's all about."

"What are you doin' here, Mr. Patterson?" I asked.

"Floyd," he said. "I just wanted to come over here and thank you boys for what you're doing. I'm proud to be an American, and I just wanted you fellas to know that. How are things going?"

"Oh, not too bad," I said. "We're hangin' in there. Say, Champ, I saw you beat Johanssen on television when you won the title back. I was just little then, but I still remember it. That was a great fight, Champ."

"Well, thank you, Corporal. How old are you now?"

"Eighteen. Be nineteen the end of next month."

"Is that your girl?" asked the Champion, pointing to the color portrait of Jenny on my desk.

"Yessir; my fiancée. Name's Jenny."

"Mighty pretty. Keep's you going, huh?"

"Thank you, sir. Yessir, she does indeed. Say, Champ, can I ask you something while you're here?"

"Sure. Shoot."

"What do you think of this Cassius Clay business? You think he should be allowed to keep the title?"

"Well, I'll tell you," he said, his whole body shifting slightly, "Clay—you know, he likes to be called Mohammed Ali now; says he's a Black Muslim—he's a heck of a good fighter. Maybe one of the best. But he's an American, too, and I think he's forgotten that. Even a champion's not above the law and the responsibilities of being a citizen. If he won't defend his country, he shouldn't be allowed to defend his title. It's not fair to you boys."

"We'd better keep moving," said one of the officers in Patterson's entourage.

"Sorry I can't stay longer, fellas," said the Champion. "I'm pleased to meet you, though. Thanks again for what you're doing. Folks back home are real proud of you. Take care of yourselves now, and I'll see you when you get back home." We shook hands again, and then he was gone.

"How about that?" I said to Amagasu. "A real champion right here in the two-shop. I shoulda asked for his autograph."

"I never heard of him," said Amagasu.

Chapter 19

"You been sayin' you wanna go swimming in the South China Sea since the day I met you," said Gerry. "There it is, sucker; go to it."

"Yahoo!" I shouted, tossing my towel aside and racing full tilt across the beach. "Last one in's a rotten egg!" I high-stepped in to my knees, plunged headfirst, glided underwater, surfaced like a breaching whale, and began stroking strongly away from shore. The water was warm, the surface flat and calm, and my body hadn't felt so buoyant and free in months — years, it seemed. I did a flip turn, pushed off an imaginary wall, came out on my back, and started slowly sculling, squirting water out of my mouth like a fireboat on the Fourth of July. Gerry paddled up beside me, and we both began to tread water.

"Salty," he said, spitting out a mouthful.

"Fuckin'-A!" I shouted, "Just like me. I'm salty! Halfway there, chump. It's all fuckin' downhill from here."

The In-Country Rest & Recuperation Center at China Beach, Danang, wasn't exactly Hong Kong or Singapore, but it gave Marines a chance to escape the war for a day or two. The facility included a snack bar where you could buy beer and soda, hamburgers and hot dogs, and listen to the juke box, an outdoor theater for movies, a small barracks for Marines spending the night, and a long stretch of wide, clean beach. Lieutenant Kaiser had given me two days off to celebrate the halfway point in my tour of duty, and Gerry and I had hopped a truck for the beach that morning. We didn't have to be back till the next evening.

Gerry and I paddled around awhile, letting the water massage our bodies and soak the dirt from armpits and toes and fingernails. We played a game of submarine, and stood on the bottom on our hands.

"I wish there were some waves," I said. "I'd like to do a little body surfing. Let's get out awhile." We stretched our towels out on the sand and lay down in the hot sun. The beach was lined with Marines in camouflage shorts and cut-off utility trousers. At either end of the beach were lifeguard towers, each with two lifeguards and a fully dressed armed Marine.

"Boy, this is weird," I said.

"What?"

"This beach. No girls; just guys."

"Whadja expect? Joey Heatherton?"

"'Course not. But the beach, you know, there's supposed to be girls. Back in New Jersey, Christ, you should see Ocean City on Memorial Day. Fuckin' fur-pie everywhere. Wall-to-wall beavers. Two piece bikinis with little hairs stickin' out around the crotch. Tits hangin' out. Legs right up to the asshole."

"Hey, shut up, will you? Jesus, you wanna blow a fuse?" I piped down, and we both lay there for awhile with our eyes closed.

"Gerry?"

"Yeh?"

"I haven't gotten a letter from Jenny in three weeks."

"Last week it was two weeks. Don't worry about it, will you? She probably went on vacation or something."

"She'd have told me about that. Anyway, she could write on vacation. It's startin' to worry me, you know? What if she's been in a car wreck or something? Jesus, I'd go nuts."

"If somethin' happened to her, somebody would've written to you."

"I don't know. When I was in boot camp, a high school friend of mine got killed in a car wreck. Suzie Brenner. We weren't boyfriend and girlfriend or nothin', but we were pretty tight. My parents didn't tell me till I got home on leave."

"You're gonna go Section Eight, you keep thinkin' like that, pal. Look, she's okay. It's probably just the mail. Talbot says mail gets sent the wrong fuckin' place all the time. Just be patient, will ya? Take it easy. I'm thirsty. Salt water's got my mouth all parched. Let's go get a beer."

"You can't go in the slop-chute in your bathing suit. Gotta get dressed."

123

"You wanna go in the water anymore?"

"Nah, I guess not. Nothin' to do without any waves. Beach is too protected here. They got great waves down by Phuoc Trac."

"Yeh, they got beau coup VC, too," said Gerry. "They even got the fish trained, I bet. Fuckin' flounder swim right up to you, blow up right in your face."

"Look, Rocky; fan mail from some flounder," I said.

"What's it say, Bullwinkle?" said Gerry.

"Just listen. Ka-boom!!!"

We got dressed and walked up to the snack bar. The juke box was playing loudly.

"That asshole Haller'd have a field day around here," I said. "Listen to that shit. They don't even sing anymore. Just get loaded up on drugs and scream and throw up into the microphone. What the hell's goin' on back there in The World?"

"Aw, Haller's okay," said Gerry. "You ever talk to him?"

"Only when I have to." I downed two beers and two cheeseburgers in two minutes. "More beer! More cheeseburgers!" I hollered, thumping the empty can on the table. A young Vietnamese woman came over to the table with another round. "Ah, sweet cheeseburger queen, the girl of my dreams," I beamed. A guy at the table next to us patted her on the backside.

"You're gonna shit your fuckin' brains out tonight, sucker," Gerry warned. "You better go easy on that pogey-bait. Your stomach ain't used to it anymore."

"I don't care, I don't give a fuck; I ain't had a cheeseburger in eight months. This is hog holiday!" I roared, piling on pickles, onions, relish, catsup and mustard. "Bury me with a beer in each hand."

"Okay, buddy, just remember you asked for it," said Gerry. "Come to think of it, so did I." He grabbed another cheeseburger for himself. "When's Lieutenant Kaiser leaving?"

"Couple of weeks, maybe three. Sometime in early September."

"What're you goin' to do about Gunny Johnson?"

"Oh, I got him pretty well under control. I did everything he said when he got here; soon as he went back to sleep, I changed it all back the way it was. He never even noticed; he's just a lifer, man; he don't really care. Long as he thinks you think he's the boss. That fuckin' crap down on the river slowed him up a bit, too. Don't talk so loud anymore."

"What's happening with Sergeant Wilson, you heard?"

"Lieutenant said they were shipping him back to the States.

That's the last I heard. They're gonna give Seagrave another stripe and make him chief scout."

"Yeh? I thought they'd give it to Walters or Newcome."

"Naw. Wally and Mogerty are good, all right, but they're too crazy. Gravey's real steady. Don't get rattled and don't cut loose. He ain't Sergeant Wilson, but you just don't find many around like him. That guy's so smart — never finished tenth grade and taught himself Vietnamese. Learned Arabic when he was on embassy duty. All kinds of stuff — and a really good guy, too. I'm gonna miss him. Anyway, Gravey's a good choice; he'll take it real seriously. We're birthday buddies, 'dja know that? September thirtieth. He's exactly one year older than me."

"Geez," said Gerry, "nineteen and he's a sergeant already."

"You watch, pal; I'll be a sergeant before I turn twenty. Be eligible in December, and I ain't even nineteen yet. They're losin' bodies left and right around here. Gotta promote somebody, and Lieutenant Kaiser's been givin' me 4.9s and 5.0s on my pro & con marks. That oughta make up for the points I lose on time in service."

"Jesus, Ehrhart, how do you rate? I'm almost twenty-one and I ain't even a corporal yet."

"That might change pretty quick."

"You know somethin' I don't know?"

"I might."

"Well. Fork over. What is it?"

"Well, listen, don't buy the champagne yet, but I think you're on the list this time."

"How do you know?" said Gerry, poking his head up from behind a fourth cheeseburger.

"Lieutenant Kaiser looked. Amagasu's on it, and he said you are, too."

"Hot damn! It's about fuckin' time."

"What the hell, man, you don't do nothin' but sit around twirlin' your tumblers all day. Big Deal. Janitor could do that."

"Fuck you."

"I can't eat any more."

"Me neither. Wanna go swimming again?"

"I'm too drunk. And too full. Sharkbait." I burped loudly.

"Come on," said Gerry. "We could swim back to The World. We could swim to Sweden! Let's go. Only take us a couple of months. Straight out there to Hawaii, then southeast to the Panama Canal and over to Africa; turn left, up to Europe, through the English Channel and we're home free! How about it? We can be there by October. Think of it: blondes everywhere! Free love! Ingrid Bergman!"

"We can use our cocks for masts!" I shouted. "Tie our jungle jackets to 'em. Here come the Vikings! Arf, arf! Shiver me timbers, Brunhilde; I'm Beowulf, and this here's my sidekick, Tonto. We're lookin' for mead an' ale. Which way's the bedroom?"

"Wanna see the Hammer of Thor, Brunhilde? I've slain thousands with it."

"Look at 'em all lyin' there smiling. Line forms to the rear; no pushing! You're next, blondie."

"What're we waitin' for? Let's start stroking."

We both sat there for awhile, looking out to sea.

"Whaddaya wanna do?" asked Gerry.

"I don't now. Whadda you wanna do?"

"My stomach's feelin' a little shaky."

"So's mine. What time is it?"

"1430."

"Movie don't start till after dark."

"You wanna stay tonight?"

"I don't know. Do you?"

"Probably be the only time we get to come up here. I hate to waste it."

"Me, too."

"Well?"

"I don't know."

We both sat there for awhile.

"Let's hitch a ride back to Battalion," said Gerry.

"Okay."

Chapter 20

We had a wonderful four-holed outhouse at Battalion that was truly one of the engineering masterpieces of the Navy SeaBees. It was really a small walk-up hooch made of plywood, with a screen door and screened-in windows all around the upper half of the walls. The bench-type seat was sanded smooth to prevent splinters in tender places, and toilet paper hung on pegs within easy reach. The outhouse was built on high stilts to allow 55-gallon drums to be placed beneath each hole; these were removed daily, doused with gasoline and burned, a process known as "burning the shitters."

Though it was well after dark, Gerry and I had hardly left the outhouse since we'd gotten back from China Beach. After a number of trips back and forth between Gerry's hooch and the outhouse, we'd both given up and decided to remain seated, saving us both a lot of time and trouble.

"I almost didn't make it that last time," said Gerry.

"Jesus, I feel awful," I said. "Whadda they put in those cheeseburgers, anyway? Drano?"

"Water bo burgers," said Gerry, "imported from Hanoi." Suddenly gunfire erupted off to the south. It rapidly built to a steady sustained pitch, punctuated by explosions that sounded like grenades, mortars and light artillery.

"What the hell's goin' on?" I said, craning my neck back over my shoulder. "Jesus, look at that. You can see right over the berm from up here. I never noticed that before."

"Looks like Hoi An," Gerry said. At that moment, a general alert sounded through the compound, the great wailing sirens like fire whistles shattering the darkness. Marines began to pile out of hooches, hotfooting it helter-skelter for the berm. "Shit," said Gerry.

"Forget it," I said. "They'll never miss us. I ain't goin' anywhere. My asshole's so sore, I can't move."

"They're really gettin' hit down there. Better lace up your boots, just in case we gotta move in a hurry."

"This is amazing. You can see right over the berm from up here. Wonder why Charlie's never taken a shot at somebody takin' a crap."

"Even the gooks got some sense of decency. Jesus, somebody's *really* takin' a shellacking."

"Looks like two different places," I said. "That one on the right's Hoi An, probably the MACV compound. That other place on the left must be the national police headquarters at Hieu Nhon."

"Yo! Get outta there. Ya fuckin' deaf? General alert," someone hollered from the bottom of the steps. It sounded like the sergeant of the guard.

"We can't," I hollered back. "We're sick." The door opened.

"You two?!" said Sergeant Barron.

"Hi, Sarge," said Gerry. "We're sick. Can't move, doctor's order's."

"We went to China Beach today," I added. "They put Drano in our cheeseburgers. We been sittin' here since 1800. Honest."

"Somebody's gotta guard the crapper," said Gerry. "If they overrun us, we'll hold out to the last roll of ass-wipe."

"Did you know you can see right over the top of the berm from up here?" I pointed out. "We'll let you know if we see 'em comin'."

"You guys are gonna get your heads blown off," said Barron. "Serve you right, too. Why'd they ever let you in my Marine Corps?"

"That's what I'd like to know," said Gerry.

"We're volunteers of America," I said. "What's goin' on down there, anyway?"

"The prison in Hoi An and the national police headquarters at Hieu Nhon are both under attack. Looks like they're probably trying to spring the prisoners. MACV says they've got recoilless rifles and B-40s."

"Well, I was close. MACV takin' anything?" I asked.

"Just enough to keep 'em pinned inside their compound. Said the gooks are all over the city. Platoon from Delta tried to get through to Hieu Nhon, and stepped right into the shit. Colonel told 'em to forget it and pull back. Listen, you can stay in here if you want to — but be damned well ready to move. They just might try to hit here."

128

"Sure, Sarge. Thanks."

The fighting continued without slackening. From where we were, four miles away, it sounded like a continuous dull roar. You could see the soft flash of individual explosions and a wild criss-crossing of tracer rounds, some of them spinning up toward the stars before dying out like Roman candles. The whole thing looked like one of those animated representations of an atom, distorted and flattened into half a globe, the horizon hiding the other half. We could see half a dozen secondary fires.

"I wonder where Co Chi is tonight," I said.

"Who?"

"Miss Chi. You know, the secretary at Hieu Nhon I told you about. The really pretty one. Long hair. Always wears a white *ao dai.*"

"Oh, yeh. The one Trinh said wanted your picture."

"Yeh."

"You think she's there tonight?"

"I don't know. Don't know where she lives. Never said anything to her but hello. Doesn't speak English — and she's real shy."

"She wouldn't live there."

"I don't know. I hope not."

"Jesus."

"Yeh."

A tremendous explosion erupted, sending fire and burning debris high into the air; two more explosions followed.

"Wanna bet the vc just blew into the prison?" I said.

"No bet," said Gerry. "Who do they got in there?"

"Who'd they *have* in there. Everybody. Vc, detainees, suspects, murderers, robbers. Like a political prison and county jail all in one. Couple thousand inmates, maybe. Charlie just got a whole new division."

We lapsed into silence for awhile.

"This is unreal," said Gerry.

"What?"

"Watching this. Like the movies or somethin'."

Neither of us said anything else for a long time. Almost imperceptibly at first, the fire began to slacken; then it dropped off noticeably until there was only sporadic gunfire. Long periods of silence were briefly interrupted by bursts of machinegun and automatic rifle fire, an explosion here and there, all of it happening far away, almost on another planet. Half an hour passed. There was no shooting at all now.

"Jesus," said Gerry. Another fifteen minutes passed.

"That coulda been us," I said. Dark forms began withdrawing from the berm. Screen doors on hooches banged softly.

"How do you feel?" Gerry asked.

"Like I just had an enema of battery acid. How 'bout you?"

"Nothin' left inside of me. I've shit everything out—stomach, heart, liver, brain, the whole nine yards."

"Wanna try to sleep?"

"I guess so," said Gerry. "But I'm takin' one of these with me." He pulled up his trousers and stuck a roll of toilet paper in one of the big thigh pockets. I did, too.

Chapter 21

"Looks like the drought's over, Ehrhart," said Talbot, grinning broadly as he handed me the mail, "Handwriting on one of those letters looks suspiciously familiar."

"Goddamn," I said, hardly breathing. It was a letter from Jenny.

"Thought so," he said. "I told you not to worry."

"Yeh, thanks, Al," I said absently. I walked out of the mail hooch and up toward the COC, holding the letter as though it were the Host. I hadn't heard from Jenny in more than a month of twisting turning nightmares and vivid daydreams played out in slow motion: automobiles wrinkling like tinfoil under the force of high-speed impact, trapped bodies screaming, sirens and ambulances, hospitals, the deathly stillness of white sheets and nurses, cancer, leukemia, knives and threats in dark alleys on moonless nights. I walked slowly to the S-2 shop and sat down. I opened the letter.

"Dearest Bill," it began, "I guess you're wondering why I haven't written. I just didn't know how to explain." What followed was less an explanation than a simple farewell. The letter was brief, alien and distant—less than half a page. "Please forgive me," it concluded. "I pray God will protect you and keep you safe. You'll always be special to me. Jenny."

I couldn't make sense of it. I was prepared for horrible bodily injury, had already imagined myself spending a life caring for a woman with one leg, a blind woman, a woman confined to a wheelchair. Death I could have understood. Anything. But this. "This isn't possible," I thought. "This isn't *possible*! Eight fucking months!" Long letters. Passionate letters. Filled with every imagineable endearment. A perfect chain, like a rosary, a lifeline, a beacon. Gone just like that? "This isn't possible," I thought.

"What'sa matter, Corporal Ehrhart?" asked Gunny Johnson. I looked up. He and Lieutenant Kaiser were both staring at me.

"What? What? Nothing."

"You're white as a ghost, boy," said the Lieutenant. "You look like you got the DTs. Are you feelin' okay?"

"What? Yeh, sure. Nothing."

"What is it?" the Lieutenant persisted. "Bad news from home?"

No! No! No! *Please*, no! "What? I don't — what, sir?"

"Go lie down, boy," said Lieutenant Kaiser.

"What?"

"Go lie down," said Johnson.

I got up and walked out into the bright hot light. I started across the sand toward the hooches, stumbled, righted myself, turned toward the berm, walked to the top and sat down, staring up the road, watching the cloud of dust rising, drifting and finally disappearing after Saunders' jeep.

Wait, Jimmy, wait. Come back. You didn't teach me about this. I'm sorry, Tranh; I didn't know. Taggart's dead now; you can come back. Please. Roddenbery, don't walk there, don't step there, come back. Without his lifelong friend, Puff could not be brave. It was an old woman; it's just an old woman; didn't even have a weapon. Imagine Grandma Conti with a rifle. The kid's got a grenade. Jesus, look out. Look at the shaved heads, look at the yellow robes, they're monks, Buddhist monks. O-oh, say can you see? I'd tie back my hair, men's clothing I'd put on, I'd pass as your comrade as we march along. Waste 'em, Ehrhart; shoot, goddamn it. God damn me. I don't believe anymore, Father. You're worse than Pilate; you're a fraud. Keep your ass down, Bobby; come back. Come back, Frank. Pay the lady. We killed her chickens, pay the lady. When we're married, Bill; it won't be long, I want to wear white. I'll wait for you. Don't go yet, Sergeant Wilson. I can't speak Vietnamese. I need you. Come back. You'll be okay, Maloney. There's your VC with a weapon, Cal. The M-16 is issue; they must have tested it. Russian rockets. Made in Berkeley. We try harder. Harder and harder. Something's happening here. This isn't possible. I enlisted. This is America. This isn't possible. Come back, Jenny, please, Mother, I'm sorry.

132

"Hey, Bill. Hey! Bill!" It was Amagasu. "You got guard duty tonight, you know that?" He scrambled up the berm to me.

"Yeh, Kenny. What time is it?"

"1800, almost. Are you okay? You been sitting up here all afternoon. What's the matter?"

"Nothin'. Not a fucking thing."

"You been crying."

"No. Mind your own — come on, Kenny, let's go."

When I reported for guard duty that night, I discovered that I'd drawn a post with PFC Haller. "Just what I needed," I thought.

"You tired enough to sleep?" I asked.

"No."

"Neither am I." I stood in the open bunker with my arms hooked over the top row of sandbags and my chin resting on my crossed wrists. The sun cast long shadows over the command post compound, and the hamlet beyond the wire, and the river, and the ricefields. The PF compound between our wire and the hamlet had never been rebuilt. The wreckage disappeared into the twilight. Two fishing boats on the river hauled in their nets and drifted off to the south. The world slid into darkness. The mountains to the west, silhoueted by the last rays of the sun, glowed purple. "For purple mountains majesty," I mumbled softly.

"What?" said Haller. He was crouched down in a corner of the bunker smoking a cigarette.

"Nothin'. Just a song I heard once." Far to the north, a line of illumination rounds popped above the horizon. Artillery in the compound behind me fired, the sound less noticeable than the vibrations transmitted through the earth into my arms. Somewhere high overhead, jet fighters whined harshly. Three silent figures moved up the road in front of me. "Listening post going out," I thought.

"It's 2200," said Haller. "You want me to take over?"

"No. I'm not tired yet. Go to sleep."

"You been standin' there staring for two solid hours. You're gonna go stare-crazy. Take a break. At least have a cigarette; I'll spell you."

"I'm all right. Back off, will you?"

"What is it with you, Ehrhart?"

"What are you talkin' about? I ain't botherin' you; don't bother me, okay? I'll wake you up at midnight."

"Hey, look, you got a reason not to like me, fine," said Haller. "I'd just like to know what it is. Wha'd I ever do to you?"

I could feel my face flush. I couldn't think of anything to say. "We got a long night, and I got a lot on my mind, so just forget it. You're okay, okay?"

"No, it's not okay. You got it in for me, and I got a right to know why."

"What right?" I said. "Shit, I don't know. You come over here, and you're playin' that fuckin' garbage you call music so loud you knock the fillings outta my teeth — you ain't even been here an hour."

"You don't like my music? Is *that* all? Why don't ya just ask me to turn it down?"

"It ain't just that. All that, 'Hey, what's happenin'? Groovy! Be cool, man!' All that stuff, Haller. I seen that peace medallion you wear around your neck. Them fuckin' hippies back home are bad enough. I don't need that shit over here, you know? You wanna be a hippie, what the fuck you doin' here?"

"Good question," said Haller. "I'm not too happy about it, I'll tell you that. I didn't have much choice — thought I didn't, at least. My old man's a bigwig in state politics. I got busted for a demonstration last year. Burned my draft card, you know? They were gonna send me to prison, but my Dad got the judge to let me off if I enlisted. Dad was a Marine — so was the judge. So here I am."

"You bullshittin' me?"

"Nope. Tell you what, though; I spend a lot of time thinkin' maybe I shoulda gone to jail after all."

"Jesus Christ," I couldn't help laughing. "A fuckin' draft card burner in the Marine Corps. Why didn't you go to Canada?"

"I thought about it, but that takes more courage than I got."

"Courage?!" I snorted.

"Yeh, courage. Think about it; I did. Leave your home, leave your family and friends, everything, never be able to come back, don't even know if you can get a job or a place to live or anything? I couldn't deal with that. Least this way, I got a chance. Only thing is, I've been thinkin', you know, since I got here — I'm gonna have to carry this for the rest of my life."

"What?"

"This. Bein' here. Bein' a part of this."

"For chrissake, Haller, you don't wanna leave the country, leave America — you owe *this much* to your country. One lousy year."

"What do I owe my country? This shit?! This fuckin' shit?! What are we doin' for our country around here? Tell me that. I'd fuckin' well like to know."

134

"Well, the fuckin' communists, you know, I mean what the hell, the communists..."

"The communists?! What, you mean like that old man you wasted down on Barrier Island, the one with his hands tied behind his back?"

"Shut up about that, man!" I spat, my stomach suddenly contracting so violently I almost doubled over. "I had orders. There it is, Haller, that's the fuckin' trouble with you. You got a smart mouth."

"I'm sorry," said Haller. "That was dirty pool. But you see my point? You see what I mean?" We were both silent for a long time.

"You know," I said, "sometimes I think I wouldn't mind it if I got blown away."

"That's crazy," said Haller.

"What isn't around here? There you are with your peace medal and your M-16, and you're gonna tell me what's crazy and what ain't."

"Hey, my rifle keeps me alive and my peace medal keeps me sane. That's not so crazy." Another long silence followed. A red pop-up burst over the south end of the hamlet. "LP comin' in," said Haller.

"I got a letter from my girlfriend today," I said. "One of those kind, you know? Dear John."

"That blonde on your desk? Geez, that's too bad. I'm sorry."

"I don't get it. She wrote to me every day. Every fuckin' day right up to the end of July. Not even a hint."

"That's tough, man. That's a real pisser."

"That's all I been livin' for, you know? Things get tough, you just keep tellin' yourself, 'Just a little longer, just a little longer, one more day.'"

"Hey, look, don't get any crazy ideas. It's a bad break, but no woman's worth blowin' it all for. Calloway — Jesus, what he did — listen, it ain't worth that."

"We were gonna get married as soon as I got back, you know? Get the hell out and forget the whole fuckin' thing, you know?"

"How old is she, Ehrhart? Seventeen, eighteen? You got lots of time. You can fix it up when you get home, maybe. Must be hard on her, too, you know; this ain't exactly the most popular war in town. Ain't like everybody's plantin' Victory Gardens back home. She's probably just confused, got a lot of pressure on her."

"We're havin' a picnic over here, I suppose. Just livin' it up, you know?"

"Give her some slack," said Haller. "Give yourself some slack."

"I know who it is," I said. "Some guy named Niles Mancini.

You ever hear a fuckin' name like that? Niles Mancini. She went to the prom with him last spring. Went flyin' with him a lot. Fuckin' rich kid, you know? Got his own personal airplane; buy her anything she wants. 'We're just friends,' she says, 'don't worry. I love you no shit, GI.' And I'm fuckin' *trapped* here. Fuckin' rat in a cage."

"Look, it's a rotten break. It isn't fair, but you can't do anything about it now, so just keep your head on."

"I ever get home, I'll kill that son-of-a-bitch. I ain't kidding. I'll kill him, man, I don't care. Jesus, she was so proud of me. Took her to the Christmas dance last winter — she even asked me to wear my dress greens. Had on a bright yellow gown that matched her hair. She was so beautiful. She *can't* just stop lovin' me. For chrissake, I do my fuckin' duty, I try to do what's right — what do I get for it? That bitch! I'll fuckin' kill 'em both, I swear to God."

"Take it easy, will you? Maybe you won't feel that way after awhile. There's plenty of fish in the sea."

"Not like her, Haller. There's nobody like her. She loved me so much. This is all wrong, man. This just isn't possible. I gotta get outta here; I'm gonna go crazy."

A gray light began to filter through the night like mist. The hooches in the nearby hamlet began to take shape. Treelines rose up soundlessly out of the darkness, and the patches of rice fields, and the banks of the river, and the dirty surface of the road. Sounds drifted over the berm from the hamlet: people rustling out of sleep, pans banging, dogs barking.

"Jesus Christ," I said. "It's almost daybreak. We been up all night."

"I know," said Haller, smiling wearily in the dim light.

"I'm sorry, man, I didn't even notice. I — you know, I'm really sorry."

"Forget it. It's okay. I know how it is. I got a girl back home, supposed to be waiting for me. Could be me instead of you. Do me a favor, will you?"

"Yeh, anything, what?"

"Just *be cool*, okay?" He drew the words out slowly. "Anything I can do, you know, anytime you wanna talk, don't be proud."

"Yeh. Sure. Randy — thanks, buddy."

Chapter 22

During the first week of September, Griffith and Amagasu both got promoted to corporal, Al Talbot was killed when he drove over a mine one morning while making the mail run to Danang, and Lieutenant Kaiser rotated back to The World.

"Ehrhart," the Lieutenant said the morning he left, "don't forget what I said. You got enough shit to deal with as it is, so keep your head out of your ass." I opened my mouth to speak, but he cut me off. "Don't argue; listen. You go home in a box, it won't change the war — and it won't make your girlfriend love you. You're young yet, boy; give yourself a chance. College, right?"

"Yes, sir," I said. I wanted to say something else, but I couldn't find the words.

"Good luck, Ehrhart," he said, shaking hands firmly.

"So long, Lieutenant. Thanks. Sir, I'm glad you made it."

"You will, too, boy. Don't forget. See you back in The World." He smiled, winked, got into the jeep, and was gone. I tried to imagine The World, but nothing would come into focus.

Lieutenant Kaiser's replacement was Captain Braithewaite, a tall powerfully built man, probably in his late twenties, who must have been a professional rugby player in a previous life. His head was shaved bald, and he sported a large droopy Ghenghis Khan moustache far in excess of what regulations allowed. He had just arrived from the States, and was not at all happy about being assigned as the S-2 officer instead of being given command of a rifle company.

"Another Stateside wonder," I said to Amagasu at the first opportunity to speak privately. "And an unhappy one at that. This oughta be fuckin' fun." We both groaned. But Captain Braithewaite quickly made it clear that he wasn't going to take his disappointment out on the troopies. The son of a high-ranking career naval officer, perhaps he'd learned to accept the random injustices of the military without breaking stride.

"So, what do you boys do for a living?" he asked in a voice filled with easy-going good humor. "Teach me something useful."

"We're United States Marines, sir," I said. "We kill people."

"Gung ho," said Amagasu.

"Which way to the front?" asked the Captain.

"Any way you please, sir," I said.

"Alpha Company's sweeping the Horseshoe tomorrow, sir," said Gunny Johnson. "You wanna go?"

"Love to, Gunny, but the Colonel wants to brief me tomorrow. You go; I'll have to take a raincheck."

"Can I go, Captain?" I asked quickly, seizing the opportunity to test the Captain before Amagasu could. "Kenny can run the shop. He's real good at it," I said, putting my arm around Amagasu and patting his shoulder proudly. "Taught him myself."

"Sure, Corporal Ehrhart. Why not?"

"Hot damn!" I thought, delighted with my swift victory. "Thank you, sir!" I said.

"Hey, what about me?" Amagasu finally managed to sputter.

"You can go next time," said Captain Braithewaite. "The war looks like it'll probably last till then — unless Corporal Ehrhart gets hot tomorrow."

"Bite the bullet, pal," I said to Amagasu.

"Stow it, Ehrhart," said Gunny Johnson. "Lieutenant Kaiser didn't let these boys stretch their legs very often, sir. They're both as antsy as a couple of colts."

"Well, that's what you're here for, isn't it?" said the Captain to Kenny and me. "We'll give you some room to romp."

"Go pack your gear, Ehrhart," said the Gunny, explaining to the Captain that we'd be riding out to the Horseshoe that afternoon in preparation for any early start in the morning. "The scouts are going, too," he added.

"Go ahead," said Captain Braithewaite. "Corporal Amagasu can look after me, right, Corporal? Say, Corporal Ehrhart, bring me back a souvenir while you're at it, okay?"

138

"Sure thing, sir," I beamed, "and thanks."

"That new captain's gonna be okay," I said to Morgan as the column of Marines moved slowly through the morning heat. "Lieutenant Kaiser was a good dude, sure enough. I really liked him, you know? But he never let me *do* anything. I was gettin' bug-fuck sittin' around the CP all the time, you know what I mean?"

"I know exactly what you mean," said Morgan. "Gimme the boonies any day. Too much bullshit back in the rear. That's why they call it the rear — all asshole." Morgan's accent reflected his Norwegian ancestry, though his family had been Minnesota farmers for generations.

"Geez, Captain Braithewaite ain't been here twenty-four hours, and Bingo — here I am. Just in the nick of time, too. That's okay." The operation was just the usual kind of sweep and clear job: search every hooch, round up detainees, blow up bunkers; a County Fair without the boiled rice and bandaids — but at least it was something out of the ordinary.

"They got a gook in a bunker, you guys," Sergeant Seagrave shouted as he hurried up to us. "Let's go." Morgan and I took off after Seagrave. Up near the head of the column, Mogerty, Hofstatter, and Wally were standing near a hooch with their rifles pointing like birddog tails. Sergeant Trinh stood nearby, along with three national policemen all decked out in brand new combat gear.

"He's in there," said Wally, pointing toward a low mound with a hole disappearing into it. "I seen him run out of the hooch and dive in."

"Is he armed?" asked Seagrave.

"Dunno," said Wally.

"Anybody wanna play tunnel rat?" asked Seagrave.

"Fuck you, Gravey," half a dozen scouts said in unison.

"Toss in a grenade," said Hoffy.

"Maybe I can talk him out," said Trinh. He bent down near the entrance to the bunker and began talking in Vietnamese. No response. He tried again. Still nothing. He shrugged his shoulders and stood up.

"Anybody got any CS gas?" asked Seagrave.

"I got a green smoke grenade," I said.

"That might do it. Couple of you guys get on either side of the hole," Seagrave ordered. "Rest of you get back. Might come out shooting." I pulled the pin on the smoke cannister and tossed it in the hole. Thick bright green smoke began pouring out. In a few minutes, a man crawled out, choking heavily and crying from the dense smoke.

Mogerty and Morgan jumped on him and pinned him to the ground. He was unarmed, and looked to be about fourteen or fifteen years old.

"Just a kid," said Wally.

"Old enough to be Cong," said Hoffy.

"Rolly," said Sergeant Seagrave, "wait until the smoke clears, then check it out. Take this," he added, handing Morgan a flashlight. "And go easy; it might be booby-trapped in there. Search the hooch, you guys."

Trinh was arguing in Vietnamese with one of the national policemen while the other two policemen kicked and beat the boy with their boots and rifle butts. "Look at those jerks," said Hoffy, "they're worse'n we are." A couple of grunts from Alpha Company, who'd been standing by watching, cheered on the policemen. Trinh finally got the boy loose and put him with the rest of the detainees in the middle of the column. The bunker had some bedding and food in it, but was otherwise empty. There was nothing in the hooch, either. We blew them both up with C-4, and moved on.

About an hour later, the column halted again — God knew why, and only God cared. We were sitting beside the trail smoking and taking it easy when Corporal Aymes and Lance Corporal Stemkowski burst out of the bushes nearby. "Come here and look what we found," said Aymes. Not fifty meters away was a small one-room temple built in a clearing among the trees. It wasn't much to look at: plain concrete and a dull red tile roof. But inside, brightly colored tapestries hung from the walls, and an ornately carved altar stood against one wall. Various kinds of pottery stood on the altar, some of it containing incense sticks. There was no one around, but someone had recently been making repairs to the roof. A sawhorse and some other equipment leaned against the back of the building.

"What is it?" asked Wally.

"It's a church, asshole," said Mogerty.

"Let's knock it down," said Hoffy, dragging the heavy sawhorse around front.

"What for?" asked Wally.

"Why not?" said Hoffy. "Grab the other end of this." Wally and Hoffy picked up the wooden sawhorse, counted to three, took a running start, and crashed the sawhorse against the wall of the temple. They both fell down and came up cursing and shaking their stinging hands. "Jesus, that sucker's solid," said Hoffy.

"Not like that," said Morgan. "Do it this way. Come on, Bill." We picked up the sawhorse and placed one end of it against the wall.

140

"Draw it back and swing it forward," he said, "like this: heave, ho!" The sawhorse banged against the wall. "Heave, ho!" he shouted again. The sawhorse banged against the wall again. "Heave ho!" everybody shouted in unison. "Heave, ho! Heave, ho!" The sawhorse broke through the wall, knocking out a hole about two feet in diameter. "Like that, Hoffy," said Morgan, dusting off his hands on his pants.

Wally and Hoffy picked up the sawhorse and positioned it about two feet to the left of the hole. "Heave, ho!" Wally and Hoffy shouted. "Heave, ho!" everybody shouted. "Heave, ho! Heave, ho! Heave, ho!" Another large chunk of the wall fell in. "Hooray!" everybody shouted. Wally and Hoffy bowed to each other, then to the rest of the scouts. Mogerty and Greg Barnes picked up the sawhorse.

"Heave, ho!" everybody shouted at the top of their lungs. "Heave, ho! Heave, ho!" In this fashion, taking turns by twos, we proceeded along one wall, knocked out the corner, proceeded down the next wall, knocked out that corner, and started down the third wall. It looked like a large mechanical beaver had gone berserk on the building. "Heave, ho! Heave, ho!" Crrrack!!! The roof shuddered. Aymes and Stemkowski dropped the sawhorse and ran.

"That fucker's ready to go, man," said Aymes.

"So do it," said Hoffy. Aymes and Stemkowski walked back and picked up the sawhorse. "Heave, ho! Heave, ho!" Crrraaack!!!! Everybody scattered as the whole top half of the temple began to heel down slowly onto the broken walls. Then the roof tore away from the one remaining good wall, banged down on the three broken walls, split in half and fell in on itself, crashing to the floor of the temple in a roar of dust and rubble. A large crowd of spectators from Alpha Company leaped to their feet, cheering and applauding. The scouts shook hands all around.

"Jesus fuckin' -A," said Morgan, "that was hard work."

"Good exercise," said Hoffy.

"Better than stealin' hubcaps," said Mogerty, who was from Detroit.

"Anything good?" asked Amagasu when I walked into the COC that evening.

"Lots of things," I said. "We didn't hit any mines goin' out; we didn't hit any mines comin' back in; I didn't get shot at, and I'm a day shorter."

"Nothing, huh?"

"Yeh, well, it depends on how you look at it. Anything goin' on around here?"

"Naw. I drove down to Hieu Nhon. You should see the place—blown to shit from that raid the other week. Not a building left standing. That ARVN platoon they had there—every one of them killed or run off."

"Yeh, I know. Sergeant Ford, that guy at Hoi An, said it looked like half the ARVN musta been VC. The gooks came right in the front gate, like somebody on the inside let 'em in. You didn't see Co Chi, did you?"

"No. There was nobody around but a few national policemen and some ARVN. You know that ARVN lieutenant that sort of speaks English? He was there. Said we're not supposed to come there anymore; just go to Hoi An instead. They only got a GP tent set up. They aren't staying there at night anymore."

"Maybe she's in Hoi An."

"I don't know. There weren't any women there at all."

"Well, I hope the VC didn't get her."

"She could be VC herself, for all we know. What difference does it make?"

"None, I guess. She's so pretty, though; I hate to think—you know? Her father's some kind of district bigwig. They might want to waste her just for the hell of it."

"Ho! Corporal Ehrhart!" Captain Braithewaite walked up from the other end of the bunker.

"Hi, Captain," I said.

"How was your day?"

"Okay, sir. Pretty quiet. I got something for you," I said, reaching into my pack. "Here." I pulled out a small clay cup glazed white and hand-painted with blue and brown clouds, green, red and brown bushes, some blue Chinese-type letters, and a thin blue line around the rim.

"What's this?"

"You wanted a souvenir, sir. Here it is. Genuine Buddhist vase. Duty free. No waiting. Get 'em while they last."

"Well, I'll be damned; you remembered. Where'd you get it?"

"Some abandoned temple we found. They won't be needing it anymore."

"Well, thanks, Corporal; that's very thoughtful. The Mounties always get their man, huh?"

"We aim to please, sir. Got one for myself, too. Thanks for letting me go out, sir. I got any mail, Kenny?"

"Just this," said Amagasu, handing me a letter. The name and return address on the envelope were unfamiliar. I opened the letter:

"Dear Bill, you don't know me, but I'm one of Jenny Kane's classmates at St. Francis Nursing School. She told me you were pretty lonely over there and might like to hear from a girl back in the states. Would you like to be my penpal? I wouldn't mind writing to you."

"Jesus fucking Christ!" I blurted out.

"What's up?" asked Amagasu.

"Nothin'," I said, crumpling the letter without reading further.

"Who's that from?"

"Florence Nightingale." I tossed the crumpled letter into the trash basket. Then I picked up Jenny's portrait. I stared at it. I took the small photo of the female guerrilla fighter out of the edge of the frame, put it in my pocket, then threw the portrait and frame into the trash basket.

"Bad news?" asked Kenny.

"Yeh. Bad news."

Later that evening, I came back into the COC, fished Jenny's portrait out of the trash basket, and took it back to my hooch, slipping it into my footlocker facedown beneath my extra pair of jungle utilities.

Chapter 23

The next morning, Amagasu and I were sitting in the S-2 shop going over the I-Sum when Sergeant Trinh walked in. We both said hello, but Trinh only nodded and continued on to the far end of the bunker where Captain Braithewaite was talking with the battalion commander and the operations officer. Trinh's usually animated round face was rigid as a mask.

"Whew!" I whistled. "He looks pissed. Wonder what's eatin' him this morning." Amagasu and I stopped what we were doing and watched as Trinh approached the three officers and began speaking. We couldn't make out what he said, but in perfect unison the three officers stood bolt upright and stared at Trinh, their mouths dropping open and their faces bulging with amazement.

"You can't just quit, man!" we could hear the Colonel say.

Trinh said something else. We couldn't hear him, but we could see his head moving in speech.

"Come off it!" said the Major. "We're *all* tired!"

Trinh spoke again, this time at some length, his voice never rising above an indistinguishable buzz.

"Where's your pride, Sergeant?" the Colonel said sharply. "We're doing our duty, and you'll continue to do yours — or I'll have you courtmartialed! What's gotten into you, Trinh? Get out of here right now, and we'll forget this ever happened."

"For chrissake, Trinh, this is *your* country!" added Captain Braithewaite.

144

"That is right!" Trinh shot back, his pitch rising with agitation. "It is my country! I have not forgotten that. *You* people have."

"You've gone yellow, Trinh!" the Major shouted. "You're a goddamned coward!"

Trinh's face lit up like a bonfire doused with gasoline. "I don't care what you think of me, but you know that is a *lie!*" he shouted. A deep silence, broken only by the static on the radios, descended upon the COC. Twenty pairs of eyes turned toward Trinh, drawn by the angry pain in his voice. "You do not know what you are doing, goddamn you! You are ruining everything, and I am not going to help you do it anymore! You are hypocrits and fools, and you are giving my country to the communists and the buzzards! Leave my people alone, you goddamned mercenaries! Take your ignorance and go home! Just get the hell out! I fight for my country, but when you are finished, I will have no country left! Go ahead and courtmartial me! Do anything you want! I do not care! I am through with your fucking war! Do you understand?! I am not going to help you anymore!"

The radios crackled. The three officers stood frozen in place. No one in the bunker breathed. Amagasu and I looked at each other. "Annunciate, Annunciate; this is Delta Six, over." My stomach danced spasmodically, as though waiting for an axe to fall. "Annunciate, Annunciate; this is Delta Six, come in please."

"Answer that radio!" the Colonel shouted. "Sergeant Trinh, go to your quarters. You're under arrest."

Trinh walked out without hesitation. The Colonel walked over to the bank of radios. The Major sat down. Captain Braithewaite stalked back to the S-2 shop, his face set, his shaved head glistening with sweat. He picked up a pile of papers, shuffled through them roughly without looking at them, then threw them down angrily. "Shit!" he said. Amagasu and I looked at each other again, and without speaking, went back to work on the I-Sum.

That night I went to see Trinh, taking with me the contents of one of my parents' Care packages. When I walked into his hooch, Trinh was sitting on the edge of his cot staring down at his feet with his forearms resting on his thighs and his hands dangling limply between his knees. He didn't look up.

"Sergeant Trinh? Am I bothering you?" I asked. He raised his head, fixing me firmly in a steady gaze as though he were seeing me for the first time. His eyes were red and blurred, his shoulders bent into a permanent droop.

"I just wondered how you were doin'. Thought you might like

some company. Want some?" I held out the package. "Got your favorite here — red licorice."

"Why do you offer with both hands?" Trinh responded. The sudden sense that I had somehow accidentally insulted Trinh seized me by the throat. I wanted to bolt and run.

"I — I don't know," I stammered. "I didn't mean anything. I'm sorry."

"Do not be sorry," he smiled wanly. "That is the way you are supposed to offer a gift. We always offer with both hands. It means sincerity, good feelings. You Americans hold something out with one hand only. To us, that is an insult — like offering scraps to a dog. You surprised me, that is all. It was nice. Sit down." He took a piece of licorice and began chewing on it thoughtfully. "I am used to being insulted by you Americans. So many little things. You do not know. That store — the laundry and barbershop — you call it the 'gook' shop; where did you ever get that word? The other day, Corporal Walters asked me to go with him to the gook shop to offer money to one of the laundry girls. 'I do not know gook talk,' he said to me — and he smiled like a big dumb puppy. I did not know if I should hit him or pat him on the head."

"Come on, he didn't mean any harm. He just didn't think."

"Yes, I know, he just did not think," Trinh said wearily. "That is what is so sad — none of you mean any harm; you just do not think. Corporal Ehrhart, I have seen you taunt Vietnamese men in the market for holding hands. You call them 'homos.' Did you know that is our custom? It means only friendship. If a woman held hands with a man in public, *that* would be something bad."

"I didn't know that, no," I said, feeling my face flush with embarrassment. "In America, it means — "

"In America, in America," Trinh laughed softly. "This is not America, Corporal Ehrhart. Such simple things, yet none of you ever bother to ask. Every day, you are losing the war in a thousand little ways, and none of you see it. The gook shop," he snorted. "What do you think the laundry girls tell their friends when they go home at night? Is every young woman in America a prostitute? Why do you think our women are?" He reached for another piece of licorice. "Your parents must miss you very much. They send you good things to eat all the time. Perhaps they have heard about Marine Corps chow," he laughed.

I laughed, too, relieved to be off the hook. "Yeh, I guess so," I said.

"Well, if you are lucky, you will be going home soon."

"Seems like forever sometimes," I said.

Trinh laughed again, though it didn't sound like a laugh. "Yes, forever," he said. I grasped for something to say.

"Do you have a family, Sergeant Trinh?"

"I have one sister left. She is a nurse. She lives — she lived with my mother in a village south of Saigon. Perhaps she will be dead, too, before long. My family has not been lucky. We Vietnamese have not been lucky."

It hurt to see Trinh so sad and subdued — and it made me very uncomfortable. I thrashed around in my head, trying to think of some safe question to ask.

"My father was killed by the Japanese when I was very little," Trinh continued in a monotone. "I never knew him. We were living in the Red River delta then, not far from Haiphong. When the communists took over the north, my mother was afraid. She thought the communists would kill us because my father once worked for the French, in the post office. That is what people were saying. So we fled to the south. My oldest sister died along the way. She stepped on a mine. I do not know if it was a Viet Minh mine or a French one. It does not matter." After another silence, he reached into a box by his feet and pulled out a letter. "It is from my sister," he said. "My mother has been killed by American artillery. I did not even get to bury her."

The mother and child I'd seen on Barrier Island back in August leaped into my head; my stomach buckled and I dropped the bag of licorice. "I'm sorry, Sergeant Trinh," I stammered. "Jesus. Jesus, I'm sorry, Trinh."

"So am I." He picked up the bag slowly and handed it to me. "I am going to miss your red licorice," he said. The six eight-inch guns in the compound roared, shaking the hooch and sending a trail of invisible whistling steel down the long corridor of the night.

"Is that what happened this morning, Trinh? Is it because of your mother?"

"That is only the end of it," he said. "What is your expression?"

"The last straw?"

"Yes. The last straw on the camel. How old are you?"

"Eighteen. I'll be nineteen the end of this month."

"Do you know how long I have been fighting? I was drafted when you were twelve years old; I have been fighting for six and one half years, and there is no end in sight. Every year it gets worse. Every year, the Vietcong grow stronger. When I was drafted, the vc fought

147

us with sharpened bamboo sticks and Japanese rifles and French rifles. Now they fight us with Russian rockets and Chinese grenades and American machineguns. You are their best recruiters. You Americans come with your tanks and your jets and your helicopters, and everywhere you go, the VC grow like new rice in the fields. You do not understand Vietnam. You have never bothered to understand us, and you never will bother because you think you have all the answers. Do you know what Uncle Ho says? 'You Americans will tire of killing us before we tire of dying.' Sometimes I think he is right — and sometimes, I think you Americans will never grow tired of killing."

"That's not true, Trinh! What do you think I'm doing here? I didn't have to come here. I wasn't drafted. I could've stayed home where it was safe, and so could the rest of us. A lot of good people have died trying to help you — and you know it, Trinh. You've known a lot of them. You people *asked* for our help, for chrissake."

"I did not ask you for anything!" he responded sharply. "Ky and Thieu and the rest of those fat, bloated bandits who are getting filthy rich from this war — *they* asked for help. They do not speak for the Vietnamese. They do not speak for me. Your President Johnson is too ignorant or too arrogant to understand such a simple truth. You help the whores and the pimps, and you take the people from the land where their ancestors are buried and put them in tin cages where they cannot fish or grow rice or do anything but hate and die — and if they do not want to leave the bones of their ancestors, you call them communists and beat them and put them in prison and kill them. You Americans are worse than the VC."

"Wait a minute, goddamn it! Don't tell me it's all our fucking fault. What about those fucking national policemen yesterday? We didn't beat up on that kid. They did!"

"If the people ruled Vietnam, those dogs would be cut by a thousand knives!" Trinh nearly shouted. "They are exactly the kind of pigs and vermin you Americans like because they do not argue with you and they grin like fools while you and your friends destroy a Buddhist temple. Your father is a priest, Corporal Ehrhart. How would you feel if I came to your father's church and broke it down? You don't understand anything, do you? Do you think I voted for Thieu last week? Did you know that a Buddhist asking for peace almost won the election, even though no newspaper in Vietnam was allowed to tell his story? Did you know that Thieu has already thrown him in prison?! And you Americans praise Thieu, and tell yourselves you are helping us. Sometimes I think you are the most evil nation on earth."

148

"I don't have to take this shit!" I shouted. "I come over here because I'm feeling bad for you, and you shit all over me."

"No, Corporal Ehrhart! You and your friends come over here and shit all over my country, and *I* will not take it anymore."

"Fuck you, man," I said, getting up quickly and turning toward the door.

"Wait!" Trinh shouted. "Wait! Don't go. Please." I stopped, but didn't turn around. My whole body shook, my lips biting down hard against tears. "Sit down, please." I walked back slowly and sat down across from Trinh, but I couldn't look at him. "I'm sorry, Corporal Ehrhart. I do not mean to accuse you. I know you are not a bad man. You are just very young." He paused. "You are very young, and you do not know. Armies are always made of the young." Trinh took hold of my hand and pressed it between both of his. He lifted all three hands between us. "It means friendship," he said. "Do not be angry with me. It is all so sad." His voice broke. The 155s across the compound punched a volley of steel into the night, a ripple of air and echoing sound filling the vacuum left in their wake. "My country is bleeding to death, Corporal Ehrhart. My beloved Vietnam is dying. I have fought hard. I am tired. Someday, perhaps, you will understand."

"What'll they do to you, Trinh?" I asked after a long silence.

"I do not know. Make me a private and send me back to an ARVN battalion, I think. Send me where there is heavy fighting. At least I will die among my own people."

We sat in silence for a very long time. I felt numb, dizzy and sick to my stomach. Trinh's hands surrounded mine with a pocket of warmth.

"I guess I'd better go, Sergeant Trinh," I finally said.

"Yes, it is late. Thank you for coming."

"Trinh, I don't know what to say. You know, I mean, I just— I'm sorry, Trinh."

"It is not your fault," said Trinh. "You are very young."

We both stood up. "Good luck, Sergeant Trinh," I croaked. "Here." I handed him the bag of red licorice, and turned to leave.

"Good luck to you," Trinh said softly. And then in a voice even softer, he added, "I hope you make it, little brother."

Early the next morning, an ARVN major and two ARVN enlisted men arrived at the command post in a jeep, and took Sergeant Trinh away with them.

Chapter 24

"Hey, you guys, listen up," said Haller one afternoon toward the end of September. "We're movin' out."

"What are you talking about?" asked Amagasu.

"The whole battalion's movin' out," said Haller. "We're goin' up north somewhere."

"Where?" I asked. "When? How do you know?"

"I heard the Colonel talkin' to Major Miles about it. They're making us a mobile strike battalion. We're leavin' this week or early next month. I don't know where we're goin'. Even the Colonel doesn't know yet. Somewhere up near the DMZ."

"I'll believe it when I see it," I laughed. "Last month, I heard we were all gettin' our tours cut by a month — twelve months, just like the army. Be home for Christmas. Right."

"I heard 'em talkin' about it just now," said Haller. "Wanna bet?"

"Scuttlebutt, Randy," I chided, "scuttlebutt."

"This is straight scoop, you turds," said Haller, offended at our disbelief.

Just then, Captain Braithewaite and Gunny Johnson walked in. "Drop your cocks and pull up your socks, boys," said the Captain. "We're going places."

"Wha'd I tell you?" Haller smirked.

"What's goin' on, sir?" I asked. "Where we goin'?"

"We don't know yet. Somewhere up around Quang Tri. And we

150

got a lot to do before we go. Got orders to travel light; we have to go through all this stuff and sort out what we need," said the Captain, sweeping an outstretched hand around the S-2 shop. "Amagasu, go find Sergeant Seagrave."

"When do we go?" I asked. The prospect of moving, especially of going north, excited me and scared me at the same time.

"We're supposed to be ready to send a lead element within four days," said the Captain. "The whole battalion'll be gone in eight to ten days."

"Here today, guano tomorrow," said Haller.

"What?"

"Bird talk," said Haller. "Never mind."

"Fuck the birds," I said. "Just get me the fuck out of this rat hole. I'll go anywhere—the sooner, the better. And they better not have any goddamned sand up there. I can't *believe* I used to play in the sandbox when I was a kid; I mean just go and sit in the stuff for the fun of it."

"What they got up there is beau coup VC," said the Gunny.

"Fine!" I said. "Fuckin' -A fine with me. Maybe we'll have somethin' to shoot at for a change."

"Yeh?" said the Gunny. "What're you gonna do when they start shooting back?"

"You're a bigger target than I am, Gunny," I beamed.

"I ain't goin'," he grinned. "I'm gettin' transferred to Regiment."

"What? Who's gonna be the two-chief?"

"They got a staff sergeant up at Regiment," said the Gunny, "just in from The World. Never worked intelligence before; they're gonna re-train him on the job."

"Oh, fuckin' swell," I groaned, "you mean *I'm* gonna re-train him. Why don't you just promote me to Gunnery Sergeant and let *me* be the intelligence chief, Captain?"

Amagasu came in with Sergeant Seagrave in tow, and Captain Braithewaite explained the impending move to the chief scout. "Tell everybody not to take anything they can't carry on their backs," he said. "Anything else they want to keep, box it up and ship it home. And you better warn 'em not to try to ship out any kind of weapons or live ordinance—no military gear of any kind. They're gonna have postal inspectors here all week checking everything."

"Don't worry, sir," said Seagrave, "if it fires, we'll take it with us. That's Mr. Charles country up there. I got a buddy in Third

MarDiv up at Con Thien. He says it's really bad up there. I'll tell you what, though, I don't mind gettin' the hell out of here. They can give this place to the devil. Damn gooks all look the same around here, you know what I mean, sir?"

"Well, don't get your hopes up, Sergeant Seagrave," said the Captain. "They're liable not to look any different up there."

"Corporal Ehrhart," said Sergeant Barron, walking into the bunker. "Just the man I'm looking for."

"I had guard duty last night, for chrissake; I'm on bunker watch tonight."

"Keep your shirt on," said Barron, "I'm about to do you the favor of a lifetime. How'd you like a free trip to Hong Kong?"

"Hong Kong? R&R? When?"

"Day after tomorrow."

"What for?"

"For the hell of it. You're about due. Guy from Bravo Company was supposed to go, but he bought the farm yesterday. You wanna go or not?"

"Well, it's kind of a bad time right now," I said, looking at the Captain. "Sir?"

"Sure, Corporal Ehrhart, go on. You need it. We'll get moved without you. Just come up to Phu Bai when you get back and ask around for us."

"I don't have any money, Sergeant Barron. Can I draw an advance?"

"Can't do it. You'll have to scrounge some money somewhere."

"I can lend you some," said Haller.

"Me, too," said Amagasu.

"Sign me up," I said.

"Okay," said Barron. "Get over to the aid station and get your shot card up to date. Pick up your orders tomorrow, and take the mail run up Wednesday morning."

"Gerry," I said that night, "can you lend me a hundred bucks?"

"What for?"

"I'm goin' to Hong Kong for R&R on Wednesday. I need some money. I'll have my mom send you a money order right away."

"I thought you wanted to go to Australia in November."

"Yeh, well, this just came up. Some grunt got his ticket cancelled, and Sergeant Barron asked me if I wanted to go in his place. I don't care if the plane lands in Borneo; I just gotta get outta here for awhile. I may be dead by November."

152

"How much money you got?"

"Three hundred and five dollars. Eighty of my own, and Randy and Kenny each lent me some."

"Here," said Gerry, reaching into a drawer. "Take this."

"Two hundred and fifty bucks?" I said, counting it. "That's too much, Gerry. You don't have to give me that much."

"Take it," said Gerry. "I was just going to send it home to Jan. Just have your mom send the money order to her. This is the only R&R you get; might as well have a good time. Eat, drink and be merry, you know?"

"Yeh, I know—for tomorrow we die."

"Fuck that part."

"Thanks a lot, Gerry; I really appreciate this."

"Thanks for asking."

"Huh?"

"Thanks for asking."

"Yeh, uh, sure."

"Really," he said. "I thought you were mad at me or something."

"What are you talkin' about?"

"You know this is the first time you been in my hooch in a month?"

"No shit? I didn't even notice."

"Well, I have. I thought you were mad at me or something. You haven't hardly talked to me or anything."

"Oh," I said. "Well, you know. I guess I ain't felt much like talkin' to anybody lately. Ever since Jenny—I don't know, my head's all—I don't know what to say or think or anything. I can't believe any of this shit."

"Pretty hard on you, I know. I'm really sorry, Bill—but Jesus, man, you can talk to *me*. We been through it all, you know?"

"Fuck, Gerry, I can't even think about it. How the fuck am I supposed to talk about it? You know what that bitch did? She's tellin' all her fuckin' friends in nursing school to write to her 'poor lonely *friend*' in Vietnam. I got a letter from one of 'em last week. Jesus, do you believe that?! I'm gonna fuckin' *kill* somebody, I ain't kiddin', man!"

"Take it easy, buddy, will ya?"

"That's what I mean. See what I mean? It just goes around and around in my head all the goddamned time. I ain't been good company lately. I been working a lot."

153

"Have you heard from her at all?"

"No. Nothin'. Not a fuckin' word. I write to her all the time — I beg, I plead, I reason, I threaten — I've tried everything. Nothin'. Like writing to a brick wall. You know, I spent a month at the goddamned language school on Okinawa and never even went to a bar, let alone a whorehouse. We're supposed to get married, for chrissake! She's probably gettin' screwed by every creep in Trenton. Free love, ain't that the hippie thing? Shit, man, line 'em all up against the fuckin' wall and let 'em have it with a Claymore. Oh, fuck it. Jesus. How's things with Jan, anyway?"

"She's okay. Still workin' in that furniture factory, but at least she's not on night shift anymore."

"I thought she was gonna go back to school in September."

"She was, but she decided to work instead — save up enough money so we can both go back together when I get home."

"That's nice. You can book it together. Get her to take your tests for you. Man, you're lucky bein' married; at least she can't just get up and walk away," I said, biting my tongue as soon as I'd said it. "Hey, I'm sorry, I know she wouldn't do that."

"Don't worry about it. I've thought about that, too. Hard not to. Jenny shook me up pretty good, too, pal. I keep reading and re-reading Jan's letters backwards and forwards and upside down, you know? Lookin' for — for what? I don't know. Bad habit. So, one good thing, anyway — I hear you and Randy are getting along pretty good these days."

"Yeh," I said, ducking my head in embarrassment. "You were right. Did I tell you he lent me some money for Hong Kong, too? You know he stayed up with me all night when I got that letter? I don't know what I woulda done if he hadn't been there. Probably blown my fuckin' brains out."

"Come on, buddy, it ain't that bad. Just ride it out, you'll see."

"Yeh, well, I don't know."

"Well, I do. It's a bitch, but it ain't the end of the world. Worry about the chickenshit later, okay? Just get yourself out of here alive. Parades for dead heroes are fuckin' boring."

"I don't think there's gonna be any heroes, Gerry."

"There's always heroes. Two kinds: live heroes and dead heroes. The live ones get the girls and the free drinks. The dead ones get buried. Let's you and me be live ones. I got it all planned."

"You heard about Trinh, didn't you?"

"Yeh, I heard. Pretty weird."

154

"I don't know, Gerry; maybe it isn't so weird. I went to see him the night before they took'im away. Jesus Christ, man, he gave me an earful. You know how long he's been in the army? Six and a half fuckin' years. Got a chest full of decorations. Guys like that don't turn chicken overnight. You know what he told me? You know all them people in that relocation camp down near Hieu Nhon that got run out of the mountains by the VC? Well, the VC were leavin' them alone, and they were leavin' the VC alone, and we went up into the mountains and dragged 'em all down here. They worship their ancestors, you know — it's part of their religion. The ground where their ancestors are buried is sacred. Like all those mounds out there, up along the highway and stuff — they're graveyards. If you take people away from the land where their ancestors are buried, they lose their souls or something. So we go and take all those people and stick 'em in that camp to protect 'em from the VC — and they end up hating us. Trinh said they all hate us. You know what else? You won't believe this. We killed Trinh's fuckin' mother a few weeks ago?"

"What?" Gerry blurted out.

"Well, not us, actually, but American artillery. You know that H&I stuff I do every night? Remember that woman and child I told you about down on Barrier Island? That stuff. Same thing. You wouldn't believe the shit Trinh told me. His father was killed by the Japs. The French killed his oldest sister. Now we kill his mother. Trinh's had it right up to the eyeballs, man. I don't blame him, either. There's somethin' really fuckin' bad goin' down here, you know that? Shit, yes, you know it, and I know it, too."

"Thin ice, pal," said Gerry cautiously.

"You're goddamned right it's thin ice, and we're standin' right in the middle of the lake."

"You know, there *are* a few VC around here — or haven't you noticed?"

"Trinh said there's more than a few VC around here. There's a hell of a lot more than there used to be. And the longer we stay, the more there are. Think about it, man. Just once fuckin' think about what's goin' down."

"So whadda you wanna do about it? You gonna quit, too? Spend the rest of your life busting fuckin' rocks in Portsmouth? You still got five months left around here, and that's all you better be thinkin' about, pal."

"Trinh said that's the whole fuckin' problem, Gerry — nobody thinks about anything."

"Forget what Trinh said! Trinh's gone. You wanna be the one to tell LBJ he doesn't know what the fuck he's doing? Go tell Colonel Glass to call the whole thing off, why don't you? Look, I'm sorry," he said, lowering his voice, "but you're gonna get yourself in real trouble if you don't back off. Just cool it. I mean it."

"Yeh, I know."

"The whole fuckin' thing's crazy. Start to finish. You don't need Trinh to tell you that — and you don't need me to tell ya to keep your fuckin' mouth shut."

"Yeh, I know, I know. But Jesus, Gerry, my whole fuckin' life, you know —"

"I know. Mine, too. Just forget it, will you? Worry about it when you get back to The World."

"I ever get back to The World, I ain't gonna even *think* about it, man. All I want is out. Oh-you-tee."

"Fine. Right now, you better worry about your ass while you still got one. Come on, let's play some rummy."

"I can't. I got eight-to-twelve in the COC tonight."

"Tonight?"

"There it is. Got a war on here. Listen, Gerry, thanks for the money. I'll tell Mom to send a check to Jan right away."

"Sure, Bill, any time. And have a good time, will ya? Screw your fuckin' eyeballs out, and come back laughin' — and bring me back a souvenir. Geisha girl, or somethin' useful like that."

"How 'bout a cheeseburger?"

"Get lost," said Gerry, throwing the deck of cards at me. "See you when you get back."

Chapter 25

The British Crown Colony of Hong Kong is made up of two parts: Hong Kong Island, and the Kowloon Peninsula on the Chinese mainland. By the fall of 1967, a lot of the Hong Kong economy was geared to the American R&R trade. The seven hotels where American military personnel stayed were all located in a six-square block area of Kowloon. The neighborhood around the hotels was loaded with restaurants, souvenir and tailor shops, and cheap bars where Chinese prostitutes were plentiful.

I arrived in Hong Kong on my nineteenth birthday. After I registered at the Ambassador Hotel, even before I went to my room, I bought a set of civilian clothing from a shop in the hotel lobby. Then I went up to my room, took off my uniform, and turned on the hot water in the bathtub. I called room service and ordered six cold beers and a bucket of ice. When the beer arrived, I climbed into the tub with a beer in each hand, and commenced to soak out 240 days worth of sand, dust, dirt, mud, sweat, pain and fatigue. I had not seen hot and cold running water in more than eight months. I ignored the cold water faucet. I played with the hot one, turning it on and off, refilling the tub whenever the water temperature got below 211 degrees Fahrenheit. I drank two more cold beers. I scooped hot water into my mouth, tilted my head back, and spit the water straight up, so that it tinkled and splashed all over my face as it fell. I got out of the tub dripping wet, urinated in the toilet and flushed it. Then I flushed it again. I flushed it a third time, just to watch the water swirl around in the bowl, then I got back in the tub. I drank two more beers. I shouted snatches of every song I could remember, until my throat hurt and my skin turned bright pink and wrinkly.

After about two hours, I got out of the tub and dried myself off with a clean white towel which I kept dropping because of the six beers I had just consumed on an empty stomach. I got dressed in my new civilian shirt and trousers, asked a bellboy in the hotel lobby to point me toward the nearest restaurant, navigated across the street, through the door of the restaurant and into a chair with a table in front of it. I ordered a steak dinner with all the trimmings. "No grease," I said to the Chinese waiter, "and nothin' outta cans." I washed it all down with several mixed drinks.

"Well, Ehrhart, it's time to get laid," I said to myself when I'd finished eating. "Jenny's not the only one who can cash in on this free love shit." I headed for the bars. It took me another five hours and a dozen more drinks in as many bars to comprehend that love was not free in Hong Kong. I had never actually made love to a woman, and I was nervous enough as it was. When it finally dawned on me that I might have to pay for it, my stomach collapsed as though it had been punched. But the hour was getting late, and I was determined, and alcohol is a great neutralizer of scruples, even after nineteen years of Christian upbringing.

A plump thirty-five-year-old Chinese prostitute who went by the name of Sunny thus became my first bed partner. Actually, she was very kind. She did all the work, and was very patient with me, and put me to sleep afterwards with a back rub.

I awoke the next morning about eleven o'clock to find myself alone with a violent headache. I got up slowly and checked my clothes for my wallet. It was still there. "Geez, she coulda rolled me easy if she wanted to," I thought as I got dressed. Suffering from guilty revulsion and the vague fear that I had probably contracted some horrible form of venereal disease, I made my way down to the hotel bar to drink my breakfast. There I struck up a conversation with another young Marine named Chuck. We soon got around to women.

"I'm tired of fuckin' slant-eyes," said Chuck, "and I don't like payin' for it."

"Me, too," I said. "Only good thing about last night was that I was too drunk to remember most of it." I didn't tell him it had been my first time.

"There's lotsa round-eyes in this town," he said. "Ya notice that? Let's got find a couple of 'em."

158

There were, in fact, quite a few Europeans in Hong Kong, but the Europeans didn't mingle with the Chinese. They frequented their own bars and restaurants. They never went into the R&R bars. So off we went in search of European women and free love. We'd storm into a European bar, order drinks, and put on our best act for the ladies. Most of them ignored us. Others said:

"I'm waiting for someone."

"Get away from me."

"My husband is a heavyweight boxer."

"You're spilling your drink on me."

When we'd taken all the abuse we could stand, we'd adjourn to a Chinese bar to repair our egos and stoke our courage for another assault on the Europeans. Then off we'd go again.

"Hi, there! Can I buy you a drink?"

"No."

"My name's Bill. What's yours?"

"Winston Churchill."

"No, it's not—oh, ha, ha! Say, that's a good one. You new in town?"

"Look, if you don't leave me alone, I'm going to call a constable."

This went on, bar after bar, back and forth, well into the evening. One woman threw her drink in Chuck's face and began screaming hysterically.

"I didn't say anything! I didn't lay a hand on her!" Chuck protested as the bartender—a very large man who could easily have passed himself off as a DI—assisted us to the door by our shirt collars.

"I ever see you blokes in here again," he said, "I'll bash yer bloody teeth in!" The door closed with a slam.

"I'd a'killed that bastard if he hadn't jumped me from behind," Chuck pointed out, leaning heavily against the building.

"Le's go back in there an' beat his ass good," I suggested.

"Where are we?" asked Chuck.

I leaned carefully out from the building, looking for a street sign. "Nathan Road," I said.

"Good! Where'zat?"

"Hong Kong."

"Which way's Chinatown? I need a drink."

"Sweet fucking Jesus, look at that!" I shouted, pointing toward a tall blond who had just stepped out of a street stall down the block from us. She had her back to us as she walked away, so that all we could see was a cascade of straight long white-blond hair falling down over a grey sweatshirt all the way to her waist, two firm smooth mounds rippling beneath the seat of her blue denim jeans, and a pair of long graceful legs. "Let's go!" I shouted.

"Aw, man," Chuck replied, "I can't take no more o' this shit." But I was already half way to her by then, careening along on a dream and eight solid hours of alcohol. In another moment, I had caught up to her. I reached out, put my hand on her arm, and turned her around.

I couldn't believe it.

She was beautiful.

She was so beautiful, I couldn't believe it.

My hand still on her arm, my mouth dropped open — and then it started working, desperately: "You're the most beautiful woman I've ever seen in the whole world, no kidding, I really mean it, my name's Bill, I been in Vietnam forever and all I wanna do is buy you a drink, one drink, and get you to sit with me for a little while, I wouldn't do anything but just look, no funny business, maybe you could talk a little too if you felt like it, I haven't talked to a real girl in a thousand years, maybe never will again, it would mean so much, you have no idea, just one drink, no tricks, honest, all I wanna do is sit and look at you for awhile and maybe talk a little, you don't have to say anything, just listen, whatever you like — "

And in the middle of my motor-mouth, I noticed she was laughing.

The magical faery queene was laughing. Not a harsh laugh. Not ridicule. Light and clear and honest, it seemed to surround me like the sound of water bubbling among rocks on a warm day, her head lifting and lilting, her shoulders rising and falling with a gentle ease that offered no resistance. I got confused and started talking even faster, then stopped talking altogether and just stood there with my hand on her arm, gazing with bewilderment into the ocean of those sparkling sea-blue eyes.

I'd forgotten completely about Chuck, who, having realized that the woman wasn't going to knock me down or spit on me or walk away or call the cops, came bounding up.

"I saw her first," I said, "get lost."

"Hey, buddies, 'member?" said Chuck. "Semper fi. Gung ho."

"You couldn't take any more, jerk; you were too tired. Why don't ya go lie down somewhere?"

"I feel better now."

"Buzz off."

"My ass."

"Wait! Please," the magical faery queene laughed. "I'll have a drink with both of you. Okay?"

We all went into a nearby bar, got a table and ordered drinks. And then Chuck began to recite everything he'd seen and done in Vietnam. He reeled off every gory detail. I hardly said anything at all. I just sat there, alternately amazed at Chuck and entranced by the white-haired faery queene with the dancing eyes. When we'd finished the first round of drinks, Chuck called for the waiter.

"No more for me, thanks," said the faery queene. Then she turned to me, waved her magic wand, and said, "Well, Bill, where would you like to go now?"

"Huh?" I said.

"Where would you like to go now?"

"Me? Uh, anywhere! Anywhere at all. Whatever you say, sure, lead the way."

"Good night, Chuck," she said, as the two of us got up to leave. "It was nice meeting you."

I followed her out.

The two of us walked to the harbor and sat down on a bench at the end of a pier. The lights from Hong Kong Island glittered above the dark water of the harbor. The lights of the the Star Ferry moved over the dark water. The black silhouettes of the big steamers and cargo ships nestled at anchor on the dark water.

Dorrit von Hellemond was twenty-three years old, a Danish commercial artist traveling around the world slowly, working a few months here and a few months there. She'd spent nearly a year in New York and San Francisco, and had been in Tokyo for a few months. She'd come to Hong Kong in April. She had parents and a younger sister back in Copenhagen. I told her about growing up in Perkasie, and about my family.

"Don't you have a girlfriend?" she asked.

"Yes. Yeh. Uh, well, no. That is, I did when I left the States. I guess I don't anymore."

"I'm sorry. Did she — what happened?"

"She threw me over for some hippie rich kid with a private airplane and a 2-S deferment. Fucking son-of-a-uh-uh, sorry. My mouth, you know? Hangin' around Marines all the time. Anyway, it doesn't matter. Geez! Gerry's never gonna believe this. I'm gonna tell him about it, and he's gonna say, 'Sure, sure, right, pal!' "

"Believe what?" asked Dorrit.

"You!"

"Me?"

"Yeh, you."

Dorrit smiled. I wanted to kiss her. "Who's Gerry?" she asked.

"My best buddy back in Nam. Gerry Griffith. He's a swell guy; you'd really like him. We pal around together, you know, pass the time. Hell of a rummy player."

"I imagine you become very close to each other over there, don't you?"

"Well, yeh, some guys. People are comin' and goin' all the time. Guy rotates back to The World; new guy comes to replace him. You think you know somebody pretty good; then he gets killed or somethin', and you don't even know where to write his folks. I don't know, you *feel* close to 'em."

Neither of us said anything for awhile.

"Were you drafted?" Dorrit finally asked.

"Me? Hell, no. I volunteered. Bad ass, you know? Meanest guy on the block."

Dorrit laughed. "You don't seem so mean. Your friend, Chuck—"

"He's not my friend," I corrected. "I just met him this morning in the hotel."

"Oh. Well, I can picture him in the Marines. But not you." She laughed again.

"Why did you volunteer?"

"Seemed like the thing to do at the time," I grinned.

"That's all?"

"Yeh, well, it's my country, you know? We're over there, and somebody's gotta do it, so I figured, well, okay. So listen, tell me about your job. What kind of stuff do you draw?"

We talked and talked for a long time. I wanted to kiss her, but it seemed sacrilegious. Like putting the make on Snow White.

Late the next morning, I woke up alone in my hotel room. I couldn't remember how or when I'd gotten back. "Jesus Christ," I thought. "Was I that drunk?" I remembered Dorrit's name, but I didn't know where she lived or worked, or how to get in touch with her. It *had* been too good to be true, I realized, the bottom of my stomach falling out. She'd felt sorry for me; didn't have a polite way to excuse herself the night before. Humoring the village idiot. I checked for my wallet; it was still there. "Don't call us," I thought, "we'll call you. Fuck! I need a drink."

I called room service, ordered three beers, and drank them as I washed and dressed. Then I went out on the town. I hit a number of bars, but I wasn't having much fun, and by late afternoon I was back in my hotel room. Soon after I got there, Chuck showed up with a bunch of beer and two army guys he'd met.

"Where's your girlfriend?!" Chuck roared. I mumbled something or other, but he wasn't taking no for an answer. He kept after me until I finally had to admit that I didn't know where she was. "Har! Har!" Chuck roared. "Thought you'd get one up on me, did you? Sucker!"

Chuck filled the two soldiers in with his version of the preceding night. All three of them were howling with laughter, and I was trying to decide whether I should throw myself out the window or throw them out the window when the telephone rang.

"Hello," I said. "What? Who?! Where? Downstairs?!" I shouted. "Come on up! No, wait, I'll be right down!" I slammed the receiver down. "Stick around, chumps," I gloated. "I'll be right back!" I bolted through the door, bounded down the staircase, and flew into the middle of the hotel lobby before Dorrit had gotten ten feet from the telephone. She was still beautiful. I tried to look calm. She was laughing.

When we walked back into the room, Chuck looked up and dropped his beer. The two soldiers suddenly sat bolt upright. All three of them looked like they'd just swallowed live goldfish. They leaped to their feet awkwardly, their eyeballs round and white, and their hands fidgeting nervously at their sides. Dorrit's long white-blond hair was pulled back into a ponytail, and her tropical eyes seemed to be laughing as I introduced her all around. She was wearing a pink minidress, and when she sat down on the bed, the hem barely covered her panties. The guys kept craning their necks, trying to get a look up under that dress without seeming to be doing so. We all drank another beer, and then Dorrit looked over to me and nodded toward the door.

"Well, gentlemen," I said with great dignity, "you will please excuse us, but the lady and I are about to dine. It *has* been jolly though, hasn't it?"

"How did you find me?" I asked Dorrit when we got out of the room.

"You told me where you were staying last night. Don't you remember?" she laughed. "We made a date for tonight."

"Oh, yeh. Sure."

We spent the next two evenings together. Dorrit had to work in the daytime. I'd sleep late, then get up and putter around among the shops and rickshaws and people in the street, trying to make the time pass until I could be with Dorrit again. We'd meet someplace for dinner, then go to a movie or to one of the outdoor marketplaces, or ride the Star Ferry from the mainland to the island and back, or visit the floating village of Aberdeen where people lived their whole lives on tiny sampans all lashed together, side by side and bow to stern.

We went everywhere. Dorrit got me out of the seedy R&R district and opened up the whole city to me. She dragged me around through back streets and alleys I wouldn't have walked through alone to save my life. "You have to see this!" she'd exclaim. "There's a wonderful old silversmith back here." She laughed at my nervous reluctance. She laughed at everything. "Come on, silly, I've been here a dozen times. You *have* to try some of these rice cookies."

The second night, we went to a fancy floating restaurant down on the harbor for a late evening snack. "You've got to try escargots," she insisted, laughing as my face wrinkled with disgust. "They're *not* just snails. Where's your sense of adventure?"

"I came to Hong Kong to get away from adventure."

"You'll love them," she said, sticking one on the end of her fork and pushing it toward my mouth.

The restaurant was very crowded. Along one wall stood a huge ornamental Chinese dragon-chair. Soon after we began eating, a large group of middleaged tourists gathered around the chair and began to have their pictures taken in pairs, each man seated in the chair and wearing the headpiece of a Chinese warlord, each woman wrapped in an embroidered robe and sitting at the feet of the man. The party was loud, rude and causing quite a commotion. They were Americans.

"Must be the Big Bottom, Oklahoma, Rotary Club," I said, wincing and trying to look English.

"Hey, you!" one of them hollered across the room. "Hey, buddy!" He headed directly toward our table, barging across the crowded floor of the dining room.

"Oh, no," I groaned.

"You're American, aren't you? On R&R from Nam, huh?"

"Yessir."

"I thought so! I'd recognize that Uncle Sam haircut anywhere. Hey, it's good to see ya, boy! Have a drink on me. Who's your lady friend here? Her, too. Hey, Charlie Chan, get over here and get these people a drink! Put it on my tab. What'll ya have?"

"Uh, thanks," I said, "we already have something."

"Nonsense, boy! Come on, drink up! Hey, Arnold, come over here!" he bellowed, waving toward the group. "Got a good old American GI here!" He slapped me on the back. "Right outta Vi-et-nam. You a Marine, by any chance?"

"Yes." Everybody in the restaurant was looking at us. "Listen, really, mister, we'd just —"

"Sure, I'd of bet on it. Tell a Marine like my own brother. I was in the Corps; you could tell that, couldn't ya? Double-you double-you two. The big one. Guadalcanal. You bet! Say, I'm proud of you boys, yeh, you better believe it. We're behind ya all the way, and don't you forget it. Those goddamned pinko peaceniks — don't you pay them no mind at all, boy. How's it goin' down there, anyway? Hey, Arnold! Those damned politicians just get off your backs, let ya kick a little commie ass, we'd have this thing over by Christmas! Right, boy? Ain't that right? Say, why don't ya come over and sit with us for awhile. Meet Arnold; he was in the Marines, too. I'll tell ya, small world, ain't it?"

"Look, thanks," I stammered. "We already have our food; thanks for the offer."

"George!" one of the women hollered, waving both arms. "Geo-orge! Come over here! It's our turn!"

"The wife," George beamed, taking my arm and trying to lift me out of my chair. "Come on, boy! Bring your ladyfriend."

"Hey, look mister!" I said sharply, wrestling out of his grip. "We'd just like to finish eating and go. Okay? It's been nice talking with you. Our food's getting cold. Okay?"

"Yeh, sure," said George, looking hurt. Then his face brightened. "Oh, sure!" he winked, leering at Dorrit. "I get the picture. Go to it, boy!" He nudged me with his elbow. "Hey, listen, now, boy, you get back to Nam, you take it to 'em real good, okay? Give 'em a good ol' Yankee what-for! Watch your ass now, ya hear?"

"Yeh, sure, thanks. Goodbye." George barged back across the dining room, bumping several tables and a waiter as he went. I drained my drink in one gulp. I looked over at Dorrit. She was studying me with her head cocked to one side. "What?" I said.

"You're blushing," she said. She burst out laughing. "I'm sorry, I can't help it. If you could see yourself..."

"Ever wish you were somewhere else?" I said. "There it is, Dorrit; the folks I'm fightin' for. Come on, let's get outta here before George gets off his chain again."

"You handled yourself very well under the circumstances, Mr. Ehrhart," said Dorrit, still trying to control her laughter as we left the restaurant. "I thought you were going to punch him."

We went back to Dorrit's apartment, and she invited me up. "I'm sorry it's so small," she said, picking up several folders and sitting down on the bed. "Sit down." The folders contained some of her artwork, and pictures of her family and Denmark, and of the other places she'd been during her travels. We talked for a long time. Finally she stretched out on the bed belly-down with her head on her arms. "Will you rub my back a little?" she asked.

"Sure." I began to rub. Her body was firm and soft at the same time. Her skirt rode high up on her thighs, leaving her pastel green panties visible, the silky material stretched taut across her buttocks. As I worked her back with my fingers and the heels of my hands, stretching and kneading the skin under her dress, her panties pulled gently up into her crotch. I could feel the line of her bra across her back, wondering if it too was green.

"I'm tired," she said.

"Oh, geez," I said, recovering myself and sitting up. "I'm really sorry. I didn't mean to keep you up so late. I better go. You gotta go to work tomorrow."

"No, I don't," she said, taking my hand. "I've taken the day off. We can sleep as late as we like. It's your last day, and I want to spend it all with you."

"No kidding?! That's swell! I better go so you can get some rest. I don't wanna waste a minute tomorrow. Call me when you get up, okay?" I gave her a quick kiss on the cheek, and bolted out the door in a hot flush and a buzz of confusion. I walked the seven blocks back to the hotel.

Early the next morning, I was awakened by a knock at the door. When I opened it, there stood Dorrit. She was laughing.

We took the Star Ferry over to the island, then took a cab to Repulse Bay Beach. "My favorite place," she said. The beach lay in a deep cove with Victoria Peak looming high over one end of the bay. We spent the whole day lying on the white sand in the bright sunlight, or playing in the calm water. Dorrit would surface-dive and swim underwater, circle around behind me, grab me by the waist, and come up spitting water into my ear and laughing. Every time she touched me, I wanted to shout. She wore a tiny bikini that barely covered her breasts and hips, and her smooth flat tummy rippled with firm muscles. The jukebox in the concession stand played a song about gentle

166

people with flowers in their hair. As we lay in the sand, I leaned on one elbow and held Dorrit's hand.

"You gotta give me a picture, you know? Gerry's *never* gonna believe this. Dorrit von Hellemond. *I* don't believe it. I'm gonna wake up any minute now in a foxhole in Vietnam."

"Stop it," Dorrit pouted.

"Now you're blushing," I laughed.

In the evening, we rode the cog-tram to the top of Victoria Peak, where we had dinner and watched the sunset. Then we went to an open-air market where hundreds of stalls and booths offered everything from sweet potatoes to Chairman Mao's Little Red Book. I found a magnificent hand-tooled Chinese brass cannon inlaid with silver and gold, and was about to buy it when Dorrit stopped me.

"Please don't," she said. "It's beautiful, but — I just don't want to think of you that way. Buy me this!" she added quickly, her face brightening as she pointed to the next stall. She picked up a delicate silk flower with yellow and orange petals and a green leafy stem. "This is what I want from you."

Late in the evening, we rode the Star Ferry back to Kowloon and walked to the hotel. I'd bought some presents for my family and for Jenny, but hadn't had time to mail them, so Dorrit was going to do it for me. As I wrapped and addressed the packages, Dorrit sat on the bed without speaking. When I turned around, she was crying soundlessly. I went over to the bed and sat down beside her. She reached across with her left hand and pulled my head down to her breasts. She made no noise at all, but I could feel her body shaking and I had to bite my lip hard to keep from crying myself. I wasn't even sure why. We sat there for a long time, clinging to each other and not talking. Reluctantly, I finally said that I'd better call a cab and get her home.

Dorrit lifted my head and cradled it between her hands. She looked me right in the face. "I want to stay with you tonight," she said. The blood began pounding in my temples. I stared at her. I tried to work my mouth, but nothing happened. "I'm sorry," she said, turning her face aside. "I wanted to give you a present to take with you. I didn't mean to push myself on you. If you don't want me to stay —"

"No, no, of course!" I shouted, bursting alive. "I just — hell, yes, I want you to stay, please stay, I had no idea, I mean, I really didn't think, I never — Jesus Christ, I gotta shave, wait a minute, I just gotta shave..." I raced off to the bathroom, lathered up, sliced my face in half a dozen places, and dumped half a bottle of Jade East cologne over my head. I could hear Dorrit laughing.

When I came out of the bathroom, Dorrit was lying in bed in a pink and yellow flowered slip with the white sheets turned down to her waist, and her long blond hair fanned out over the white pillow, and her mouth still open in a sparkling laugh—but there was no sound coming out, and her sea-blue eyes burned like sapphires, and both of her arms were stretched up to meet me.

Bang! Bang! Bang! "Time to go!" someone was shouting as he pounded on the door. "Your bus waiting! Time to go!"

I picked up my wristwatch from the nightstand and looked at it. Eight a.m. I looked over at Dorrit, who was lying beside me with her eyes open. The strident high-pitched voice and the pounding at the door continued: "Time to go, sir! The bus waiting!" Bang! Bang! Bang! I got up slowly, my head throbbing from too little sleep. I went to the window and looked down at the street; there was a green military bus waiting to take me to the airport, where a plane waited to take me back to Vietnam. I turned around and looked at Dorrit again, who was sitting up in bed now.

"I ain't goin' back," I said. I walked over to the door and opened it. "Stop bothering me," I told the bellboy. "Beat it. Understand?" I hung the 'Do Not Disturb' sign on the outside knob, closed the door, walked back to the bed, and knelt down on the floor at Dorrit's feet. "I ain't goin' back," I repeated. I laid my head in her lap, put my arms around her hips, and held on tight.

"You have to go back," said Dorrit, stroking my head.

"The hell I do. The whole thing's crazy. I'm tired of it. Let's go to Macao. We can hop the ferry this afternoon and start all over again. You can find a job easy. And I'll find something. Diggin' ditches. Something. I don't care."

"Please, Bill," Dorrit suddenly sobbed, "please, don't make it any harder for me. You *have* to go back."

"*Why?!*" I burst out vehemently. "What the hell for? Go back there and get my brains blown out? You got *any* idea what's goin' *on* down there? For chrissake," I snapped, pointing to the yellow and orange silk flower lying on top of Dorrit's dress, "you think *that's* me? You think that's what I am? You wanna know somethin'? So far I've killed two armed vc—maybe one more—and I've blown away a six-year-old-boy, and an unarmed sixty-five-year-old grandmother, and a fifty-year-old man with his hands tied behind him. They oughta toss me in jail and throw away the key for what I've done. So whadda they do?! They promote me to *corporal*, for chrissake!"

"Bill, please, don't—"

168

"No, Dorrit, listen to this! You're tellin' me I gotta go back; I'll tell you what I'm goin' back to. You think that guy Chuck was just tryin' to impress you or something? You think he made up all that stuff? That's what's goin' down there! You know how we interrogate people, Dorrit?"

"Bill! Please!" Dorrit cried, her voice pleading. But I was on my feet now, my back turned to her, my voice rising to a shout.

"Listen! Listen! We take the flash suppressors on our M-16s and stick 'em into the top of the foot, lean on the rifle butt, and twist. You know, like imagine a big screwdriver stickin' into your foot right here." I wheeled around, bent down, and jabbed my finger into the tendons and bones behind Dorrit's big toe and second toe. "And this ain't like armed guerrillas. This is just Mr. Joe Blow, the rice farmer, and his wife. I've seen feet split right in half like that. Works like a charm. Only they don't know nothin' to talk about except they want us to go the hell away and leave 'em alone, that's all. Only we don't wanna hear that, so we split the other foot, too. Nice, huh?

"You know what we do, we get sniped at from some ville?" I leaped to my feet again, pacing wildly around the room. "Some guy — maybe don't even live there — takes a couple of potshots at us. We call in an airstrike. Couple of snake-eyes, couple of napalm canisters — instant French fries, level the whole ville. Then go in and count up the bodies. Oh, yeh, the brass likes body counts. Anything dead is vc. And you know what, Dorrit? I can make it read like we scored a great victory against the forces of communism and evil. It's easy! Call somebody's house an enemy structure. Call a bombshelter an enemy fortified position. Call a helpless old man a de-tai-nee. Bingo! Facts and figures. We win. Not only *can* I do it — I *have* to do it! They don't *wanna* know the truth, Dorrit. They got the whole thing all worked out, Dorrit, and you better not be the one to tell 'em we ain't gettin' nowhere.

"And we *ain't* gettin' nowhere," I went on, my voice crackling harshly as I waved off Dorrit's attempt to interrupt me. "No fuckin' place at all. Oh, there's vc around somewhere — I know because they keep killin' my buddies. But I'll be damned if we can find 'em. Round and round and round, just chasin' our own tail. Crazy, Dorrit — and it's makin' *me* crazy. You know the first night we met, you asked why I volunteered? You wanna know why I volunteered? I was gonna be a hero. Oh, yeh. Before I even signed the papers, I had it all figured out. I could see myself in a dress blue uniform with medals all over it, standin' there at attention for the national anthem at a Pennridge High

169

School football game — all the girls I ever wanted fawnin' at my feet, and every guy that ever gave me a bad time headin' for the exits double-time.

"And look at me now. Look at me, Dorrit!" Dorrit's eyes were red, her cheeks wet with tears. I kneeled down in front of her, put a hand on either side of her face, and made her look at me. And then I began to cry, too. Long and hard, my body suddenly going slack and shaking limply from the force of the sobs that tore at my stomach like rough claws. For a long time, I couldn't talk. We held on to each other tightly, Dorrit gently rocking me like a baby. "If there's a God in heaven," I finally said, my voice a hoarse whisper, "I'm gonna burn in hell forever."

"Oh, no, no, no," Dorrit crooned, "it's not your fault. It's not your fault."

"Who's fault is it? I'm through, Dorrit. Please let me stay with you. Please don't make me go back."

We both cried some more, then Dorrit lifted me off my knees and lay back on the bed, drawing me to her and nestling my head between her arm and breast. When she spoke, her voice sounded hollow and far away, as though she were in a trance.

"Please try to understand," she said. "Please. I care very much for you. I would do anything to keep you here with me if I could. You are too gentle and kind a man to suffer what you are going through. But you know what will happen if you do not. Where could we go? You don't have a passport. You can't even get to Macao without a passport, let alone anywhere else. How long do you think it would take to find an American deserter in Hong Kong? A week? A month? A year? And if they never found you? Are you willing to stay here for the rest of your life? Can you live like that? Can you ask me to live like that? How would you get a job? Who would hire you? Can you lie for the rest of your life? Can you prove your lies? What about your parents? You would never be able to see them again. Are you ready to turn your back on them forever?"

"But I just *can't* — "

"No, Bill. You *must* listen to me. You *must* go back because that way there is a chance, at least — and that is the only way. I can't live the way you are asking — and you can't either. You have only five more months. Maybe it seems like a long time — I *know* it seems like a long time — but five months is nothing against the rest of your life. There is too much ahead of you to throw it all away now. I won't let you do that. I care too much for you. *Please* go back." She paused for a moment. "I promise you I will see you again when it's all over." She wrapped me in her arms, and kissed my eyes and cheeks and temples and lips. "I promise you," she said again. "We'll be together again someday soon, and perhaps then things will be different, and we can find a real beginning."

Chapter 26

The bus was long gone by the time I had gotten my act together and was ready to leave. I had to flag down a cab. I left Dorrit standing on the curb in front of the hotel, and barely made it to the airport just as my plane was loading. We landed in Danang a few hours later.

I couldn't get a flight out of Danang that day, so I had to spend the night in the transient barracks by the airfield, sleeping badly to the unfamiliar deafening roar of afterburners from the jet fighters and bombers rocketing off the runway only a few dozen meters away. The next day, I managed to hop a C-130 as far north as Phu Bai, but got stuck again, and had to spend another night in a transient barracks. In the morning, I talked a CH-46 crewman into getting me aboard his helicopter for a flight north to Dong Ha, and from there hitch-hiked the seven miles south to the battalion's new position near the hamlet of Ai Tu, fourteen miles below the Demilitarized Zone between North and South Vietnam.

I arrived exhausted and grumpy. Already Dorrit and the vision of Eden were taking on the blurred quality of a dream. By the time I reached Battalion, my clothes and skin were coated anew with the dust and grit of Vietnam, as though I had never left. "Don't bother me," I told one and all, turning aside all inquiries about my R&R. "Where do I sleep?" I hastily threw up a one-man poncho-tent, dug a shallow fighting hole beside it, crawled into the tent, and fell asleep.

Plopfwhoosh. Plopfwhoosh. "Mortars!" I thought, opening my eyes in the darkness to the sound of mortar rounds leaving their tubes.

Plopfwhoosh. Plopfwhoosh. Plopfwhoosh. My heart suddenly dropped into my stomach, my body already diving for the fighting hole before I was awake enough to tell myself to move. Shouts of "Incoming! Incoming!" rose all around me as I hit the hole, tucking myself up under my helmet and flak jacket in a fetal position. Plopfwhoosh. Plopfwhoosh. You could hear the rounds gently rising through their high trajectories, the tone of the dull whistle changing audibly as the first rounds hit the top of their arc and began the descent toward earth. Other rounds were still going out: plopfwhoosh, plopfwhoosh. A dozen more rounds left their tubes before the first rounds began impacting. Plopfwhoosh, plopfwhoosh, plopfwhoosh. I waited for the rounds to start dropping in, my body shivering, my teeth chattering uncontrollably, my thoughts frozen into a soundless scream.

Shells began to burst all around me, louder than the loudest fireworks of a Fourth of July fantasy, the blasts stifling the scream that had never emerged from my throat. You could hear jagged pieces of hot steel tearing at the darkness. Cascades of dirt and sand, and clots of debris, rained down into my fighting hole, pounding an irregular rhythm against my helmet and flak jacket, striking my arms and legs. I curled up even more tightly, burying my face in the dirt, my whole body tight as steel wire, my fingernails digging into the palms of my clenched fists. Jesus, shit, Mother, fuck, fuck, stop it!!

We took twenty or thirty rounds in two, maybe three, minutes. When the explosions finally stopped, a familiar eerie silence fell over everything, broken only by groaning men and screaming men and frantic shouts of "Corpsman!" I could hear Sergeant Seagrave nearby, moving among the scouts' positions: "Anybody hit? You guys all right?"

I stuck my head up. "Yeh. I'm okay."

"Welcome back. Come on." None of the scouts had been hit, but other Marines nearby had been. We spent the next helf hour locating the wounded and getting them to the aid station while two helicopters out of Dong Ha beat the air overhead, criss-crossing the countryside with powerful searchlights, occasionally firing long bursts from their heavy machineguns, though we never did find out what they were firing at. Shadows, most likely; just shadows.

The attack had begun about 0130. I finally settled down enough to lie down again around 0330. When I crawled back under my poncho tent, I noticed it was riddled with shrapnel holes. Several holes were large enough to put my fist through. The interminable dry season had finally broken in mid-September, and we'd been getting rain every other day or so. "Watch it rain tonight," I thought. It did.

Chapter 27

The next morning, I had a chance to look around at my new home. However crude had been the battalion command post down near Hoi An, it had been civilization compared to this: no berm, no straight rows of strongback hooches, no COC, no mess hall, no cold showers, no walk-up four-holers with toilet paper within easy reach, no electricity, no nothing. Marines were encamped in random fashion all over the place, living in poncho tents, two-man field tents, under tarpaulins, and in jury-rigged contraptions of tin and cardboard. Several heavy coils of barbed concertina wire marked the compound's perimeter.

About a mile to the west, low foothills began to rise toward the mountains and rain forests on the Vietnam-Laos border. The coastal plain was much more narrow up here, and I'd noticed the day before, on the ride down from Dong Ha, that the land was much more sparsely populated, though abandoned fields and several large abandoned Catholic churches indicated that there had once been more people in the area.

The battalion was providing security for the Navy SeaBees, who were constructing a new landing strip to supplement the airfields at Phu Bai and Dong Ha. The new airfield was going in on a strip of land between Highway One and the river which flowed only ten meters from where I'd slept. I hadn't even noticed the river the night before. The heavy construction equipment of the SeaBees clanked and roared, churning everything to a fine powdery dust.

I checked in with Captain Braithewaite, and met the new S-2 chief, Staff Sergeant Bochman—a smallish man, taller than me but thinly built, with a heavy black moustache and a big nose. Then I went back to the scouts' positions along the river. Amagasu and Morgan were sitting by the river bank.

"Where is everybody?" I asked.

"On the other side of the river," said Morgan. "They went to see if they could find anything from last night."

"Fat chance," I said. "What are you doin' here?"

"Blister," said Morgan, lifting his bare foot to show me an ugly red open sore.

"Listen, you guys, I don't need any more bullshit like last night," I said. "What we need is some real fortifications. I got an idea." I explained my plan, and the three of us began digging like gophers.

First we dug out a rectangular pit large enough to sleep three and about eighteen inches deep. Then we filled a couple of hundred sandbags, lined the pit with them, and added three more layers above the ground, making a total inside vertical wall of about three feet. To the head and foot walls we added two more rows of sandbags, each shorter than the one below, to form a crude sloping roofline so that rain water would be carried off. We scrounged a two-by-four from the Sea-Bees to use as a roof beam, and hooked two of our ponchos together over the roof beam to form the roof. Since my poncho was no good for the roof, we used that one for a ground cloth. We scrounged a Coleman gas lantern and hung it from the roof beam, removed a few sandbags from one wall to form an entrance, and there it was: an architectural masterpiece. We were sitting there admiring our work when the rest of the scouts came in.

"Find anything?" asked Amagasu.

"Nothin'," said Sergeant Seagrave.

"What the hell is that?" asked Walters.

"Only the finest fortified bedroom in Southeast Asia," I said. "Sleeping quarters, reading room and fighting hole all in one."

"Next time the gooks hit us," added Amagasu, "we going to sleep right through it like babies."

"Hey, Hoffy," said Walters, "let's build one of them. Mogerty, you in? Where'd you get the sandbags?" Within a few minutes, the rest of the scouts had scattered in twos and threes, and were busily digging holes and filling sandbags. A combat Levittown began to rise along the west bank of the river.

"You seen Gerry around?" I asked Amagasu.

175

"He's still down south somewhere with the rest of the baggage. Should be in today or tomorrow. The lucky stiff gets a hooch when he gets here. Has to keep his safes dry. Do you believe it? The fucking safes get it better than we do."

"You're the one that wants to be an American," I pointed out.

"So, Bill, whadya do on your R&R?" asked Seagrave. "You bring back a dose of the clap?"

"Danish women don't have venereal disease," I said.

"What the fuck?" asked Seagrave. I took out the photograph and told them about Dorrit, though I left out my near-desertion.

"Lies, lies!" Hoffy insisted.

"You wish," I replied.

"You get that for *free*?" Wally asked in disbelief.

"Absolutely."

"Oh, man; oh, man," Wally moaned, pumping his entrenching tool like a huge penis. "Get me back to The Wooorld!"

"College girls!" Aymes shouted. "Turn me loose on the coeds."

"Where you gonna find a coed?" Hoffy asked. "Much less a fuckin' coed." He howled at his own joke.

"Hey, you wait, motherfucker," said Aymes. "I ain't gonna be in this Green Mother forever. I'm goin' to college—already applied. UCLA. California girls! Wahoo!"

"You really apply to college already?" asked Hoffy.

"Sure. Gotta apply now if I want to start next September. You think I'm gonna spend the rest of my life in this fuckin' Green Mother-fucker?"

"Well," said Hoffy slowly. "I might."

"You?!" Wally howled. "They'll *throw* you out. Shit, man, you already made corporal twice—and you been busted back down twice." It was true. Hofstatter was one of those characters who could do anything you asked of him in a tight situation in the field—and often didn't wait to be asked—but as soon as the pressure was off, he was immediately into some kind of trouble.

"So?" said Hoffy. "Half you guys ain't even made corporal once. I get three squares a day, and a paycheck every month."

"You can't be a lifer," Aymes pointed out. "Who ever heard of a lifer-private? I think they really do boot you out after awhile."

"To begin with, Hoffy," Mogerty added, "you don't get square meals out of round cans. And private's pay ain't worth havin'. And if you stick around here long enough, you're liable to get your fuckin' brains served up on a platter."

176

"So what am I supposed to do out there in The World?" Hoffy asked. "Join the fuckin' Peace Corps? Can't do nothin' but clean rifles and fill sandbags. Don't nobody laugh, but I never even finished high school; flunked a couple of times, and then quit."

Wally opened his mouth, and Seagrave immediately clapped a hand over it. "You know you can get one of those GED high school diplomas while you're still in, don't you?" said Seagrave.

"Yeh, I know," said Hoffy, shrugging his shoulders. "Maybe when I get back to the States."

"You really goin' to college?" Morgan asked Aymes.

"Hell, yes. I only enlisted to get in on the GI Bill. Two years and out; that's all I want."

"I'd sure like to go to school," said Morgan. "I don't know. I did pretty well in high school, but my dad needs help on the farm. He had a stroke a couple of years ago; don't get around like he used to. We got a dairy farm up north of the Twin Cities; been in the family since my great-granddad. I guess I'll end up there. It ain't such a bad life, really, but you're workin' all the time."

"I'll tell ya what I'm gonna do," Seagrave piped in. "I'm gonna find me a Cajun Queen, catch a mess of crawfish down on the bayou, and eat an' fuck for the next twenty years! Hey, Ski, you wanna come to Louisiana with me? Show ya some easy livin'."

"No, thanks, Gravey," said Stemkowski, taking off his bush hat and wiping his face with it. "I got all the Cajun Queen I need back home. My girlfriend's already in college—gonna be a nurse. I'm thinkin' about goin' to medical school."

"Medical school?" Hoffy jumped in. "I seen the way you open C-rats. Hack, hack, chop! Oh, what's this? Hemorrhoids? Nurse, pass the meat cleaver."

"Aw, fuck off, Hoffy," Stemkowski shot back. "Not everyone's as dumb as you are."

"Hey, don't get riled. You know I'm just teasin', don't ya. You wanna go to medical school, that's fine. Do it. You'd make a good doctor, I bet. I'll give you my bunions and stuff; you fix 'em up, okay?"

"Yeh, okay," said Stemkowski, tousling Hoffy's hair.

"Wally, whatta you got planned?" I asked.

"Me? I'm goin' back to Texas; gonna cook up a big pot of chili hot enough to sweat out every last ounce of this dump. And I'm gonna eat every bite of it real slow. Wash it down with a lot of tequila. Then maybe I'll go on up to Detroit and help Mogerty steal hubcaps. Hey, Mo, what does 'Mogerty' mean, anyway?"

"It means what it says," Mogerty replied. "Mo-Ger-Ty. You know? I'm from the Motor City." Wally looked at Mogerty with a puzzled expression. "Think about it," said Mogerty, grinning.

Wally thought about it for a few moments, his brows wrinkling and unwrinkling, then he gave up. "Let's go swimmin'!" he beamed. "Last one in's a gook motherfucker." Clothes began flying in all directions.

"Hold it!" Seagrave hollered. "Not all at once. Couple of guys gotta stay up here and post lookout. Take turns. I'll take first watch. Who else?"

"Me," said Amagasu.

"Okay," said Seagrave, "hit it. But don't get greedy — everybody takes a turn up here."

After a morning of digging, and filling and stacking sandbags, the cool water of the river felt gloriously liberating. The clouds had broken and the sun was shining. The water was clean. Stripped down to the buff, we splashed and flopped around like seals. The current was so swift that you had to swim upstream just to stay in place. Just a few meters offshore, the water must have been at least five meters deep; I dove for the bottom, but couldn't touch it. Though the river was about forty meters wide, we all stayed close to the west bank since the east bank was ungarrisoned and unguarded.

The sharp slap of bullets striking water came a split-second before the sound of the shots. "Sniper!" several guys hollered at once.

The warning was unnecessary. With the first report, the splash-party broke up, scouts heading for the riverbank like frantic tadpoles. I was out of the water and half way up the sandy bank when someone hollered, "Aymes is still in the river! He's hit!" Still scrambling up the bank, I looked back. Aymes lay face-down in the water, his arms floating limply on the surface of the river, the current already carrying him swiftly south. I raced back down the bank, dove in, and swam after him. Seagrave and Amagasu had opened fire immediately, and now other Marines, attracted by the gunfire, lay on the top of the riverbank firing toward the trees and bushes on the opposite bank. I swam after Aymes, holding my head up as high as I could to keep him in sight, stroking for all I was worth.

The level of fire quickly rose to a bristling storm of small arms and exploding grenades from M-79 grenade launchers. I reached Aymes and grabbed for his chin as I had been taught to do only two summers before in Red Cross Life Saving. I pulled his head up, reached across his chest with my other hand, and took him in a cross-chest

178

carry. As I did, a red-gray ooze spilled down over my arm and I almost threw up. It was Aymes' brain. There was a hole the size of my fist where his right eye should have been. The current swept us out toward the middle of the river. Already we were a hundred meters south of where we had been swimming.

"Throw me a line! Throw me a line!" I hollered. I couldn't tell if we were still taking fire. I used Aymes' body as a shield. A rope fell across us; I fumbled for it and caught hold, tied it around Aymes' chest, and held on as we were pulled ashore. A corpsman was already waiting. "Forget it, Doc," I said as we hauled Aymes' body out of the water and up over the top of the bank to safety. "He's dead." The firing had stopped. I looked across at the opposite bank, but there was no one there. I went down to the river again, knelt down, and washed the remains of Aymes off my arm and shoulder. I was still stark naked. I threw up in the river, watching the slime drift away swiftly in little swirls and widening streaks. I washed the sour taste out of my mouth. Seagrave was there when I turned around.

"Nice try," he said.

"Guess we don't go swimmin' anymore, huh?"

"Guess not," said Seagrave, putting his arm around my shoulder. "You okay?"

"Yeh." We walked back to where I'd left my clothes. Wally was livid with rage and helpless frustration.

"Look at this fuckin' piece of shit!" he stormed. He had his M-16 broken open at the breach. A shell casing minus the rear end was stuck in the chamber, and another round had been driven in on top of it. "Goddamn these fuckin' pieces of shit! Goddamn it! Goddamn it!" He threw the rifle down hard, hurling it with all his might. It broke in half. "You motherfuckin' gook bastards!" he screamed toward the opposite bank of the river.

"You know," I said to Seagrave as I got dressed, "you oughta talk to Captain Braithewaite, Gravey; see if he can get us M-14s with selectors. I'd rather have the extra weight and know the damned thing's gonna fire when I need it."

"Hey, buddy!" I turned around, and there was Gerry. He slapped me on the back. "How was R&R? What's goin' on here?"

"What are you doin' here?" I asked.

"Just got in about ten minutes ago. I heard the shooting. What's goin' down?"

"We were swimmin' in the river. Sniper got Aymes. Right through the head."

179

"Jesus. They didn't waste much time rollin' out the red carpet, did they?"

"You shoulda been here last night. We got mortared. Pretty heavy — twenty or thirty rounds — I didn't count 'em. I was too busy holdin' on to my ass."

"I think we found the war."

"Yeh? Looks like the same old shit to me. Hit an' run, hit an' run. Jesus Christ, I'm tired of this."

"You okay?"

"Yeh, I'm okay. Just shook up, that's all. I fished Aymes out of the water. Christ, his brains spilled out all over me. Big fuckin' hole in his head. Christ. Come on, let's get outta here. You got stuff to unpack?"

"Whole shitload. Got the whole S&C shop with me."

"Gravey, you need me right now? I'm goin' with Gerry; help him get set up, okay?" Gerry and I walked over to the hooch that was to be the S&C office.

"You seen Haller yet?" he asked.

"No. He's around here somewhere, I guess. I just got in last night. Took me two days to get from Danang."

"So tell me about your R&R? You have a good time?"

"You're not gonna believe it, man. It was glorious. Fuckin' amazing." I told him about Dorrit, producing the photograph to go along with the story.

"Are you kidding me?" he spluttered, dropping a pile of papers and taking the picture out of my hand.

"It's the God's honest truth, Gerry. Like a goddamned Hollywood movie, except it really happened."

"You stole this off of some drunk, didn't you?" he said, waving the picture. "Come clean. What kind of sucker you take me for?"

"Like hell I did. I slept with that lady. I did *everything* with her. It was paradise, man; fuckin' paradise."

"*She's gorgeous!*"

"She's more than that, pal. She's the closest thing I'll ever get to the angels."

"You shoulda stayed right where you were, you fool."

"I thought about it, pal," I said slowly. "I fuckin' well thought about it."

"You ever gonna see her again?"

"I hope so. She promised me she would, and I think she meant it. I don't know; I'll still have fifteen months left in this fuckin' Green

Mother when I get outta here. I don't know what I'm gonna do. Maybe she'll come to the States. I'll figure somethin' out."

"What about Jenny?"

"What about her? Wasn't me did the Dear John number. Hell, I don't know. I don't know what to think. I'll tell ya, Gerry, you got no idea how close I came to packin' it all in and stayin' there in Hong Kong. Straight scoop."

"Well, I'm glad you didn't buddy. You'd of got yourself in a shitload of trouble if you had."

"Yeh, I know. That's what Dorrit said. I was all set to do it. Probably spend the rest of my life wishin' I had. You know what finally changed my mind? I could see you wanderin' around without me like a goddamned stupid cow. Mooo! Get your ass blown right off, I ain't here to tell ya where to hide it."

Gerry started to react, then closed his mouth again, grinned and grabbed me by the arm. "Good to see you again, Bill," he said. "What's it look like around here?"

"What you see is what you get. Been here eighteen hours, and already I've been shot at and mortared. We'll probably get overrun tonight. One good thing, though — I won't be cooped up in the COC anymore. We ain't got one. No daily intelligence summary. No H&I lists. No bunker watch. Don't even have a typewriter. Too bad, huh?"

"I'll lend you mine."

"Like hell! Don't even tell Captain B you got one. Fuckin' pushin' papers gives me a headache. Captain B says me and Kenny are gonna be mostly scouts from now on. Fine with me. I'll take the boonies any day — only thing you gotta worry about is stayin' alive. You know, I bet folks back in The World would think I'm kidding."

"Looks like we're all in the boondocks around here."

"At least you got a hooch. You know who's got a hooch? The Colonel, the XO, and you. Pretty fancy company you're keepin' these days."

"Influence. I got influence. Gunny Johnson's replacement show up yet?"

"Yeh. Staff sergeant named Bochman. He looks all right. I don't know. I just talked to him for a little while this morning. Never been in Intelligence before; been an Admin man for eight years. Said he was gonna get out, but they offered him another stripe and a change of jobs if he'd re-up, so he did. Imagine that. He coulda got out, so he ends up in Vietnam instead. Lifers! Jesus. I wouldn't stay in for four stars and a fat job at the Pentagon."

"I thought you were thinkin' about tryin' to get an appointment to Annapolis?"

"Don't jerk me off. When'd I tell you that? First night we did guard together? Where you been the last five months?"

Chapter 28

I had, in fact, considered applying for an appointment to Annapolis. For five or six years, from the time I was nine or ten, I had wanted to go to Annapolis. Joe Belino, an All-American quarterback for the Midshipmen in the early sixties, had been an idol of mine. I'd had a Naval Academy decal on my bicycle and an Academy pennant on my bedroom wall. I'd built plastic models of ships and carrier-borne aircraft, and carefully hand-painted them.

The notion had somehow lost steam by my junior year of high school, a victim perhaps of girls, beer and a driver's license, my thoughts dwelling less and less on Midshipmen and more and more on Saturday nights. After that footloose crazy fantasy-come-true summer of living on my own in California between my junior and senior years of high school, I'd applied to UCLA in the fall of my senior year, having forgotten completely about the Naval Academy.

But by then, Vietnam had become something on the order of a real live shooting war, and I'd enlisted, knowing full well that I would end up in Vietnam.

My DIs at Parris Island had first reintroduced the possibility of my going to Annapolis. Because the Marine Corps comes under the Department of the Navy, ten percent of Academy graduates may opt for commissions in the Marines. In addition, a certain number of appointments to the Academy are made each year from the enlisted ranks of the Navy and Marine Corps. I'd been an honors student in high school, and the DIs had thought I'd make a good candidate for

Annapolis. Of course, I'd have to serve a tour in Vietnam first, but they'd assured me that with my high school record and a good combat record, I'd be a shoo-in for the Academy once I got back to the States.

So I'd gone to Vietnam with that notion banging around in my head, along with a lot of other vague notions. I had had, in fact, only two clear thoughts when I'd arrived in Vietnam: coming home again, and marrying Jenny. Beyond that, my future, in my own thoughts, had neither substance nor form. Dreams rose to the surface like bubbles, and floated off, leaving nothing behind. Once the challenge had been met, everything else would take care of itself. The intensity of that belief increased exponentially with each passing month. March 5, 1968 — the date of my rotation home — loomed like a neon gateway to liberation.

As the patrol moved soundlessly through the damp overcast night, I thought about Gerry's reminder of a possible appointment to Annapolis, almost laughed out loud, then felt a rush of acute embarrassment at the realization that I had once actually told him I was considering it. It felt as though I had been caught insisting with a straight face that the world was flat. For without my even noticing, over the previous nine months, a new thought had emerged slowly and hardened into a concrete resolve: I knew that once I left Vietnam, I would never again go anywhere that required a uniform and the forfeiture of my right to come and go as I chose.

Even the fact that I would still have fifteen months more to serve in the Marines, once I left Vietnam, could make no dent in that resolve. Like every other incongruent fact, like Jenny's Dear John letter, like the shadowy fear that America was no longer home, it was simply relegated to the unsolvable equation of the future lying somewhere out beyond the neon gate. Facts were easy to ignore in Vietnam; it was a way of life. When facts got in the way, you could conjure a dream by force of will, and make the future bright again. A reconciliation with Jenny and a stateside reunion with Dorrit posed no contradiction at all; an infinite number of dreams can dance on the head of a pin.

We were about forty-five minutes out on a four-hour patrol route that would take us southwest into the foothills and back to Battalion when it began to rain. It was cold. The monsoon had begun so slowly that I had hardly noticed it. But now, after months and months of violent unbroken heat, sixty-five–degree rain felt like late autumn hurrying toward winter. Sergeant Seagrave halted the patrol, allowing us to don rainsuits or ponchos, a few scouts changing at a time while

184

others stood at the ready. The ponchos were ungainly and awkward, the loose folds getting in the way of equipment and making more noise than one cared to make at night in the field. Rainsuits were much better. Nothing more than rubberized pants and jackets, they fit the body snugly. They were nonporous, causing you to sweat even in cold weather, but they sealed in body heat and didn't get in the way. Because of my seniority, I'd gotten first pick of Aymes' gear when we'd divided it up. I'd taken his rainsuit. The patrol moved on through the rain.

We were just at the base of the hills, the low white mounds of a large Vietnamese burial site on either side of us, when the horizon behind the hill directly in front of us began to flicker and dance with orange-white light. Plopfwhoosh, plopfwhoosh, plopfwhoosh. "Jesus Christ," someone whispered hoarsely, "they're hitting the airfield again." Plopfwhoosh, plopfwhoosh, plopfwhoosh. The mortar tubes were just behind the hill, less than 1000 meters away. And they were really pouring it on, even more heavily than the night before. The patrol was in between the mortar positions and the airfield, and you could hear the rounds passing overhead. Behind us, shells began exploding in the battalion compound.

The shelling took on a dreamlike aura. The flashing explosions lit up the silhouettes of tents leaping high into the air in slow motion to collapse into darkness and distant noise. I thought of the night before, lying in the midst of the chaos, but in place of the terror came only a curious sense of discomfort. I thought of the night Gerry and I had watched the Vietcong bombard Hieu Nhon and Hoi An. I wondered if Co Chi, the beautiful shy young woman who had worked at Hieu Nhon, was still alive. Directly under the arc of the shells, I thought about shortrounds, my head involuntarily flinching. I thought about Gerry and my stomach tightened: "Don't hit Gerry," I thought. "Don't hit Gerry."

The firing stopped. The last shells exploded in the rainy darkness. The silence swept over the graveyard, deeper and more resonant than ever. Rain beat noisily against my rubber rainsuit.

"Let's go get 'em!" someone whispered. It sounded like Hoffy.

"Hold on," said Sergeant Seagrave. "Stay down. They're gonna have a chopper up in a few minutes. We go anywhere near those gooks, the chopper's liable to take us for the fuckin' VC. Wally, get on the horn; find out what they want us to do."

A new fear seized me. I thought of the night before, of those two helicopter gunships with the powerful searchlights and barking snarling machineguns. From the air, would we look any different from the Vietcong? I looked around for cover, but the graveyard offered nothing. Not even a headstone. Only the low flat gravel-topped mounds. "We're gonna get wasted by our own people," I thought. "Jesus fuck!"

Through the rain came the beating whine of helicopter blades, and then we could see the searchlight sweeping down through the rain as the helicopter began to work the whole area systematically. And then another thought: would the vc rush the compound in the confusion. I tried to look around and press myself flat at the same time.

"Wally, you got Battalion?" asked Seagrave, an edge of urgency in his calm voice. "Gimme the receiver. Annunciate, Annunciate; this is Annunciate Two Sierra. We got a chopper overhead. Do you have radio contact? Who the fuck does? Well, find out. You better tell somebody we're out here, goddamn it! That's a roger. Affirmative. Negative, goddamn it! Get him the hell away from us!"

The gunship was almost directly overhead, coming in fast at less than five hundred feet. I plastered myself to the ground, trying to look like a Vietnamese burial mound. The spotlight passed right over me. "Jesus, Jesus, motherfucker!" I waited for the gunfire. Nothing happened. When I looked up, the light was two hundred meters away.

"Have you got him yet?" Seagrave barked into the headset. "Yeh, yeh, roger, Annunciate. Mogerty, where's the map? Gimme the map." Seagrave lit a small red flashlight and pressed it against the map. "Annunciate; this is Two Sierra. Our position is approximately Yankee Tango 465837. Victor Charlie at Yankee Tango 576838. You got that chopper yet? Wave him off, will ya?"

"Here he comes again," said Walters.

"Hurry the fuck up!" Seagrave spoke into the radio. A single 81-millimeter mortar fired in the battalion compound. The round drifted lazily up into the night. The gunship drifted off toward the west, still poking at the earth with its spotlight. An explosion erupted behind the hill.

"Annunciate; this is Two Sierra," said Seagrave. "On target. Keep 'em comin'." Moments later, a long volley of mortar fire softly erupted from Battalion.

"Lot of good that stuff's gonna do now," said Morgan, who was lying beside me. "Those gooks are long gone by now." Shells began exploding on the other side of the hill.

"We goin' after 'em?" asked Hoffy, who had crawled over toward the radio.

186

"No," said Seagrave.

"What the fuck, man," Hoffy growled. "They're right there, for chrissake!"

"Battalion says hold tight. We're supposed to stay in position here, keep a lookout till 0500, then go back in."

"Goddamn it!" said Hoffy.

"You wanna stumble into a Main Force Company in the middle of the night?" said Seagrave. "Whattaya think you are, fuckin' John Wayne?"

"I don't give a fuck if there's a regiment of NVA out there," said Hoffy. "Just gimme a goddamned fight — "

"Hoffy!" Seagrave snapped sharply. "Just shut up. Now. Circle up, gentlemen, and break out your umbrellas. Port and starboard watch."

"When we finally got back in, debris was lying everywhere. The mortar barrage had really torn the place up good. Captain Braithewaite was waiting for us outside the general-purpose tent that served as the command center. "Everybody okay?" he asked.

"Yeh," said Seagrave.

"Captain, why the hell didn't you let us go after those little cocksuckers?" Hoffy blurted out. "We coulda nailed 'em."

"Hoffy, will you shut the fuck up?" said Seagrave impatiently.

"Corporal Ehrhart," said the Captain, "looks like you're the acting two-chief again."

"Sergeant Bochman — "

"He's dead."

"He just *got* here!"

"The way it is," said the Captain, shrugging his shoulders helplessly.

"Wow," I said. "How bad did we get it, sir?"

"Four KIA. Fifteen or sixteen wounded. Lost some SeaBees, too; I don't know how many. You guys go get some sleep. Don't bother getting up early — except you, Corporal Ehrhart. You've got to write the report up."

"We don't have a typewriter, sir."

"Use Admin's. The Colonel wants a report. I'm sorry. You can have the rest of the day off if you do the report first thing."

"Yessir. Sir, I'm glad you're okay."

Captain Braithewaite smiled, then winked. "Thanks, Corporal. Go on now, get some sleep."

I immediately raced over to the S&C hooch. My stomach almost turned inside out: the whole rear end of the hooch was splintered and collapsed. I rushed inside.

"Gerry? Gerry!"

"Wha? What? Who is it?" came the sleepy reply through the darkness. I could see a form lying on the floor.

"Gerry? It's me — Bill. Are you okay?"

"Yeh, yeh, whadda you want? Lemma sleep, will ya? Christ, I been up half the night."

"Go back to sleep, you blockhead." I walked out of the hooch, pulling the door shut behind me, but the door frame was bent and the door wouldn't close.

"Bill?"

"Yeh."

"You okay?"

"Yeh. Go to sleep." When I got back to our fortified fighting hole-bedroom, Amagasu and Morgan were standing in the middle of what was left of it. It had taken a direct hit. Rain continued to fall steadily.

Chapter 29

Somehow, the SeaBees and their attendant security force managed to build things faster than the Vietcong could knock them down again. By late October, though the runway itself had not yet been laid, the land for the airstrip had been cleared and graded, and a number of support buildings had been constructed. Others were nearing completion. A spacious COC, much larger than the one near Hoi An, lacked only a roof. Several high observation towers stood over the battalion's position like giant Martian machines out of the Classics Illustrated version of *War of the Worlds*. Gerry's hooch had been repaired; other hooches had been built for Admin, Sick Bay, Supply, an armory and a kitchen; and Morgan, Amagasu and I had rebuilt our riverfront villa.

The Vietnamese, too, had a construction boom underway. Though the area we were now in was far less populous than farther south, there were civilians around, and they wasted no time cashing in on the American presence. The day I'd arrived at Ai Tu, I'd noticed a hastily constructed ramshackle tent just across the road from the compound. As the weeks had passed, the tent had been replaced by a more or less permanent building made of tin, plywood, cardboard and canvas salvaged from our own garbage and held together with wire, spit and prayers to the local deities. Then the building became two buildings, then three, and finally four: one each for a laundry, barbershop, souvenir stand and snackbar.

The entire boomtown was unofficially tolerated by the battalion commander, in spite of the fact that it undoubtedly employed more than one Vietcong spy. After a mortar attack, Sin City would be placed off limits for a few days, but invariably the restriction would be quietly forgotten again. The battalion had no official barber, and haircuts had to be obtained somewhere because Marines with long hair do not exist.

If you asked the little old bearded fellow in the souvenir shop for the special photo album, he would sell you a collection of photographs of Asians luridly engaged in various X-rated activities bound in a plastic booklet entitled "The Views of Vietnam." How the Vietnamese managed to lay hands on canned Coca Cola and American beer — items we could not beg, borrow or otherwise obtain through regular channels — baffled everyone. Clearly, the supply sergeants at the big bases in Danang, Phu Bai and Dong Ha were making a killing off the war in Vietnam.

The battalion's fourth intelligence chief since I'd gotten to Vietnam arrived toward the end of October in the form of Gunnery Sergeant Krebs, a grizzled veteran of Korea, Lebanon, the Dominican Republic and a previous stint in Vietnam. In fact, he'd been back in The World less than three months when he'd requested a transfer back to Vietnam. "Too much spit-and-polish bullshit stateside," growled the Gunny by way of explanation. Like all field Marines, he carried two canteens. One of the canteens, however, was always filled with scotch. He wouldn't tell anyone where he got the stuff, but he loved to share it with the troopies while telling stories of the days when he'd been our age, so we never bothered to press him about his source.

Greg Barnes rotated home in late October, the first scout to get out clean on his regular rotation date in as long as anyone could remember. To replace Barnes and Aymes, we picked up two new scouts from the rifle companies. "Hell," Jon Thurston observed on his first day as a scout, "Vietnam ain't nothin' but a Tennessee squirrel-shoot with big squirrels." He was a genuine hillbilly, kind as could be and obviously having the time of his life. The other new scout, Marino P. Falcone, an Italian whom we dubbed Frenchy, came right off the streets of Newark, New Jersey. Both new guys were nineteen years old.

Thus, the month of October passed in an alternating progression of warm sunshine and chilly, clammy rain as the last of the dry season reluctantly gave up the ghost and the rising monsoon took its place. We patrolled nearly every day, sometimes in the morning, sometimes in the afternoon, sometimes at night. Sometimes we set up ambushes and waited, and sometimes we humped through the boondocks for hours on end. We made contact only once, exchanging shots with armed phantoms we never really saw, searching the nearest civilian hooches in the aftermath, rounding up the inhabitants for questioning, and blowing up three of the hooches with dynamite because there was nothing else we could do.

On the last day of the month, Captain Braithewaite told us to be ready to move out the next day for a long stay in the field. Three of the four rifle companies and a large command group, including the scouts, would be heading up toward the DMZ for a major operation against North Vietnamese regulars suspected of infiltrating south.

Chapter 30

I'd been hearing about the mythical North Vietnamese Army ever since I'd arrived in Vietnam, but I'd never actually seen or engaged them. With the exception of the operation which had cost Bobby Rowe his life, an operation I hadn't gone on, we'd thus far been fighting the Vietcong. The VC had two types of forces: the ragtag farmer-by-day-fighter-by-night guerrilla bands, and the more organized Main Force units, both consisting of men and women recruited in South Vietnam. The NVA, on the other hand, were reportedly much better equipped and better trained, and operated in units much more like the conventional companies, battalions and regiments deployed by the Americans and ARVN.

In spite of rumors I'd heard that there was actually very little practical difference between North and South Vietnamese communists, the NVA had an aura about them. The Vietcong were collectively called "Charlie" in troop slang, but the North Vietnamese were called "Charles."

As we loaded onto the trucks that morning of November first, a deep fear rumbled in my stomach, but there was a certain undeniable excitement at the prospect of finally standing toe-to-toe with the myth. The trucks were to take us to a point northwest of Dong Ha, and from there we would patrol in force up to the DMZ, pivot around Con Thien, and loop back south to a point northeast of Dong Ha. The operation was scheduled to last about two and a half weeks.

We made contact before we even reached Dong Ha and

could disembark from the trucks. Hoffy spotted them first as he stood in the truckbed gazing forward out over the cab. "Look at them goddamned beggars up there," he shouted, pointing up the road across the tops of the trucks in the column ahead of us. I leaned out over the side of the truck to look. A knot of hooches straddled the road a few hundred meters ahead, and on either side of the road danced a cluster of small children, their arms outstretched, darting among the slow-moving trucks, looking for handouts. "Christ, they're everywhere. You can't get away from 'em! Let's give 'em a surprise," Hoffy grinned, reaching into his pack, extracting a heavy can of C-rations and hefting it like a baseball.

"Yahoo!" shouted Wally. He reached for his pack. Everyone else did, too. I took out a can of chopped ham and eggs. I didn't like the canned ham and eggs anyway.

"Everybody down," commanded Hoffy. "Wait till I give the word." As the truck rolled slowly along toward the hamlet, it must have appeared to be empty. "Now!" shouted Hoffy.

The scouts roared into action, rising out of ambush and opening fire in a hail of bloodcurdling shouts and flying cans: The Little Rascals Meet Uncle George, the Wild Man from Borneo. Tiny Asian eyes suddenly went round as quarters and white as virgin snow. Tiny mouths flew open. Tiny arms and legs flew every which way in a pandemonium of screaming frightened children caught flat-footed out in the open and heavily outgunned. Cans bounced off chests and shoulders and heads; bodies went down like sandbags.

But when the dust cleared, we could see the survivors fighting each other for the spent missiles. "They don't quit, do they?" said Morgan with a touch of admiration.

"Anybody throw 'em a John Wayne?" Hoffy roared, referring to the little can openers that came with each C-ration meal. We were still laughing when we got to the disembarkation point and had to start walking.

We walked through intense humidity beneath an overcast sky all that day and all the next day and all the next day. Periodically, it rained. The terrain alternated between rugged foothills covered with head-high vegetation and soggy overgrown ricefields infested with enormous leeches. The whole area from Dong Ha north to the DMZ was completely devoid of civilians, though abandoned fields and the remnants of hooches, orange groves and banana stands indicated that the area had once flourished.

Crossing an open, wide valley on the third day, we came across the burned-out hulls of two Ontos, armored tracked antitank vehicles that carried six 106-millimeter recoilless rifles. They were gutted and rusted, and had been stripped of their guns. "This is where one of our battalions got their asses kicked last summer," said Major Miles, the operations officer. I remembered reading about that one: a deadly ambush by a large force of NVA that had inflicted heavy casualties on several companies of a Marine battalion before finally being driven off by airstrikes and heavy artillery fire. We passed the two skeletons without stopping, eyes nervously sweeping the surrounding hills.

By the evening of the fifth day, we'd still seen no sign of the enemy we'd come to find. It was like shadow-boxing. Each round, you step into the ring, and bob and weave and dance and jab and hook at nothing; and when the round ends, you go to your corner breathing hard with sweat running down into your eyes, and you can hear Howard Cosell sitting nearby at ringside telling the viewers at home that your opponent is still far ahead on points; then the bell rings for the next round, and you step wearily out into the center of the empty ring, and begin bobbing and weaving and jabbing.

It was raining when we stopped for the day and dug in. I immediately set up a one-man poncho tent. The two-man field tent, commonly known as a pup-tent, was standard issue, and in boot camp a great deal of effort had been spent in teaching us to erect the pup-tent correctly. It required two people, each with a shelter half and the requisite number of tent pole sections, tent pins and support ropes. These items were much too heavy to bother lugging around in the field, especially considering that the tent was too small for two people anyway, was impossible to construct correctly except under ideal conditions which never presented themselves in Vietnam, and would collapse in the middle of the night if not constructed properly.

Any sensible Marine discarded his shelter half and accessories immediately upon issue. I had done so on the advice of Jimmy Saunders. In fact, one always tried to stay as far away as possible from anyone with a shelter half, for it was widely held that anyone who lacked the sense to get rid of his shelter half would sooner or later manage to get you killed. Sensible Marines slept under ponchos while in the field.

The poncho was not very useful as a piece of raingear, but it made a dynamite one-man tent. To make a one-man poncho tent, you needed only your lightweight, easily transportable poncho, four little sticks, one stick about two feet long, and a bit of string. First you pulled the drawstring on the face hole of the poncho hood tight, closing off the hole. Then you laid the poncho out in a loose rectangle on a flat

194

bit of ground, and staked down the four corners with the four little sticks. Then you reached inside under the poncho with the big stick, poked it up into the poncho hood and stood the stick upright, which would lift the poncho up from the center and stretch it into a taut four-sided pyramid. Finally, you took the string and ran it from the center grommet on one side of the poncho to a nearby tree or bush and secured it, lifting one side of the poncho slightly to form an entrance just high enough to crawl under. And that was that; you were ready to curl up around the center stake and go to sleep. If you wanted to get fancy, you could throw in a little brush or a few banana leaves for a mattress. The whole process took five minutes, maybe ten if you wanted a mattress.

I'd finished my tent and was digging my fighting hole when Father Ligon, the battalion chaplain, approached me. I'd deliberately avoided the Chaplain for months. It wasn't that I disliked him; he just made me uncomfortable.

"Hello, Corporal Ehrhart; how's it going?" he asked cheerfully.

"Not bad, Father," I replied, "can't complain." We exchanged small talk while I finished digging a shallow, narrow fighting hole just long enough to lie down in and deep enough to get below ground level, anything more being wasted effort.

"How's that girlfriend of yours—Jenny, isn't it?" he asked.

"She threw me over a couple of months ago, sir," I replied. "Haven't heard from her since, except for a birthday card that didn't say anything. Hooked up with a draft dodger by now, I suppose."

"Oh," said the Chaplain, "I didn't know. I'm sorry."

"So am I, sir."

"You know, Corporal, I don't mean to put you on the spot, but I do miss the talks we used to have when you first got here."

"Yessir."

"You were more faithful than my Catholic boys," he laughed.

"Things change, Father."

"What happened, Corporal Ehrhart? What's wrong? Is it because of your girlfriend? Is that it?"

"What's wrong, Father? Take a look around. And you're askin' me what's wrong? Look, I'm sorry, sir; I'd rather not get into it."

"You can talk to me, son; that's what I'm here for."

"Man to man?"

"Of course. Making me a major wasn't my idea."

"Father, when I enlisted, I thought I was doing the right thing. I thought I was doin' right by my country—gonna help the Viet-

195

namese, and all like that. I really believed it. I guess that sounds pretty corny, doesn't it?"

"Not at all, son; not at all. We all want to believe we're doing the right thing."

"Well, I don't believe it anymore. I don't know what to believe, but I sure don't believe that. We're not doin' anybody any good around here, and any fool can see that. Well, anyway, the point is, there I'd be, goin' to chapel every week and prayin' to God to forgive what I'm doin', knowin' all the time I was just gonna go out and do more of the same thing the next day. Father, any God worth his salt isn't gonna buy that for a minute. It got to where I could almost hear Him up there while I was prayin': 'Don't hand me this crap again, you turkey. Just don't bother me unless you're serious.' After awhile, I couldn't even open my mouth. Everytime a thought pops into my head, there'd be that voice."

"God's always ready to listen and forgive, son. He's always been ready to comfort people like us, and He still is. I really don't mean to preach a sermon at you, but you mustn't let your own fear keep you from Him."

"Father, that's not right. You can't just say you're sorry, and then go out and deliberately keep doin' the same stuff over and over again. You got no business tellin' guys like me it's okay to deal like that."

"I'm not saying it's okay, Corporal Ehrhart, and I never have. I can't presume to judge men. But you boys are as much a part of Jesus' flock as anybody else; maybe you're the part He cares about most. Jesus broke bread with publicans and sinners, didn't He? Can I do any less, and still be a priest?"

"Well, if you're just here to look after the sheep, how come you got that?" I asked, pointing to the M-16 Father Ligon held.

He looked down at the weapon and shook his head slowly. "I'd be happy not to have to carry one of these, and I hope I never have to use it," he said, "but I'm afraid the vc don't make exceptions for Catholic priests."

"I understand that, sir, but that's the point. You've got an excuse. Colonel Glass has got an excuse. General Westmoreland has an excuse. President Johnson has an excuse. I'm up to my earlobes in everybody's excuses. Either you're a Christian, or you're not a Christian. There's nothing ambiguous about 'Thou shalt not kill.' "

"You're right, of course," said Father Ligon. "But it's just not that simple. Nobody's perfect, son. We're human beings. God made us

196

in His image, and He knows we're going to fail. That's what Jesus Christ is all about."

"That just don't get it, Father. These guys believe in you. They trust you. You tell 'em they're gonna be forgiven, and they just keep on prayin' and shootin' and prayin' and shootin', and thinkin' they're gonna go to heaven. You think God gives a big rat's ass about communists and democratic elections and domino theories? I just hope to high heaven there ain't any God, because we're all in a whole lot of trouble if there is."

"Corporal Ehrhart, have you ever thought about applying for a discharge as a conscientious objector?"

"Oh, no; no way. End up in Portsmouth for twenty years? I don't want any trouble. I've got enough trouble as it is. I got four more months to go in this cesspool, and then I'm gettin' out clean."

"But if you're really this troubled, maybe I can help you. If you're really sincere, I can talk to the Colonel."

"Listen, Father, you said I could talk straight with you, so I am. But this is just between you and me, and I'm trustin' you to keep it that way. I've got a good record, and I've only got four months left. It's gonna be hard enough to live with myself for the rest of my life. And then get drummed out of the service on top of that? I'm not gonna stick that kind of albatross around my neck. No, sir."

Father Ligon sighed deeply. "Well, that's your decision," he said. "If you change your mind, let me know. But think about this, will you? Don't let what men do in God's name turn you away from God's love. Just because we fail to live up to what God asks of us doesn't mean He won't forgive us. It's God's world, after all; He knows what we're up against."

"Well, that's a heck of a way to send somebody to sea, isn't it, sir? Knock a hole in the bottom of the lifeboat, and then tell 'em, 'Do the best you can, folks; good luck.'"

"I'm afraid I just can't seem to find the right things to say to you, can I?"

"I guess not, sir. I'm sorry. Really; it's nothin' personal. You're a nice man, Father."

"I'm sorry, too, son," said Father Ligon, his voice sounding very tired and lonely. "I just don't have all the answers. God works in mysterious ways sometimes, I suppose."

It was dark now. A roaring sound like a freight train rose up out of the south and beat through the darkness overhead, the sound of 175-millimeter artillery shells. "Long Toms," I said, using the

197

nickname for the 175s, "headed for North Vietnam. You can't hear 'em fire, and you can't hear 'em explode; you just hear 'em tearin' up the stars."

"I guess we'd better turn in," said the Chaplain. "If you change your mind about having me talk with the Colonel, let me know. Good night, son."

"Good night, Father."

That night, it rained hard. I woke up in darkness, lying in the two-inch-deep river the hillside had become. The ground was rocky and wouldn't absorb the water, and there was nowhere to go to escape the run-off. I spent the rest of the night sitting up, awake and shivering. Daylight waited for the last possible moment to arrive, and when it did, it was cold, gray and foggy.

Chapter 31

I lost track of the days after awhile. Each day was the same as the ones on either side of it: you walked all day, up hills and down hills and between hills and across flooded uncultivated overgrown fields and through thickets and forests and wild meadows; and sometimes it rained and sometimes it didn't; and at night you took off your boots and burned the leeches from your feet and legs with a cigarette, and then you put up your one-man poncho tent and dug your fighting hole and tried to sleep for a few hours; and the next day you did it all over again. By the middle of the second week, we were nearly as far north as the DMZ, and still there'd been no sign of enemy activity.

After the night I'd ended up sleeping in the river, I'd contracted a bad cold and a vicious case of the runs. For several days, I had to blow it out my backside every fifteen minutes. This required asking someone to cover me while I stepped out of the line of march, stripped off enough gear to free my trousers, and squatted. There is nothing so vulnerable as a Marine with his pants down—especially with Wally or Rolly or Hoffy standing there howling with laughter while my face contorted from the spasms in my bowels and my rear end contracted violently. I couldn't eat at all, and after the first day nothing remained in my bowels but the terrible seizures and a slimy liquid that I had to take seriously or turn my trousers into a walking nightmare. My pucker-hole was as sore as a bride's box on the morning after her wedding night.

To cure myself of the runs, I'd traded all my food for peanut butter and crackers. I forced myself to eat the peanut butter and crackers three times a day because if you have the runs, nothing will plug you up any better or more quickly than C-ration peanut butter and John Wayne canned crackers. After several days, the peanut butter and crackers took effect, leaving behind my cold and a wicked rash.

Unfortunately, I had to continue to eat peanut butter and crackers for several more days because I'd acquired a lifetime supply of the stuff, and the only things anybody was willing to trade me were chopped ham and eggs, and date pudding. To argue that I'd given them things like pork steak, beef stew and canned pears did no good. In a capitalist society, price is determined by demand, and peanut butter and crackers were not in demand. "Don't any of you mother-fuckers ever ask me for a goddamned favor," I pointed out repeatedly to anyone within earshot. "I'll see you rot in hell first!" I prayed and prayed that Seagrave or Haller or Amagasu or somebody would be afflicted by the disease that had allowed me to corner the market on peanut butter and crackers, but nobody else got sick.

The arrival of the resupply helicopters on the tenth or eleventh day out finally brought me relief. By then, my intestinal virus was ancient history, and I could think of nothing but pound cake, peaches and chicken dumplings. I dove head-first into the loaded cargo net before it had even touched the ground. "Hot dogs and beans!" I shouted. "Ham and limas! Fruit cocktail!" I didn't even notice Gerry until he began beating me in the face with a stack of letters.

"Whatsa matter with you?" he asked, pulling me off the pile of C-ration cartons.

"Outta my way!" I roared. "I want cookies and cocoa!"

"I got mail for you," he said, pinning me to the ground with his knee. "Here, take it, will ya?"

"What are you doin' here?" I asked, noticing Gerry for the first time as I struggled to get at the boxes of food.

"I got tired of sitting around the rear, so I invented a couple of top secret messages for Colonel Glass, and hopped a chopper to deliver 'em. What's goin' on around here?"

"Nothin'," I said, opening a can of meatballs and beans, and stuffing my mouth with the contents. "I got a cold; I got the runs; I got jungle rot from my asshole to my knees; I'm starved to death; and we ain't seen a goddamned thing. Whaddaya got here?" I asked, pointing to the letters.

"A letter from your dad, and one from your mom; one from Dorrit; one from Sadie Thompson. Who's Sadie Thompson?"

"Friend of mine back home," I said in between mouthfuls of food. "I never told you about her? Last time I was home on leave, she took me to a Quaker Meeting—she's a Quaker. So after I get over here, Father Ligon tells me Quakers are pacifists, don't believe in war or nothin'. Wow. There I am sittin' in this Quaker church in my dress green uniform, proud as a peacock. *I* didn't know."

"You got a letter from Jenny, too."

"No shit?" I said, my stomach suddenly tightening. I put down the can of food I was holding, took the letters from Gerry, and started flipping through them slowly. I tried to look calm as I fumbled to open Jenny's letter, the first I'd gotten from her in two months. "How ya been?" I asked.

"Okay. We got mortared again, and Jan broke her leg."

"Yeh? What happened? She okay?"

"Yeh, she's okay. She fell down a staircase. Got a cast on up to her hip."

"Well, you don't have to worry about her cattin' around on ya for awhile," I said. "Shit!" I crumpled up Jenny's letter, struck a match, and set the letter on fire.

"More bad news?"

"No news at all. Nothin'. 'Hi. How are you? Nursing school is fun. Hope you're okay.' Whoop-de-doo. Yeh, I'm okay, all right—no thanks to you. Jesus Christ."

"Take it easy, will ya?" said Gerry as I opened Dorrit's letter. "You're under four months. Just get there, then worry about it."

"Yeh."

"What's Dorrit have to say?"

"This is more like it," I said. "Says she's lookin' forward to seein' me again. Wow, man. What a woman." I polished off the last of a can of ham steaks and a tiny loaf of canned white bread. "Good stuff," I said. "Just like Mom's. You stickin' around for awhile?"

"Yeh, couple of days, I guess, till the Colonel sends me back."

"Hey, dammit! Where's my watch?"

"What watch?"

"The one I had right here," I said, waving my naked left wrist and pointing at it with the can of jelly I held in my right hand. "Shit! I musta lost it somewheres back there."

"Why don't ya go back for it?"

"Funny boy."

"Just a thought."

"Shit. Some gook NVA's gonna have himself a nice wristwatch."

"Send a bill to Uncle Ho."

"Jesus Christ. First my girlfriend. Now my watch. Probably lose my ass before I get outta this cesspool."

"I'd settle for a million-dollar knee job."

"Saddle up!" someone shouted. "Let's move!"

About two hours later, we crested a hill and suddenly found ourselves on the edge of an unearthly landscape that looked like the surface of the moon, or No Man's Land in 1916 France. Enormous craters, thirty to forty feet across and twenty feet deep, had turned several hundred square meters of forest into a quagmire. Stumps of uprooted trees pointed twisted roots skyward, while the jagged splintered carcasses of other trees stuck up at the edges of the craters. The trees around the rim of the disaster area had been stripped clean of their leaves and branches, and many of the trees leaned precariously away from the area of impact. The column of Marines began to back up as each new man broke out of the forest into the wasteland and came up short, staring wide-eyed.

"Keep moving! Keep moving!" someone hollered repeatedly.

"Holy Moses!" Gerry gasped.

"What the hell happened here?" I thought out loud.

"Arc Light," said Gunny Krebs. "B-52s. Remember that racket last night?" I nodded slowly. I'd been abruptly awakened by a violent rumbling and shaking of the ground beneath me; I'd thought at first it was an earthquake, and I'd been scared out of my wits, but others who'd been awakened had said it was just the B-52s up on the DMZ. "This is what you were hearing," the Gunny continued. "They come in at 30,000 feet, three planes to a mission, ten tons of bombs to a plane. They're so high up, Charlie can't even hear 'em comin'. Anybody underneath 'em gets planted."

"God almighty." I took a last look at the eerie devastation.

"God's almighty wrath," said Gerry.

"And we dispense it," said the Gunny. "Don't worry; they'll do the same for you if they get the chance."

"I'll leave them alone, if they'll leave me alone," I said.

"Why don't we make 'em a deal?" said Gerry.

The column skirted the edge of the carnage, small patrols searching the craters for any sign of NVA dead, then we slipped back into the forest. A mile or so further on, we stopped for a rest. The Gunny passed his special canteen among the scouts. "Can Gerry have a swig?" I asked, taking a mouthful of scotch and wincing at the bite of the alcohol on my tongue.

202

"Sure," said the Gunny. "Any friend of yours is a friend of mine. You guys see that blue ridgeline out there?" he asked, pointing north. "That's North Vietnam. The Ben Hai River's down there, but you can't see it from here."

"Are we in the DMZ?" asked Amagasu.

"You wanna know how far north you are?" said the Gunny. "See that hill there?" He pointed south across a slowly rising meadow toward a low double-crest about 1500 or 2000 meters away. "That's Con Thien."

We all sat there, puffing cigarettes and silently contemplating the magnitude of this revelation. Con Thien, we all knew, was the hottest spot in Vietnam. One of a series of Marine Corps positions strung out along the southern edge of the DMZ, Con Thien was the northernmost outpost in South Vietnam. For months, the little battalion-sized "Dien Bien Phu" had withstood a daily bombardment of upwards of 500 North Vietnamese artillery shells per day. Every big gun in the southern half of North Vietnam seemed to be zeroed in on Con Thien. Back in September, the post had nearly been overrun several times, and had made the cover of *Time*.

"That's Con Thien?" I finally said.

"That's it," replied the Gunny.

"Where the hell's all the gooks? Let's see some fireworks."

"They heard you were comin', Bill," said Mogerty. "They got outta town while they still could."

Just then, Captain Braithewaite came over with a stack of what appeared to be leaflets tucked under his arm. "Ehrhart; Gunny; come over here a minute," he said. He handed each of us one of the leaflets. It was a single sheet of white paper, folded in half to make four pages. It contained photographs of the October 27, 1967, demonstration in Washington and the mass march on the Pentagon. It also contained excerpts from some of the speeches, along with the names of the speakers. The last page said: "U.S. Soldiers, join your brothers and sisters back home. Put down your weapons. Resist your officer [*sic*] and oppressors. Refuse to fight the criminal imperialist war. Demand peace now." Under the text on that page was a photo of youthful American demonstrators carrying a large banner reading: "Liberate Vietnam — Stop the War." Beneath the photo, in very small type, was printed: "National Front for the Liberation of South Vietnam," the formal title for the political arm of the Vietcong.

"Where did you get these?" asked Gunny Krebs.

"The point platoon brought 'em in," said Captain Braithewaite.

"They were scattered all over the woods up ahead. Look at 'em. They're not even wet. They haven't been there overnight."

"Where the hell's the gooks, Ehrhart?" said the Gunny, parroting my question of a few moments earlier. "Just because you don't see 'em..."

"This fuckin' demonstration wasn't even three weeks ago!" I said. "Where the fuck did they get this stuff?"

"From Jane Fonda and Dr. Spock, probably," said the captain. "Get rid of these things. Burn 'em."

"I'd like to cut off Dr. Spock's balls and stuff 'em up Jane Fonda's cunt with a bayonet," I said. "What the fuck!"

Just about the time we saddled up and started to move again, the high swift whine of incoming artillery split the air, Marines instantly scattering all over the ground face-down to the sharp unnecessary shouts of "Incoming!" A split-second later, five or six dirty white puffs of smoke erupted on the forward face of Con Thien, followed immediately by the sound of the explosions. After waiting a few minutes to see if more shells were coming, we were up and walking.

We walked all the rest of that day. By late afternoon, we'd crossed in front of Con Thien, turned south, and reached a point several thousand meters southeast but still within sight of Con Thien, where we dug in for the night. In the morning, we found out that we'd be staying in place for the day to rest, so Gerry and I decided to take a stroll up to Con Thien to do a little sightseeing.

Con Thien, commonly referred to as Disneyland in troop slang, had to be the most godforsaken chunk of real estate on the face of the earth. Though one got the sense from newspaper accounts that it was a commanding bastion perched atop a great natural citadel overlooking the whole DMZ, and though the outpost did occupy the highest elevation around, it was in fact little more than two low hills at the top of a long gradual slope that fell away slowly on all sides. As Gerry and I approached the outpost, it looked lush and green like the surrounding terrain, but the closer we got, the more the green faded into dull brown.

By the time we reached the outer wire of the perimeter, we could see that men and machines had long since stripped away or trampled most of the vegetation within the wire, leaving only scattered patches of something that bore an anemic resemblance to prairie grass. We soon learned that these pathetic patches were minefields laid within the perimeter to slow down and channel the NVA in the event they managed to breech the outer wire.

204

Wherever Marines dared to walk within the perimeter, which was perhaps a thousand meters across at most, there was nothing but mud. Oceans and rivers of it, thick and deep and brown. The Marines there lived in sandbagged bunkers dug into the earth like the burrows of nocturnal animals. Everybody looked like actors in a realistic war movie: they had hollow eyes and permanent shell-shock; they talked in hushed voices, and moved as if in a dream, constantly peering up at the sky and back over their shoulders. The bunkers were all run down and beat up from weathering and long use and incoming artillery, and the mud was littered with empty wooden artillery shellboxes, old C-ration cartons, and spent brass from bullets. I'd never seen anything like it in my ten months in-country. We stayed just long enough to have our pictures taken in front of a bunker by a stubble-faced Marine who couldn't understand why we wanted our pictures taken at Con Thien, and couldn't make up his mind if we were funny or dangerous.

"Jesus, that's as long as I ever want to spend in that dump," said Gerry as we walked back to our battalion's bivouac.

"Did you see those guys?" I added. "They looked like ghosts." A stick of incoming abruptly ended the conversation, exploding in a rippling series inside the perimeter behind us. "Let's get the hell out of here!" I shouted. We ran all the way back to Battalion.

Gerry hopped a resupply helicopter out the next morning, having run out of excuses to give the Colonel for remaining. Four days later, the rest of us finally reached Dong Ha by shoe-leather express, loaded onto waiting trucks, and arrived back at Ai Tu with seventeen days' worth of stubble on our faces, seventeen days' worth of crud on our bodies, still wearing the same socks we'd put on seventeen days earlier, and mildly amazed at the progress the SeaBees had made in our absence. The metal corduroy runway had been laid, and several camouflage-green C-130s sat at one end of the strip.

"Well, I'm sure as hell glad to see somebody makin' a little progress around here," said Morgan. "Do you believe that shit? Two weeks on the DMZ, and we don't even *see* a goddamned gook."

"Seventeen days," I said.

"Look at it this way, Rolly," said Frenchy, "we didn't lose nobody, either."

"Yeh, shit," said Hoffy. "We shoulda kept goin' north at the river. Some fuckin' war! First they say fight, then they tie one hand behind your back, slap a ball an' chain on your ankle, and blindfold ya."

"You go to North Vietnam, Hoffy," said Sergeant Seagrave. "I like it fine right here."

"We're winnin' hearts and minds, Hoffy," added Mogerty, picking up a copy of *Stars 'n' Stripes* and waving it at Hofstatter. "Don't you read the newspapers?"

"Only when there's nothin' better to do," said Hoffy. "And there's always somethin' better to do. Brush your teeth. Fuck off. Sleep. Where they get the bullshit they put in there, anyway? Pull it outta their assholes or somethin'."

"If you can't trust your local general," I said, "who can you trust?"

"Stars and Stripes forever," said Mogerty.

"They oughta call it *Excuses 'n' Assholes*," said Hoffy. "Hey, don't ya get it? Excuses are like assholes, you know — everybody's got one." He howled at his own joke.

"Beer call!" shouted Gunny Krebs, appearing around the corner of a tent with a case of beer. "Two cans apiece. Compliments of Uncle Sam."

"Stuff's piss-warm," said Stemkowski, opening a can with his John Wayne opener and draining half of it. "Two fuckin' weeks in the boondocks, and they give us warm fuckin' beer."

"Seventeen days," I said.

"You don't want it," said Sergeant Seagrave. "Give it here."

"My ass," said Stemkowski.

"Listen up, you guys," said the Gunny. "You know we just been out on four major combat operations?"

"What the fuck you talkin' about, Gunny?" asked Sergeant Seagrave.

"We ain't been out on *one* operation, boys; we've just been on *four* of 'em," the Gunny laughed. He pulled out a typed sheet of paper from his pocket, unfolded it, and began reading: "November 1st to November 10th, Operation Lancaster; November 11th to November 12th, Operation Kentucky One; November 12th to November 14th, Operation Kentucky Two; November 15th to November 17th, Operation Kentucky Three."

"Couple of 'em were kinda short there, weren't they?" said Sergeant Seagrave.

"Four little Indians, all in a row," said Gunny Krebs.

"There it is!" shouted Hoffy. "That's the kinda shit they put in the newspapers. Send a bunch of Jarheads into the boonies, let 'em stumble around for awhile, give it a fancy name, and write it up in the papers. Fuckin' unbelievable." He picked up the newspaper Mogerty had been waving at him, and began tearing it into six-inch squares.

206

"I'll tell ya what *this* stuff's good for," he said, taking one of the squares and pretending to wipe his rear end with it.

"Hi, guys!" said Gerry, appearing at the same tent corner where the Gunny had just materialized.

"Fuck you."

"Go to hell!"

"What are you so fuckin' cheerful about?"

"Guess where you guys are goin' next week," Gerry beamed.

"Crazy!"

"Cleveland."

"Siberia."

"Disneyland!" Gerry roared with delight. "All expenses paid."

"Con Thien?!"

"Give that man a kewpee doll!" said Gerry.

"Ooooh, nooo!"

"Oh, yes," Gerry laughed.

"What's so fuckin' funny about that, Griffith?" growled Stemkowski.

"*You* guys are goin'," Gerry grinned. "I'm not goin' anywhere. I'm stayin' right here with Battalion Rear. Don't forget to send me a postcard of Mickey Mouse." Gerry disappeared around the corner of the tent in a hail of oaths, catcalls and empty beer cans.

Chapter 32

As the trucks pulled in through the narrow break in the thick coils of concertina marking the outer perimeter of Con Thien, the grunts inside the wire poked their heads up out of their holes like little prairie dogs. They waved their arms, and laughed, and shouted, "Welcome aboard, motherfuckers; make sure you wipe your feet!" We waved back half-heartedly. "Assholes," Hoffy muttered. An hour later, as the former tenants of Con Thien disappeared back down the road toward Dong Ha, a thousand brand new prairie dogs violently hurled middle fingers after the receding trucks.

I was lucky, though; I got one of the best bunkers in the whole place: a large rectangular structure built almost entirely underground, about fifteen feet by seven feet, and five feet high inside. Most of the interior sandbags were in good condition. The roof consisted of heavy wooden planks covered by several layers of sandbags covered by a canvas tarpaulin that kept the rain out nicely. The far end of the bunker, the end away from the tunnel-like open entrance, had double-deck planks built in like bunk beds that could sleep four, two on top and two underneath. Most of the mud floor was covered with duck-boards, and there was plenty of room to stow gear and C-rations, with space left over for a kind of boxcar living room.

The bunker lay about halfway down the back slope of the western hill, the side of the hill facing away from North Vietnam, only a few dozen meters up from and to the side of the huge sprawling bunker that served as the COC. The NVA gunners could only hit our bunker with high trajectory mortars because the low trajectory artillery shells, if they cleared the top of the hill, would carry on down into the valley below us. Of course, we still had to contend with the mortars because Charles was always trying to lay one onto the COC, but our location increased our odds by half.

I shared the bunker with Seagrave, Walters and Morgan. Thurston, Falcone and Amagasu had a bunker just up the hill from us. Mogerty, Hofstatter, Stemkowski and a new scout named Bob Davis found a home on the other side of the valley from us. This valley quickly became known as Death Valley—as in "Yea, though I walk through the valley of the shadow of death"—because it was a favorite target for the NVA gunners. It ran almost directly north and south between the two hills of Con Thien, forming a wide open alley for incoming on its way to the battalion aid station and the helicopter landing zone. Though we were to spend many hours over many days trying to determine why two of the most important facilities at Con Thien had been located in the middle of a shooting gallery, we never did come up with an explanation that satisfied anyone.

That first afternoon was unseasonably clear and bright, with a sky full of puffy white clouds, and, in spite of occasional incoming, Morgan and I decided to stroll up to the observation post at the top of the hill and check things out.

Looking out over the valley of the Ben Hai River, we could see the last few thousand meters of South Vietnam falling gently toward the river like Land's End, the blue land on the other side of the valley rising away northward in a soft slow wave toward the horizon. Just beyond the wire, thick grass grew in wild meadows that looked as though they might once have been ricefields. Hedgerows of trees and bushes crisscrossed the meadows in parallel and perpendicular lines, and heavy forests grew farther out. Far to the west, we could see the jagged mountain range that ran north and south down the Vietnamese-Laotian border. Every imaginable shade of green and blue shimmered in the sunlight in stark contrast to the dark colorless mud within the wire. We peered toward the east, and then toward the west, looking for Gia Linh and the Rockpile, the two outposts we knew were only six or seven miles to either side of us, but we could see nothing beyond the thick green forests.

"How the hell are we supposed to stop the gooks from infiltratin' the D?" said Morgan. "They could build a superhighway out there, and we'd never know it."

"They probably already have," I said.

Morgan snorted through his teeth. "Jesus," he said.

"He ain't interested," I said.

By late afternoon, a steady rain had begun to fall from low boiling clouds that seemed to come out of nowhere. The top of the hill on the other side of Death Valley, no more than 200 meters distant, disappeared. That night, Seagrave, Walters, Morgan and I sat around a hissing Coleman lantern inside our bunker listening to the rain beat against the tarp. Suddenly Wally burst out of a private fog like a man zapped by a cattle prod. "Hey, holy fuck!" he blurted out. "When I was a kid, my mom used to get pissed as hell at me for makin' mud pies. Now I'm livin' in one! Jesus, just think about *that*!"

"You know," said Sergeant Seagrave, after a long pause, "it's amazing what you can get used to. You almost forget what it's like to live like a human being. I'll bet LBJ wouldn't be dickin' around so much if he hadda live here for awhile."

"I heard his son-in-law's in the Marines," I said. "Got a nice fat job as a general's aide or somethin'."

"Figures," said Wally.

"I wouldn't mind this so much if we were gettin' somewhere; but this," said Morgan, sweeping his hand around the bunker in a slow gesture intended to encompass all of Vietnam, "this is just Mickey Mouse."

"Why do ya think they call it Disneyland?" said Seagrave.

"I'd like to send some of this fuckin' mud to some-fuckin'-body in Washington," said Wally.

"Don't do it," I said. "They'll just send us more chocolate chip cookies."

"Arrrgh!" Morgan bellowed.

"Anybody wanna go visit Mogerty and Hoffy and them?" Wally suggested.

"Get my ass blown off so I can sit in their rat hole instead of ours?" I said. "No thanks. You seen one rat hole, you seen 'em all."

"The gooks won't shell us at night," said Seagrave.

"Says you," I said.

"No, they won't. They never do up here. One of those guys we just relieved told me. They're afraid their muzzle flashes'll give their positions away. They only fire in the daytime up here."

"Fine," I said. "I still ain't goin' nowhere. It's cold, dark, rainy and muddy out there. You can go if you want. My mother raised me better'n that."

"Well, whaddaya wanna do?" asked Wally.

210

"Let's go to sleep," said Seagrave. No one could come up with a better idea, so we all crawled into our bunk beds, and after a good deal of tossing and turning and grunting into something resembling comfortable positions, we got some blankets spread out and settled down, cramped but otherwise snug.

A scraping sound came out of the darkness at the other end of the bunker. It got louder. It got a lot louder.

"What the fuck is that?" said Wally. Seagrave, who was sleeping in the upper outside bunk next to me, struck a match. The sudden light froze three pairs of glowing red eyes that glared at us from the stack of C-rations in the far corner.

"Rats!" Seagrave hissed. Wally screamed. Morgan shouted. Several boots went flying toward the pile of cans and boxes. "Goddamn it!" Seagrave roared, forgetting about the match until it had burned down to his fingers. The bunker was instantly dark again. The scratching sounds resumed.

"Flip a grenade down there," said Morgan.

"It's Willard!" I shouted. "Help, help, do something! We'll all be eaten alive!"

"I'll fix 'em," said Seagrave. "Come on, Bill."

"Me?"

"Yeh; come on."

"What are you gonna do?"

"You'll see; come on." We both crawled out of the bunk. "Light a match," said Seagrave. "Here, use this candle." Seagrave knelt down, opened a can of peanut butter, and put it on the duckboards between his knees. Then he took out his bayonet and held it in both hands six inches above the open can. "Blow out the candle, and keep quiet."

"You're crazy," I said.

"Just be quiet, damn it!"

For awhile, nothing happened. Then the scratching sounds began again. The distinct sound of metal being nudged across wood came through the darkness, followed by a heavy *thunk*. "I got one! I got one!" shouted Seagrave. "Light the candle!" I did. Pinned to the duckboards by Seagrave's bayonet, its head still in the can of peanut butter, was a five-inch rat with a six-inch tail. It was very dead.

"Hey, lemme try that," said Wally. We spent the next two hours skewering rats, ending up with a grand total score of Marines 5, Rats 0. The rats finally gave up, and after another round of rustling and jostling for position, we settled down again to sleep. The damp bunker grew quiet.

"Gravey," said Walters.

"Yeh?"

"Were they VC rats or NVA rats?"

Morgan giggled. Then Wally giggled. I started laughing. Then everybody broke up. "Get your fuckin' elbow outta my ribs," said Seagrave.

"Bill," Wally said. "You're the assistant intelligence chief; interrogate those rats."

"They're dead," I said.

"Torture 'em till they talk," said Wally.

"The only good rat is a dead rat," said Morgan.

"Go to sleep," said Seagrave.

"Good night."

"G'night."

"G'night."

"Good night, ladies," Wally sang softly, "good night, ladies; good night ladies; I'm going to leave you now."

"Shut up, Wally," said Seagrave. The bunker grew quiet again.

"Uncle Floyd's Guaranteed Louisiana Rat Traps," Wally intoned through the darkness in a voice like a television announcer. More giggles.

"Uncle Floyd's Guaranteed Vietcong Rat Traps," said Morgan.

"Uncle Floyd's Guaranteed NVA Rat Traps," I said.

"Hee, hee!" the three of us giggled in the darkness.

"Shut the fuck up, will yaz?" said Seagrave. "I'm tryin' to sleep."

"G'night."

"G'night."

"G'night."

The bunker got quiet again.

"Gravey," I said. "You gotta get up and lemme out. I have to piss."

"Goddamn it, Bill!"

"I'm sorry; I gotta piss."

"Let him out, quick!" Wally pleaded. "I'm right below him. It'll drip down on me."

"Hey, it's rainin' in here," Morgan shouted. "It's rainin'. It's *warm* rain! Hey!"

"Lemme out!"

"Let him out!"

"Jesus fuckin' -A Christ!" said Sergeant Seagrave.

Chapter 33

I was disappointed to discover the next morning that the COC contained a typewriter, which meant that I was back to doing the daily intelligence summary again, this time by the light of a Coleman lantern while sitting at a tiny fold-up field desk in a musty corner of the COC while radios crackled all around me in the dim light. The news was softened, however, by the realization that the I-Sum consisted of little more than the number of incoming rounds we'd taken during the previous twenty-four hours. In addition, my daily trips to the COC allowed me to trade thoughts with Randy Haller, whom I'd seen very little of since we'd left Hoi An.

Most of the time, however, we'd just sit around our own bunker, or visit the other scouts, and play cards and talk and just pass the time while waiting for the next barrage of incoming to arrive. And when it did, we'd all double up inside our flak jackets and helmets, and put our fingers in our ears, and hold our breath, and shiver, and hope like hell none of the stuff landed in our neighborhood.

You didn't walk around outside any more than you had to. Getting caught in the open by incoming was both harrowing and physically uncomfortable. Because the telltale whistle of the rounds didn't afford you much warning, and the heavy mud made it impossible to run, you'd just have to flop yourself down right where you were and try to bury your body in the mud like a pig wallowing down on the farm. Then you'd have to spend the next few hours trying to scrape the mud off your one pair of jungle utilities, and out of your nose and rifle.

There weren't too many places to go anyway, except maybe to the helicopter landing zone to get the mail, when the weather was good enough to allow landing, or over to the supply dump to get a few more cases of C-rations. And it was almost always raining.

Nighttime was very different. The guy who'd told Seagrave that the NVA didn't fire at night had been right, and after a few nights, we actually got used to feeling more or less relaxed. I discovered that after sundown, my teeth didn't grind so much and my jaws stopped aching from the constant effort of clenching my teeth to keep them from grinding in the daytime. I wondered if the gaunt, sallow fellows Gerry and I had seen a few weeks earlier had also changed character at night.

Of course, there was always the possibility of getting hit by a ground assault some night, but our bunker was far enough inside the wire that we would have plenty of time to tighten up before some NVA soldier flipped a grenade through the door. Nighttime actually got to be sort of fun. I soon came to look forward to it through the long daylight hours of ducking and cringing.

About the fourth or fifth night, Mogerty, Hoffy, Stemkowski and Davis came pouring into our bunker in the middle of a rat-trapping session. "Get on the bullshit band!" shouted Mogerty, all excited. "They got tunes on!"

"Get outta here, you assholes," said Wally, wrapping his arms protectively around his PRC-10 radio. "You're trackin' mud all over our goddamned house."

"Come on," said Mogerty, "turn on the radio. They're playin' music on it. We were just listening to it in the bunker next to ours. Somebody's playin' music. Turn it on, turkey."

On military radios, there is a frequency way up at the top of the band that is left unassigned at all times, and is supposed to be used only in emergencies. It was regularly used, however, as an open conference line among enlisted men, and anybody with a spare radio and a little time to kill would get on the air and try to find somebody else from Podunk, Iowa, or Bumfart, Maine. "Hey, hey, hey; this is Cool Albert from Detroit," you could hear on any given night, "Any Motor City Soul Brothers out there, man? Who knows a good joke?" Thus the frequency had acquired the nickname of the Bullshit Band.

After much cajoling, bribery and threats, Wally finally consented to turn on the radio. Nothing but static. "Fuck you guys," he said.

"Put on the whip, and run it out the door," said Hoffy. "You can't get nothin' in here with a tape antenna." Wally took out the ten-foot long whip antenna, plugged it in, and stuck it out of the bunker. He fiddled with the radio. "Baby, baby, where did our love go?" Diana Ross and the Supremes crooned from the speaker, quite audible in spite of the crackling static.

"Hot damn!" shouted Morgan.

"Wha'd I tell you!" said Mogerty.

"Run next door and get Kenny and them, Rolly," said Wally. "Let's have a party!" The song ended and a voice came over the box:

"Diana Ross and the Su-premes," said the voice. "Ain't they wonderful? Eat the apple and fuck the Corps; that's what I always say. And who am I? Why, I'm Dancin' Jack, your Armed Forces Bullshit Network DJ, comin' to you from somewhere deep in the heart of the heart of the country. Do I have any more requests out there, you jive motherfuckers?"

"You got 'Dancin' in the Streets'?" another voice broke in.

"All right! Martha and the Vandellas," said Dancin' Jack. "Anybody out there in radioland got 'Dancin' in the Streets'?"

"Yo!" came a third voice. "I do."

"Well, spin it, comrade!" Another song began: "Callin' out around the world, there'll be dancin' in the streets..."

"How are they doin' that?" asked Wally.

"Must be guys down around Dong Ha and Camp Carroll with turntables and tapedecks and stuff," said Mogerty. "All you gotta do is put your headset up to the speakers and the airways fill with music."

"Yahoo!" shouted Hoffy, snapping his fingers and shaking his shoulders in time to the music. Morgan piled back into the bunker with Thurston, Frenchy and Amagasu in tow.

"Anybody wanna get high?" asked Mogerty.

"You got some booze?" asked Thurston.

"Uh, uh," said Mogerty, "marijuana." He took out a small vial and opened it.

"Where'd you get that?" asked Seagrave.

"Buddy of mine in Alpha Company."

"Well, let's smoke it!" Wally volunteered. Mogerty rolled a fat reefer, lit it and started it around, then rolled another and lit it. I'd never seen marijuana before, let alone smoked it. When the first reefer got to me, I passed it on without taking any. I was suddenly beginning to feel very uncomfortable.

"Smoke it," said Wally, drawing in a great lungful of smoke. "It's good for you. Put hair on your chest."

"I don't know," I said hesitantly. "I never used drugs before."

"Bullshit," said Hoffy. "Whaddaya think booze is?"

"And this stuff's better'n booze," said Mogerty. "It don't give ya a fuckin' hangover."

"Who all's cherry in here?" Hoffy asked. Amagasu, Morgan, Thurston and I tentatively raised our hands.

"Not me!" said Wally, grinning broadly and holding up a joint. "I just popped mine."

"Always a first time for everything," Hoffy roared.

"How long you been smokin' this stuff?" I asked.

"Since yesterday," said Hoffy. "Like I said, there's always a first time for everything. Can't think of a safer place than Disneyland. The gooks get far enough to overrun this bunker, we'll all be a lot better off if we're stoned outta our fuckin' minds."

"If God didn't want you to smoke it, Bill," Mogerty added, "he wouldn't have invented the stuff. He *gave* it to us. You don't have to refine it, or distill it, or nothin'. Just pick it and smoke it. There's a message in that."

I still wasn't convinced. I had visions of pink furry monsters chasing me relentlessly as I ran screaming into the dark night beyond the safety of the bunker, there to drown helplessly in the universal mud. The Beatles crackled over the radio: "Yesterday, love was such an easy game to play; now it seems as though it's gone away; oh, I believe in yesterday." I took a puff. It was harsh, and made me start coughing.

"Hold it in," said Hoffy. "Draw it straight into your lungs and hold it."

"If I get crazy," I warned, half pleading, "somebody better hold me down."

"For chrissake, you won't get crazy," said Hoffy. "Whaddaya think this is, LSD?" I took another puff, then a much deeper drag, and passed the reefer on. "There, see?" said Hoffy. The smoke had a sweet pungent taste and made me a little lightheaded. Otis Redding was sitting on the dock of the bay, and I could see the tide rolling away as the joints went around and around; the music played on into the night, and everybody in the crowded bunker began to carry on five different conversations at once; and then everybody was laughing, and the music was playing and playing, and fingers popped in time, and bodies swayed, and the laughter and the night and the smoke rolled on and on like waves against a beach on a far-off tropical island inhabited by Dancin' Jack. Whatever anybody out there in radioland wanted to hear, somebody else seemed to have it: rock 'n' roll, blues, jazz, soul,

216

country. Inside the bunker, we sprawled all over each other, and laughed at everything and nothing, and ate two whole cases of C-rations, pitching the empty cans and cartons out into the darkness beyond the entrance, and tried to play cards, but all we could find was a 52-card deck of aces of spades, so we played poker, and everybody ended up with five aces, which was the funniest thing in the whole world.

"So, Ehrhart," said Hoffy, leering into my face by the eerie light of the Coleman lantern, "how do you like Mary Jane?"

"Huh?"

"Mary Jane, my boy; the marijuana."

"Oh," I said, peering out of a fog. "Oh, wow. But it's illegal, ain't it?" We both burst out laughing.

"What have you done in the last ten months that *ain't* illegal, Ehrhart?" Hoffy roared, and we both laughed harder, rolling over and clutching our sides. The driving beat of the Rolling Stones came thumping through the static. The whole bunker shouted in unison:

"Baby better come back, maybe next week; can't you see — I'm all — a-loosin' sleep; I can't get no! Satisfaction!" Clap, clap, clap-clap-clap. "Oh, no, no, no!!!"

Chapter 34

The next morning, everybody slept late. Dancin' Jack hadn't signed off the air until well after 0400, and there was nothing to get up for anyway. We were all in the rack when Gunny Krebs crawled in.

"Happy Thanksgiving!" he said cheerfully.

"So what?" said Sergeant Seagrave. "Go'way, Gunny; we're tryin' to sleep."

"Is that any way to talk to a gunnery sergeant?" asked the Gunny in mock indignation. "Come on, get up; here, have a drink on me." He reached for his famous canteen as Wally, Gravey, Rolly and I tumbled sleepily out of our bunks and collapsed on the duckboards. "It's Thanksgiving," said the Gunny.

"I got a headache," said Morgan.

"Impossible," said Wally, groping for his boots.

"That's my boot," I said, yanking a boot out of Wally's hands.

"We already celebrated," said Seagrave, reaching for the canteen. He took a swig and passed it along. "What's up, Gunny?"

"It's Thanksgiving dinner time, gentlemen; grab your messkits and get it while it's hot."

"What?" I said.

"We got Thanksgiving dinner over at the aid station," the Gunny elaborated. "They just flew it in on a couple of choppers. Turkey, stuffing, all kinds of good stuff — got it all in big tubs down there."

"More Mickey Mouse," said Seagrave. "Jesus Christ, who's fuckin' idea was that?"

"General Robertson's," said Gunny Krebs. "Benjamin Franklin's. How should I know? Captain Braithewaite says you're supposed to go eat."

"That's Death Valley out there, Gunny," I said. "What the fuck do I wanna go trompin' around out there for? I don't want no dumb turkey anyway. We got everything we need right here." I pointed to the pile of C-rations in the corner, then hauled out the case of Louisiana Red Rooster hot sauce we'd scrounged off the SeaBees before we'd left Ai Tu. "Want a bottle? I'll give you one if you tell whoever sent that turkey to go stick it up his ass."

"Send the goddamned bird to the Baton Rouge VFW," added Seagrave. "Tell 'em it's on me."

"Listen, boys, this isn't my idea," said the Gunny. "Captain says you're supposed to eat Thanksgiving dinner. It ain't his idea, either. Do I have to make it an order?"

"You just did," I said. "Sorry, Gunny; don't get mad. Fuckin' ridiculous, that's all."

It was raining. The mud in Death Valley was a foot deep if you kept to the high ground; the soft spots could swallow you whole. We plodded through the rain like Brer Rabbits on a giant Tarbaby, ducking and wincing in painful anticipation of incoming while the dark mud sucked and clawed at our legs. The passage to the aid station took forever. We were all nervous wrecks by the time we arrived. I couldn't stop flinching. Father Ligon, his prematurely bald head glistening, greeted each new diner at the door of the aid station. "Happy Thanksgiving!" he beamed. "It's good to see you. God bless you." When he got to me, you could see the words 'God bless you' begin to form on his lips, then disappear. "Hi, Corporal Ehrhart," he said, smiling softly. "It *is* good to see you."

"It's nice to see you, too, Father," I said, shaking his hand.

"How are you doing?" he asked.

"Okay. I'm okay, I guess."

"You let me know if there's anything I can do for you."

"Sure, Father; thanks."

I moved on toward the makeshift serving line among the litters and medical equipment where messmen began to fill my messkit with turkey, stuffing, mashed potatoes, sweet potatoes, corn, string beans, cranberry sauce, and pumpkin pie. The messkit was too small; the entire menu ended up in one indistinguishable heap rising high over the tin dish. It looked like someone had gotten sick.

By the time we managed to struggle back to our bunker, the

food was very cold and heavily diluted with rain water. All four of us sat there, too overcome by the enormity of the little disasters piled in front of us to say much, every now and then taking a bit of something or other and trying to guess what it was. "I think this is a drumstick," said Wally, holding one end of a six-inch long solid object and banging the other end on the duckboards.

"Happy Thanksgiving, fellas; mind if we interrupt your meal for a few moments?" Without waiting for an answer, a strange man in jungle utilities with no insignia crawled into the bunker. He had a notepad, and he was followed by another stranger with several cameras dangling from his neck.

"Whadda you want?" Seagrave stated without looking up.

The man with the notepad explained that they were from some magazine or other, and that they were doing a feature story on Thanksgiving at Con Thien.

"A little something to warm the hearts of the folks back on the homefront, huh?" said Seagrave.

"Yeh, something like that," said the journalist, half smiling.

Seagrave looked up at the two strangers with a face empty of expression. "Get the fuck out of our house, assholes," he said. "Now." He shoved a defiant forkful of food into his mouth. The two strangers disappeared into another dimension. Morgan giggled. I giggled. Wally beat rhythmically on the duckboards with the turkey drumstick, and started humming softly. Graves grinned slowly, then burst out laughing, spraying the mouthful of food all over the wall in front of him.

We were looking for a large container to put the rest of our Thanksgiving dinner in, hoping to salvage it for rat bait, when Amagasu came sliding into the bunker, having slipped on the mud just outside the entrance.

"Shit!" said Amagasu, slamming into the duckboards with a thud, one side of his body newly coated with mud.

"Behold, the Emperor of Nippon!" I said.

"Bullshit," said Kenny. He pulled a wad of letters out of one pocket. "Choppers brought in mail," he said, dumping the letters on the duckboards and scrambling out again, intent upon reaching the safety of his own home up the hill.

I got only one letter, from my mother, but the envelope also contained a newspaper clipping. I looked at the headline: an article about the Surgeon General's continuing research into the cancer-causing effects of cigarettes. The letter said, "I hope you're not smoking too much; it's really not good for you. Please read this article."

I was sitting just inside the entrance to the bunker, and was right in the middle of the article, when half a dozen rounds of incoming shrieked down Death Valley and exploded less than a hundred meters away, sending me diving headlong away from the entrance as a scattergun-load of shrapnel peppered the roof and side of the bunker. Curled up in a fetal ball and still cringing, I looked at the letter again and burst out laughing.

"What the fuck's so funny?" asked Seagrave, who sat hunched over like a turtle, his teeth still set against the blast.

I waved the letter wildly in the air. I tried to speak, started coughing, caught my breath and tried again. "My mom says I shouldn't smoke because I might get lung cancer in twenty or thirty years," I stammered between gasps of air and laughter. "Might kill me." Just then, another half dozen rounds came barreling in and went off in a multiple roar that punched my eardrums, rattled my fillings, and shook the bunker heavily, knocking dirt down from the ceiling. The four of us were still laughing when Thurston, Frenchy and Amagasu came scooting in to find out what was so funny.

Chapter 35

A couple of days later, Captain Braithewaite said he needed two scouts to go along with Charlie Company — not to be mistaken for 'Charlie' as in Vietcong — on a sweep outside the wire. I was getting tired of doing nothing but sitting around in the mud, so I volunteered myself and talked Rolly Morgan into going along. We got up early the next morning, well before dawn, and began the 300 meter trek through the mud to Charlie Company's command post. it was pitch dark and raining, and you couldn't see where to walk very well. We both kept getting stuck in the mud, and hanging our clothes and equipment up on the barbed wire surrounding the interior minefields, and finally I got stuck up to my knees. Both of them.

"God-fucking-dammit!" I shouted. "I'm stuck."

"This was your idea, Bill," said Morgan.

"Aw, fuck you! Gimme a hand." I stretched out my arm toward Morgan; he grabbed it and pulled — and I fell over face-first. By the time we reached Charlie Company, I was covered with mud from head to toe, and had a fierce desire to get my hands on Ho Chi Minh or Lyndon Baines Johnson or anybody else who didn't have to live in the mud as a matter of course.

The company cleared the outer wire just about dawn, then humped around in the meadows for an hour or two several hundred meters north of Con Thien, never losing sight of the place. The rain had let up. We found a line of trenches connecting a series of open bunkers where the NVA forward observers would sit with their field telephones and call target adjustments back to their gunners. Nobody was home at the time, so we just blew up the bunkers with C-4. Then we moved over toward the west, still less than a thousand meters beyond our wire. There were paper leaflets strewn all over the field, and Marines began picking them up like colored eggs at an Easter Egg Hunt.

"Look at this, Rolly," I said, handing one to Morgan. "It's a fucking Christmas card!"

Printed on heavy white paper stock in seven different colors — orange, purple, black, green, yellow, blue and brown — was a Christmas card from the Vietcong. The front panel carried a candle and tree design, and the greeting: "Merry Christmas." Inside was a drawing of a young woman gazing at a photograph of a uniformed man. Along the righthand margin of the drawing was the caption: "Will you return safe and sound?" The fine print on the back panel said, "National Front for the Liberation of South Vietnam."

"Thoughtful little fuckers, ain't they?" said Morgan.

My stomach tightened. "These things are hardly wet," I said. "Where's the CO?" I spotted the company commander and trotted over to him. "Captain, these things are hardly even wet; they haven't been here more than a few hours. You better have the men spread out and keep moving, sir. I'd guess the gooks are drawin' a bead on us right now."

"Keep your interval!" the Captain shouted. "Keep moving!" Platoon commanders and platoon sergeants repeated the command, the company beginning to move again like a slow worm crawling through the grass. We were sweeping on line through an open field with hedgerows on three sides when the dull sound of mortar rounds leaving their tubes brought instant cries of "Incoming!" from forty or fifty throats all around me. Everybody hit the deck as the rounds began exploding on the open side of the field between us and Con Thien.

Fear like a stalking cat seized me as the NVA gunners began walking the rounds back toward us, cutting us off from the safety of Con Thien. I forced myself to get up and look for cover. Guys all around me began to scamper out of the open toward the hedgerows. Three quick explosions erupted, sounding very different from the exploding mortar rounds.

A set-up! The whole hedgerow was sewn with exploding booby-traps. A man ran into the hedgerow just in front of me, and came flying out in pieces. I hit the deck. "Jesus Christ! Jesus Christ!" I thought. Mortar rounds were falling among us now. Guys were running for cover, and guys were lying all over the field, and rounds kept exploding, and men shouted meaningless orders, and men hollered for corpsmen. No more than sixty seconds had elapsed since the first mortar rounds had left their tubes. I lay there trying to hide and trying to look around at the same time. There was nothing to strike back at. I couldn't stay where I was, and I couldn't move. Fear clawed and scratched and bit until my thoughts bled white; my stomach was the size of a ping-pong ball.

I could hear the four-deuce mortars open fire from Con Thien, the big 4.2-inch rounds thundering overhead and exploding among the trees well out on the other side of the hedgerow to the northwest. Maybe the observation post on the hill had spotted the NVA firing positions. The NVA fire seemed to trail off, then stopped altogether. Our own mortars kept pounding away, and finally, after ten or fifteen minutes, two tanks came clanking out from Con Thien. By then, there was little left to do but pick up the dead and look after the wounded. The tanks drove up and down the hedgerows, setting off the rest of the boobytraps—I counted at least nine more explosions—while we just sat and stood around waiting for a medevac helicopter to come for the casualties.

You could hear some of the wounded moaning, and one guy who'd had his thigh ripped open was still screaming, but the vitality of his cries indicated that he was not fatally wounded in spite of the bone-shivering screams. It was always the quiet ones who were close to the edge. I lit a cigarette, took a few puffs, and calmed down enough to notice that I'd wet my pants. After awhile, the medevac showed up with two F-4 Phantoms flying cover. The wounded and dead were loaded onto the helicopter, which rose up again and beat noisily away to the south. Then the two F-4s swooped down one at a time and tossed a few 500-pound bombs into the bushes about 200 meters in front of us, wheeled up and away, and were gone in a mighty roar. The silence swept in across the DMZ. It was raining again.

"That was a swell little operation," said Morgan as the company trudged slowly back up the hill toward Con Thien, the rest of the day's patrol cancelled. "Controlling infiltration!" he spat. "We can't even step outside the fuckin' wire without getting our butts kicked."

"Who says we're supposed to control infiltration?" I replied. "We're just target practice for the gooks. Uncle Ho and LBJ got a deal between 'em: we supply the targets; they supply the artillery. Gives everybody jobs. It ain't infiltration we're supposed to be controlling; it's inflation."

"Wouldn't surprise me none," said Morgan.

"God's honest truth. I read it in the *Wall Street Journal*."

"Got a cigarette? Mine are soaked. Christ, I thought we'd bought it out there."

"So did I. I pissed my pants."

"Yeh?"

"Yeh. Don't laugh. And don't fuckin' say nothin' to the guys."

"Don't worry; in this rain, ya can't tell anyway. If I'd a had breakfast before we left, I'd a probably shit in mine."

"Nice day, huh?"

"You volunteered us."

An hour later, Morgan and I got back to the COC to discover that Falcone was dead, and Wally, Seagrave and Stemkowski had been wounded and evacuated. A group of scouts playing cards in our bunker had heard the firing, figured it was our patrol getting hit, and had headed down to the COC to find out what was going on. Before they'd reached the COC, a cluster of incoming had caught them in the open. Frenchy had been killed instantly. Wally had been hit in the shoulder and arm; Seagrave in the thigh; Stemkowski in the head and chest. Later that afternoon, we got word that Wally and Seagrave were okay and would probably be back in a few weeks or a month. Mike Stemkowski died aboard the medevac helicopter.

"Sure is empty in here," said Morgan that night as we sat alone in the bunker. "You wanna ask Kenny and Jon to move in?"

"I don't know. I wouldn't mind havin' Kenny around, but I don't think I can take Thurston. He's nice enough, but I don't like where his head is. Out on a squirrel-shoot back in Kentucky or wherever the hell he's from. I think he's really enjoyin' himself over here. Gets on my nerves." I pulled out one of the Vietcong Christmas cards from my pocket, struck a match and lit it. As the flames got near my fingers, I dropped the fragile ashes into the mud and crushed them under my boot. "I guess Ski ain't gonna make it to medical school," I said. "You know, there's Ski with a girl waitin' back home, and he gets it. Bobby Rowe—'member him?—got a wife back home; he gets it. I ain't got a scratch, and my girl tells me to go take a hike."

"Look what happened to Calloway," Morgan pointed out. "Things just happen, that's all."

"Yeh, I guess so." Neither of us said anything for awhile. "I wish to hell I'd never heard of Vietnam," I finally said. "You know what I might do if I ever get back to The World?"

"What?"

"Buy a ticket for Hong Kong, and go. Just go."

"Why Hong Kong? Oh, yeh. You got time to do when you get back, don't you?"

"Yeh. Fifteen months." Another long pause.

"You ever wanna come stay on my Dad's farm for awhile," said Morgan, "just get away from things for awhile, you'd be welcome any time, you know. I'll teach ya how to milk cows. You could stay as long as you like. We always need a little extra help."

"That's nice, Rolly. Thanks."

"I mean it. You come any time."

"Yeh. Thanks, Rolly. Really. That's good to know."

"You wanna listen to Dancin' Jack for awhile?"

"No. I guess I'll turn in. You can listen if you want. It won't bother me."

Chapter 36

"Hi, guys!" Gerry grinned, poking his head into the bunker.

"Gerry!" I shouted. "What are you doin' here? Get your ass in here before you get it blown off." We slapped each other heartily. "Good to see ya, buddy," I said. "What are you doin' here?"

"I got tired of waiting for my postcard, so I came up to get it. So where is it? Let's have it."

Morgan tore the lid off a box of C-rations: "Meal, Combat, Individual/Pork, Sliced, Cooked With Juices/B-1 Unit/Universal Folding Box Co., Inc., Hoboken, NJ 07030." He handed it to Gerry. "Here," he said. "We been meanin' to send it, but we didn't have a stamp."

"This ain't Mickey Mouse," said Gerry.

"The hell it ain't," said Morgan. "What's in that box?"

Gerry lifted the long box he'd brought in with him. It was shaped like a flower box, only larger. "Dunno," he said. "It's for you." He held it out to me.

"A care package from your mom!" shouted Haller, who had moved in with us after Seagrave and Walters had been wounded. "Food! Open it." I took out my bayonet, cut the string and tape, and opened the box. Inside was the top of a pine tree, about two feet long, with all the branches carefully folded up along the trunk and held securely with a ribbon wrapped around the bundle like a barber pole.

"A real live Pennsylvania pine tree," I gasped.

"It's a Christmas tree!" said Haller. "Incredible!"

"I don't believe it," I said.

"Your mother's amazing, Ehrhart," said Gerry.

"Will you look at that," I said, lifting the tree out of the box and cradling it like a baby. It was embarrassing. My eyes were getting watery. I blinked hard a few times. "I don't believe it," I said.

"Let's put it up!" said Haller, who immediately began clearing a space in the corner among the pile of C-ration cartons. I emptied out the rest of the box, which contained a little homemade stand for the tree, and a box of ornaments and tinsel. In ten minutes, we had the whole tree decorated.

"What do we put on top?" asked Haller.

"I got just the thing," I said. I rooted around in an ammo box and came up with a six-inch high paper angel with a paper base that just fit over the top branch of the tree.

"Hey! Where'd ya get that?" asked Haller.

"Friend of mine sent it to me last week," I said. "Sadie Thompson. She's a Quaker."

"Perfect," said Haller, straightening the angel unnecessarily. "Good old Sadie. Thanks a lot. Fuck all those guys with their tinfoil trees; we got a *real* tree!"

"We oughta sing a Christmas carole or something," said Gerry as we all sat there admiring our tree. He started to sing "Silent Night," and the rest of us sheepishly joined in, but we hadn't gotten two lines into the song when voices began cracking, and everybody looked away from each other and began to laugh with embarrassment.

"Yeh. Well," said Morgan. "So, Griffith, speakin' of Christmas, you get your Marine Corps–issue Christmas cards yet?"

"No. What are they?"

Morgan reached into his ammo box and pulled out several cards and envelopes. On the front cover of the top card was a gold Star of Bethlehem with gold rays beaming down on a gold manger scene. Along the righthand margin was the red, white and blue diamond insignia of the first Marine Division. Inside, the card read: "On Earth, Peace to Men of Good Will."

"Jesus," said Gerry.

"Of course," said Morgan. "Everybody gets six cards and six envelopes. Absolutely free."

"On Earth, Peace to Men of Good Will," Gerry read. "Onward Christian Soldiers."

"You know what Sadie said to me before I came over here?" I said, touching the angel lightly. " 'Try not to kill anyone.' "

228

"Merry Christmas," said Haller

"Yeh," I said. "I haven't written to her in six months. What the hell am I supposed to say?"

"Well, you could tell her about the Christmas tree," said Morgan. "Tell her what ya did with her angel. That oughta make her happy." We sat back again, nobody saying anything, just looking at the tree. Incoming exploded over on the other side of the perimeter, sounding very far away. Then a salvo shrieked in and went off down in the valley nearby. We all ducked involuntarily, but none of the ornaments fell off.

"Welcome to Disneyland," I said to Gerry.

"How much of that do you get?" he asked.

"Anywhere from twenty-five to two hundred fifty rounds a day. Just goes on all the fuckin' time," I said. "How long you stayin'?"

"Just overnight. I brought some stuff up for Colonel Glass. Gotta catch a chopper out in the morning. Battalion Rear's movin' in a few days; I gotta get packed up."

"Where we goin' this time?"

"You guys ain't goin' anywhere for awhile; you'll be here till Christmas, at least. Rear's movin' down southwest of Quang Tri, about eight miles south of Ai Tu."

"Anything been goin' on down there?" I asked.

"Not much. We been mortared a few more times, but now the airfield's in, the gooks go for the runway and the planes mostly. They blew up a C–130 last week. Anything goin' down around here — besides all that racket?"

"That's it," I said. "They shell us all day long, and we listen to Dancin' Jack all night long — "

"Who?"

"Dancin' Jack. You'll see tonight."

"And we kill rats," added Morgan. "We got twenty-three so far." He pointed to the makeshift scoreboard carved into the roof beams.

"That's all we do," I went on. "That's it. You know we lost Frenchy and Ski, and Wally and Gravey got hit — "

"Yeh, I heard."

" — and we ain't so much as seen a gook, let alone shot at one. Same old shit, man, I'm tellin' ya, only there ain't no civilians up here to beat up on, and instead of mines and snipers, it's artillery and mortars — with an occasional rocket thrown in for good measure. I got eighty-two days left, man. Eighty-two fuckin' days." I knocked on the wooden duckboards. "You know what I'm gonna do? First thing when I get back to The World, right in the airport, anywhere, first chance I get, I'm gonna find the prettiest girl I can, and I'm gonna buy her a Coca-Cola. And I'm gonna sit there and watch her drink it through a straw."

"What's the point?" said Haller.

"I dream about it all the time — I used to dream about it; now I can dream it without even closin' my eyes. Me and a beautiful girl sittin' across from each other in a booth with leather seats, not sayin' anything, just smiling. Smiling and smiling until the soda's all gone. And then we get up and go our own ways, and we remember each other for the rest of our lives."

"I can think of a few things I'm gonna do with a beautiful girl or two or three when *I* get back to The World," said Haller, "and they don't include Coca-Cola."

"You got no class, Randy," said Gerry.

We had a party that night. All the other scouts piled into the bunker, including a new guy named Zag Bannerman — we'd only gotten one replacement so far — and a lot of other guys stopped in to see the real live Christmas tree because already word had begun to spread far and wide, and a glimpse of a real decorated pine tree in the midst of the filthy colorless world of Con Thien was worth a trek through the mud and the rain. Gunny Krebs stopped by with his canteen, and Captain Braithewaite. Even Major Miles, the operations officer, and Lieutenant Colonel Glass, the battalion commander, made the pilgrimage. I sat beside the Christmas tree, beaming like a proud father, and fielding envious compliments with the humility of a grand pooh-bah. "How about that, sir?" I'd say to the officers. "Eat your hearts out, suckers," I'd say to the enlisted men.

The next morning, Gerry headed down to the landing zone to wait for a helicopter out. "See ya in a couple of weeks," he said, putting the palm of his outstretched hand over my ear and giving my head a shake.

"Next time you write Jan, tell her I said 'hello,' will ya?" I hollered after him as he shuffle-trotted down the hill into the valley. He threw his hand up in the air in a gesture of acknowledgment, but didn't turn around, intent upon keeping his footing.

About an hour later, a corpsman crawled into the bunker. "Which one of you guys is Ehrhart?" he asked.

"Yo," I said.

"WIA gave me this," he said, holding out a mud-caked

wristwatch. "Said I was supposed to give it to ya — said it was real important — you lost yours, or somethin'."

"Gerry?" I said, my stomach wrenching so heavily that I nearly doubled over. "Gerry?! What happened? What happened? Where is he, Doc?"

"Gone. We just put him on a chopper. Don't worry; he's okay. He's gonna make it."

I slumped back against the sandbag wall, rested my head against it, and took a few deep breaths. "What happened?"

"Shrapnel in the knee," said the corpsman. "Looks like a million-dollar job; free ticket home. He got caught by incoming down at the LZ. Might lose his leg — I don't know — but he's gonna make it. He was right near BAS when he got it, so he didn't lose much blood. Listen, I gotta get back. I just brought this up cause he said it was real important; he made me promise."

"Yeh. Yeh, it is," I said. The corpsman turned to leave. "Hey, Doc, thanks for comin' all the way up here."

"Yeh, sure."

"Keep your ass down," I shouted after the corpsman as he disappeared out the entrance. I looked at the watch in my hand. Almost absentmindedly, I started to clean the mud off it.

"Damn," said Randy. "Gerry ain't even been here twenty-four hours, and he gets zapped."

"Guy's all busted up like that," I said, not really talking to anyone, "remembers I lost my watch." Gerry's watch was still running. I put it on. Then I crawled way back into the top bunk and lay down, turning my face away from Haller and Morgan.

Chapter 37

We left Con Thien on the twenty-third of December in a driving rain, each man aboard the trucks silently hoping that the convoy would get out of range of the NVA gunners on the other side of the DMZ before another volley of incoming arrived. Each of us suspected that there was a round out there somewhere with his name on it, and that time alone had cheated fate out of delivering it. No one talked much. We had taken a beating in the thirty-three days we'd been there, and except for trading artillery fire with the North Vietnamese, we had been able to do nothing about it but hide like the rats who had shared our bunkers. No one was sorry to leave.

The new battalion command post below Quang Tri City sat on a low hill indistinguishable from all the other low hills around it, except that we sat on top of it. The four rifle companies set up positions throughout the countryside around us, forming a box several miles across. The area contained more civilians than up around Ai Tu only eight or ten miles north, but still far less than the Hoi An area. The perimeter of the battalion command post was marked, as at Ai Tu, only by heavy coils of concertina wire with no berm. A general purpose tent, surrounded by a four-foot-high sandbag wall, served as the COC, and the troops lived in whatever accommodations we could construct.

The scouts got hold of a general purpose tent, but Randy Haller scrounged a smaller three-man tent from an antitank company not far from us, and invited me to move in with him. "Imagine that," he said, "an antitank battalion in Vietnam, and the gooks don't even have any tanks." For our convenience and comfort, we summarily designated the three-man tent a two-man tent, scrounged two cots from the battalion aid station, and made ourselves at home. From our veranda, a patch of grassy earth flanked by the two shallow fighting holes we'd dug for ourselves just outside the entrance of the tent, we could see a two-acre lake in a valley nearby, and a large Catholic church on the side of a hill about a mile to our west. The church was abandoned, and one of its two spires had collapsed, whether from artillery or neglect we couldn't tell.

You could hardly tell it was Christmas time except that we were issued a few cans of warm soda and beer, and everybody got an unusually large number of Care packages from friends and relatives back home, consequently suffering for days from the massive dose of alien substances like rum-balls, butter cream candy and fudge. C-ration toilet paper — you got a little roll with every meal — was worth its weight in gold. We dumped a good half-ton of chocolate chip cookies into the lake, tossing in a few grenades as well to make sure that the cookies couldn't be retrieved and recycled.

A twenty-four-hour Christmas truce was announced by Washington and Saigon, and though everyone I knew thought it was silly to call a one-day truce in the middle of a war no one intended to stop fighting, we were perfectly happy not to run a patrol that day. We still didn't dare relax because we had no idea whether or not the Vietcong would keep their word. They hadn't given their word to *us*, or to anyone any of us knew, so we weren't taking any chances. Christmas day, in fact, while tossing chocolate chip cookies into the lake, we decided we'd better test fire our rifles just to make sure they still worked, and we'd set about firing at cookies that were still floating, trying to sink them.

Hoffy's rifle jammed almost immediately; Amagasu's jammed also. Christmas truce or no Christmas truce, how could you relax when you couldn't trust the Vietcong and your own people sent you hardware like the M–16. "You cocksuckers!" Hoffy screamed, tossing his rifle into the lake. Amagasu said something in Japanese. Christmas day came and went without incident.

It rained nearly every day, and when you were wet all the time, even temperatures of 55 and 60 made your joints ache with cold — especially after the long hot dry season when temperatures had been twice as high. At night, you went to bed in wet clothes, but if you put your poncho over your blanket, the rubber kept the heat sealed in, and after awhile you would warm up from your own body heat. You were still wet when you woke up, since moisture condensed on the inside of the poncho, creating a permanent cycle of heat and moisture, but at least you could sleep without shivering. It wasn't so bad.

Within a few days, the whole battalion slipped into a regular routine much like the one we'd been in around Hoi An: patrols, patrols, patrols, day in and day out; guard duty and listening posts; mines and snipers, though neither were as heavy as down south; detainees and daily intelligence summaries. Captain Braithewaite finally got what he'd wanted ever since he'd arrived: command of a rifle company; and I got my fourth S-2 officer in less than a year: Captain Broderick, fresh from The World, a man with no sense of humor. Seagrave and Walters returned on the last day of 1967.

That night, on the stroke of 1968, flares of every imaginable kind and color burst into the dark sky from every Marine outpost all the way south as far as we could see, all the way north to the DMZ, and all along the DMZ. From the top of our hill, it looked like all of Vietnam was celebrating the American new year. We'd been specifically ordered not to fire flares by the senior Marine general in Vietnam because the flares would compromise our positions, according to the written order. But we all knew the Vietcong knew exactly where we were, and it was New Year's Eve, and you always celebrated New Year's Eve, and we didn't much care what any general thought, anyway. "Happy New Year!" we all shouted, sending pencil flares and pop-ups into 1968.

"Who's shooting off those flares?" Captain Broderick hollered, storming out of the COC into the darkness in the general direction of the scouts' positions.

"Those guys over there, sir," said Sergeant Seagrave, pointing in six different directions at once. "We didn't get a good look at 'em." I started to giggle, then felt my lungs collapse sharply as Seagrave belted me in the ribs with his elbow.

"Goddamn it," said Captain Broderick, stalking off.

"Yessir," said Sergeant Seagrave.

The next day, Haller and I celebrated the new year a second time with a picnic thrown together from the contents of several Care packages: salami, cheese, saltines, raisins, chocolate, and cookies shaped like trees and stars and Santas — all laid out on top of a box of 81-millimeter mortar shells.

"Happy New Year," said Haller.

"Sixty-four days, Randy," I pointed out between mouthfuls washed down with warm Pepsi. "Sixty-four days, and I'm gone forever." The sun even made a brief appearance, and we both decided that it was a favorable omen sent by the gods to carry us into the new year.

The rumor-mill, however, immediately began to contradict the sign of the gods. Rumors began flying thick and heavy that we were about to be sent to Khe Sanh, an outpost much like Con Thien out on the western end of the DMZ. Intelligence reports indicated a massive build-up of NVA troops in the hills around Khe Sanh. Because we were the only mobile strike battalion in all of I Corps, the northern-most military zone of South Vietnam, we seemed to be the most likely candidates to reinforce the place. Our battalion's job since October had been largely that of troubleshooter. Having just gotten out of a similar situation at Con Thien, no one was happy. A sergeant in artillery communications broke down in the COC one afternoon, suddenly crying and shouting, "I can't go there! I've only got two months left! For God's sake, I've got a wife, and a baby I've never even seen!" It was embarrassing, like watching somebody have an epileptic seizure in a movie theater, and it was unnerving because the sergeant was only voicing what everyone else was thinking.

Then the U.S. intelligence ship *Pueblo* was captured by the North Koreans, and within a few days, the rumors had us about to depart for North Korea on what promised to be a suicidal rescue attempt. "Jesus Christ," said Walters. "I'd rather go to Khe Sanh." Tensions ran high; good friends got into fistfights over packs of cigarettes and cans of pears and fruit cocktail.

But orders never came. Only the days came and went in an endlessly familiar succession of uneventful patrols and uneasy nights. The rain fell, and rumors of war washed over the battalion like waves on a calm beach from an offshore storm, and I continued to count the days and hope. I'd made my short-time calendar when I'd reached 90 days to go: a *Playboy* centerfold, the December 1967 playmate, on which I'd drawn 90 little numbered squares. Each day, I filled in one of the squares. The calendar hung from a nail in the COC where the S-2 shop was, and some days I'd let Major Miles fill in the square because he had the same rotation date as I did. "One more day," he'd say as he penciled in the square. "We're almost ready to trade this gal in for a real one, Corporal Ehrhart."

"Yessir," I'd say, and we'd both smile a secret smile. Captain Broderick thought we were silly, but he'd only been in Vietnam a couple of weeks.

Toward the end of the month, the battalion received orders to move to the big Marine base at Phu Bai on January twenty-ninth for a month of rest and refitting. "Hot damn!" I shouted at Haller when he delivered the news to our tent. "A month! That's it! That's all for me! The war's over! By the time you guys get sent back out, I'll be on that big Freedom Bird, headin' for The World!"

"Gimme a break, will ya?" said Haller.

"Don't feel bad, pal," I said, grinning from ear to ear. "I'll send ya a picture postcard. What would ya like? Coconut trees on a beach in Miami? The Golden Gate Bridge? You name it."

"Don't count your chickens before they hatch," said Haller. He caught himself immediately. "Hey, sure. Yeh, send me a picture of the Golden Gate."

"I'm gonna miss you, Randy."

"Yeh. Well, we got some time yet."

"Too much time! Man, I can just *taste* it! Bein' back in The World — wow, Jesus, you know?"

"So don't lose your cool, now, buddy; you're in the home-stretch."

"You know, Randy, I still can't believe I didn't like you. That goddamned music of yours," I laughed.

"Hell, that was nearly a year ago. Wait'll ya hear what they must be playin' by now. Probably make my stuff sound like Lawrence Welk."

"I don't give a big rat's ass *what* they're playin' back in The World — once I'm there! Before I got to know you, Gerry used to tell me..." My voice trailed off. "Geez, I sure miss him. We coulda spent a lot of time together this month."

"Wonder how he's doin'," said Haller.

"I thought he'd have written by now," I said. "I hope he's okay."

Two days before we pulled out, U.S. Army helicopters began swarming all over the hill next to us, depositing load after load of soldiers like insects depositing eggs.

"Jesus Christ," said Hoffy. "We're gettin' replaced by the Doggies. Humiliatin'."

"I don't give a fuck who replaces us," said Wally.

"They're bringin' in a whole brigade," I said. "Six battalions to cover the same area we been holding by ourselves. First Air Mobile Cavalry Division."

"First Air Mobile Cavalry Division," said Hoffy, rolling his eyes and exaggerating the words. "Shit. Talk about a PR job. Those assholes

236

can't even hump a mile without crappin' out. You know them fuckers got more choppers in Nam than the entire Marine Corps? Shit. Fly everywhere they go. We had equipment like that, we could end the war in a week."

"Don't bet on it," said Sergeant Seagrave.

"Fuck the war," I said. "Thirty-eight days and a wake-up. I'm so short, I gotta use a step-ladder to get into my boots." As if to find out if I was telling the truth, half a dozen boots rained down on me.

That night, Haller and I were awakened by intense small-arms fire, some of it actually ripping through our tent only inches above us. "Jesus Christ, we're getting overrun!" I hollered. I was up and into my fighting hole in a split second, dragging my rifle, cartridge belt, helmet and flak jacket with me.

But when I stuck my head up and took a look around through the darkness and the noise of flying bullets, all I could see was the Army compound on the hill next to us, the entire perimeter lit up like neon by the flashes of hundreds of small-arms weapons. We didn't seem to be taking any fire at all, except the fire that was coming from the Army positions. "Gravey!" I hollered. "Gravey, what the fuck's goin' on?"

"I don't know," I could hear Seagrave holler back. "Just stay down. They must be gettin' hit over there." I looked and looked, but I couldn't see any incoming fire. Off to my right, within our perimeter, I could hear shouts of "Corpsman!" I hadn't heard anything out of Haller since we'd jumped into our holes.

"Randy," I called.

"Yeh."

"You okay?"

"Yeh. Jesus, what are they doin' over there?"

"Damned if I know." After fifteen minutes or so, things got quiet again, and I slipped into the COC to find out what I could. Captain Broderick told me not to bother him then, but as I was leaving, Major Miles explained that the Army compound had been hit with eight or ten rounds of light mortar fire.

"Mortars?!" I said. "Did you see what they did over there, sir?"

The Major shrugged his shoulders, pointed to the short-time calendar on the wall, and said, "Just keep counting, Corporal Ehrhart. How many days we got? Thirty-seven and a wake-up?"

A mortar is a high trajectory weapon. You can set it up on the back side of a hill, and lob rounds over the top of the hill and onto a target several thousand meters away without even being seen; and you can't be shot at by flat trajectory weapons like rifles and machineguns

237

because you're protected by the hill. The odds are that your target doesn't even know where you are. There are only three reasonable responses to that kind of attack: sit there and take it, which is often all you can do; try to figure out where the enemy mortars are located, and return fire with your own mortars; send out a reactionary ground force, or helicopters if you have them.

The Army had chosen response number four.

The next morning, we found out that the Army's random fire had killed one Marine and wounded three others. "Those worthless shitbirds," said Hoffy that afternoon as a group of scouts sat on the hilltop looking over at the Army perimeter. Helicopters continued to arrive, depositing more and more eggs. "Like a bunch of scared kids. You woulda thought there was a whole Chinese division attackin' 'em. I'll bet the gooks laughed their asses off. Wanna go over there and kick a few heads in?"

"Whadda you expect?" I said. "Couple of friends of mine joined the Army while I was still in high school. Got sent to Fort Dix, New Jersey, for boot camp. Christ, they were back at school two weeks later in dress uniforms with three-day passes. You know they got candy machines and televisions and stuff in their barracks? Go to the slop-chute, go to the movies week nights. In boot camp, for chrissake! No wonder they can't fight their way out of a paper bag."

"All that chickenshit stuff they used to do to us in boot camp?" said Mogerty, "don't seem so much like chickenshit from here."

"I wouldn't wanna do it again," said Wally.

"Me, neither," I said, "but I'm sure fuckin' glad somebody bothered to train me before I got here."

"Hey, Bill," said Haller, who had come up and was standing off to the side of the group. "Come here a minute."

"What's up?" I said.

"Just come here a minute, will ya?" I walked over to him. "Come on over to the tent; I gotta show you something."

"What is it? What's the big secret?"

"Just come on. That girl from Hong Kong; her name was Dorrit, wasn't it?"

"Yeh. Why?"

"Dorrit von Hellemond?"

"Yeh. What's goin' on?" We went into the tent. Haller unfolded the copy of *Stars 'n' Stripes* he was carrying, and turned to a back page.

"You better read this," he said. "I didn't think you'd want me to show it to you out there." I took the newspaper:

POLICE SEEK KILLER
IN BRUTAL SEX MURDER

HONG KONG (AP) — Hong Kong police are searching for the killer of a beautiful Danish girl who was found raped and murdered on a lonely back street in Kowloon Monday morning.

The girl, Dorrit Vonhellemond, 23, a commercial artist from Copenhagen, had been slashed about the face with a knife. Her throat had been cut and she had apparently been tortured with lighted cigarettes.

Police are looking for a man, identified only as caucasian, who was seen with Miss Vonhellemond the previous afternoon. They declined to say if he was a suspect, saying only that he is the last person known to have been with the girl before her body was found.

I looked at Haller. "They spelled her name wrong," I said. "It should be small 'v' and capital 'H'."

"Sit down," Haller said, gently pushing me down on the cot.

"You know, she used to drag me all over that city. Dragged me through the weirdest out-of-the-way places, scared out of my mind. She wasn't afraid of anything. I don't think it ever even crossed her mind to be afraid. Randy, she was— " My voice cracked, and a black wave rose from some dark place within me.

And when the wave finally broke, I screamed. "THIS IS IN-SANE!!!" I grabbed my head between my fists, slid off the cot, and rolled into a tight ball on the damp ground, drawing my knees tight against my stomach, sobbing. There was nothing inside me but pain: iron, red hot.

Somewhere in a dream, I could hear Haller's voice: "He's okay. Don't go in there. Leave him alone right now. He got some bad news, that's all. I'll explain later. Don't let anybody in. Tell 'em to go away."

When I got up, it was dark out. Randy was sitting on his cot looking at me. He handed me a canteen. "Scotch," he said. "Gunny Krebs gave it to me." I took two huge gulps, almost gagged, but managed to keep it down. I passed it to Haller, who took a drink. He handed it back, and I took another drink and handed it back to him. "You okay?" he asked.

"Yeh."

Haller threw the tent flap back. Morgan and Amagasu were sitting on the ground right outside. "He's all right," said Haller. "Give this back to Gunny Krebs, will you?" He handed the canteen to

Morgan. Morgan and Amagasu stood up. Morgan stepped into the tent, put his hand on my shoulder, letting it drop slowly. Then he and Amagasu turned and walked away.

The next day, we got on a CH–53 helicopter and flew to Phu Bai.

Chapter 38

The huge sprawling base at Phu Bai was the best thing the Marine Corps had ever done for me, as far as I was concerned. Other units were stationed there permanently to provide such services as base security, so we didn't have to worry about guard duty or listening posts or things like that. The battalion wouldn't be running any operations or patrols, so I didn't have to worry about daily intelligence summaries or detainees or things like that. In short, we didn't have to do much of anything but hang around and take it easy for awhile. After four solid months in the field, that was okay with me.

We lived in strongback tents with electric lights once again. We had showers and walk-up, sit-down outhouses. There was an outdoor movie theater, and a crude enlisted men's club that dispensed semicold beer for a reasonable price. We were issued new jungle utilities and socks, and replacements for wornout field equipment. "I won't be needing this junk," I said to the other scouts, fending off blows and catcalls as I reminded them how short I was. But I took the new field equipment anyway because it felt nice to have something that was stiff and new and clean for a change.

About the only thing we didn't get was new rifles — or rather old rifles. Sergeant Seagrave once again tried to trade in the scouts' M-16s for the older but vastly more dependable M-14, but he was told that the M-16 was standard issue and there was nothing to be done about it. Nevertheless, we couldn't complain, especially after living the entire month of January expecting to get sent to Khe Sanh or North

Korea at any minute. For two solid days, we played cards, drank beer, stood under the showers until we turned pink and the hot water ran out, and slept a lot.

Early on the third morning, January thirty-first, Gunny Krebs came into our hooch and woke us all up. "We gotta saddle up," he said.

"Leave me alone."

"Turn out that light."

"Where's your canteen?"

"Come on, boys, get up," said the Gunny.

"What's goin' on?" asked Sergeant Seagrave, rubbing his eyes.

"MACV compound in Hue's takin' sniper fire and 60-millimeter mortars," said the Gunny. "They just called down for an assist. Don't sound like much, but we're sending two companies up to check it out."

"But it's the Vietnamese new year," I protested. "It's Tet. What happened to the goddamned truce? Supposed to be a three-day truce, ain't there? Christ, we didn't bother them on *our* new year."

"Why don'cha ask 'em about it when you get there, Ehrhart?" the Gunny said, laughing at his own joke. I didn't think it was funny; I wanted to sleep. "Let's go," he said again. "Trucks are loadin' out on the road in fifteen minutes. Take three days' worth of rations. Anybody need ammo, get over to supply right away."

"Je-sus Christ," Wally moaned. "This green motherfucker. Nice fuckin' rest they give us."

"Quit your bitchin', Wally," said the Gunny. "We'll be back in a day or two — maybe be back by tonight. Come on, fellas, let's move out."

When we got out to the trucks, it was still dark. Captain Broderick pulled me aside. "Not you, Corporal Ehrhart," he said. "You're too short. You don't have to go."

"Aw, what the hell, Captain," I said. "Thanks, but I might as well. Won't be nothin' to do around here with everybody else gone. Please."

"You sure?"

"Yessir. Gimme somethin' to do for a couple of days. I'll go nuts sittin' around here all alone."

"Okay. Climb aboard."

We loaded into the trucks, and the trucks rumbled into the darkness up Highway One toward Hue, eight miles north. Less than an hour after we had awakened, with dawn just breaking, the convoy entered the south side of the city, the silhouettes of two- and three-story buildings visible ahead of us. We passed a Shell gasoline station.

And then all hell broke loose.

Enemy soldiers dug in close by on either side of the road, behind walls and inside buildings and on rooftops, let loose a withering fusillade that struck against the sleepy convoy with the force of a sledgehammer crushing a cockroach: automatic weapons, small-arms, rockets, recoilless rifles, mortars, grenades. Everything. All at once. Men began to scream and topple over in the trucks before we could even begin to return fire. Orders and shouts broke off in mid-sentence as hands flew to faces attached to heads already snapped back by the impact of bullets. Marines scrambled pell-mell out of the trucks, diving wildly for anything that offered cover. The noise drowned everything, even your own thoughts.

I lay in a ditch, pushing the barrel of my rifle up over the low top and firing wildly, not daring to look for a target, only trying to make somebody duck out there. Slowly, almost imperceptibly at first, we began to fight back. The shock of the ambush had caught the whole column completely by surprise, but the recognition of certain death gave way to training, discipline and the instinct to survive.

We knew the MACV compound lay straight up the road, perhaps seven blocks ahead near the south bank of the River of Perfumes that bisected the city east to west. We knew that it hadn't yet been overrun and that if we could reach it, we might find sanctuary. We crawled and fought our way down the first block. I leaped out of the ditch and threw myself behind a low wall, tossing a grenade into the window of a nearby house. Sergeant Seagrave dove headlong into the wall beside me, his helmet crashing against the stones. I thought he'd been hit, but he came up grinning and swearing. "Beaucoup VC out there, ain't there?" he observed almost calmly. "Cover me." Then he was up and gone, leaping over the wall and diving for a stone column ten feet ahead while I stuck my head up and sprayed the facing building with bullets.

We fought our way up the next block. And the one after that. All day long, we inched up the street. Casualties were appalling. Wounded and dead Marines lay everywhere; other Marines struggled to drag them out of the street toward cover. Disabled and burning trucks and jeeps stretched back down the street behind us. Gunny Krebs toppled over between Morgan and me, blood gushing from holes in his face, neck and chest. We stripped him of what was left of his rifle ammunition, took his .45 automatic, tossed his body onto a truck, and raced back to the wall we'd been hiding behind.

"Shit!" Morgan shouted. "His canteen!"

"Forget it!" I said, grabbing his arm to restrain him. He flew back against the wall.

"Shit!" he shouted, even louder this time. His forearm was bleeding from a two-inch shrapnel wound. I wrapped it up with my bandage.

"You okay?" I asked.

"Yeh."

"Let's go. That wall up there. Cover me."

Hour after hour, it continued. Minute after minute. Half a block. Another block. Taking fire from all sides. I had never imagined there could be so many NVA in the whole world. And they had to be NVA. The Vietcong had never had anything like this: the recoilless rifles, the heavy machineguns; not in these numbers. The mythical NVA were real, and they were all in Hue City, and they were all trying to kill me.

We finally reached the MACV compound. A block north stood a narrow two-lane bridge spanning the river. We could see the walls of the Citadel, the Imperial City, on the other side. Instead of turning into the MACV compound, we continued on toward the bridge. Two quad-.50s — trucks with four .50-caliber machineguns swivel-mounted together on the truckbed — drove out onto the bridge and started over, their guns clattering hoarsely. Several other trucks followed them. Marines charged out after the trucks in a headlong dash for the other side, 300 meters away.

Out on the bridge, I could see water on either side of me. I fought the urge to leap off the bridge into the water and float away to sea. I ran as fast as I could from one steel support to the next, firing at both riverbanks. On the north side, the two quad-.50s broke left and right, firing steadily up at the thick stone walls of the ancient city of emperors. Both of the guntrucks were hit by rockets or recoilless rifles almost immediately. Major Miles lifted a dead Marine to throw him up on one of the other trucks, then he collapsed, the body collapsing on top of him.

"Fall back! Fall back!" someone was hollering. I didn't stop to find out who. We left the two wrecked quad-.50s and at least one other truck, and withdrew to the south side of the river, taking our dead and wounded with us. Night was falling. We headed for the relative safety of the MACV compound.

We had been fighting continuously since dawn. Continuously. There had been no respite. It had taken us fourteen hours to go the seven blocks to the army compound. Holed up there, counting heads, we soon realized that our initial force of three hundred fifty men had been reduced by about half, many of them — like Morgan and Mogerty — wounded though still able to fight. Captain Braithewaite, commanding Alpha Company, had taken a .50-caliber machinegun bullet through both thighs in the first burst of fire that morning, shattering both of his thigh bones. Gunny Krebs was dead. Major Miles was dead.

We also learned that night that relief would be limited. In honor of Tet, the NVA and Vietcong that morning had unleashed an offensive that spanned the length and breadth of South Vietnam. From what we could gather, every major American installation and every district and provincial capital lay under seige or was under direct attack. The whole country, however, was of little concern to us. We had a big enough problem right where we were.

"Captain Broderick," said Sergeant Seagrave that night, "the gooks hold the whole fucking city! There must be a couple thousand of 'em, for chrissake. Nice of them MACV turds to let us know." Captain Broderick's jaw worked beneath his skin, but he couldn't think of anything to say. "Those gooks didn't roll in here yesterday," Seagrave continued. "How the fuck did they get 'em all into this city without anybody knowin' about it? Where the hell's the ARVN? Where's the fucking police? Jesus Christ, sir."

"I don't know," said Captain Broderick.

"*Somebody* around here ain't on our side," said Seagrave. "I'll tell ya that, sir. Don't take a fool to figure that one out."

"Hearts and minds," said Mogerty, who had a bandage on his left upper arm. "Winnin' hearts and minds."

"So where the fuck's Westmoreland's light at the end of the fuckin' tunnel?" asked Hoffy.

"That's enough," said Captain Broderick.

We took fire all night long. No one slept. The next day, we consolidated our position around the MACV compound, then set out to retake the city, building by building, block by block. It seemed like an impossible task. No one mentioned it. Occasionally, a helicopter would come whomp-whomping into the landing zone set up by the river, dropping off ammunition and food and taking out casualties. Only those that could no longer fight, but could still be saved, were evacuated. Few helicopters were able to get through, and space aboard them was limited. Anybody who could still walk, see, and fire a rifle stayed behind. So did the dead: body bags stuffed with Marines lay stacked around the landing zone like cordwood.

The whole thing was like the war movies I'd watched with intense delight as a boy. Men shouted and ran and crawled around on their elbows and knees with their rifles cradled in their arms; weapons barked and stuttered; smoke and debris erupted in fiery columns; whole slabs of buildings crumbled and collapsed to the street.

But the screams were real, and when men fell down they didn't get up, and the sticky wet substance splattering against your leg was somebody's intestines. One more minute. One more hour. Days were beyond imagination.

The fighting was made more difficult by the fact that we were in the third-largest city in South Vietnam. After nearly a year in rural areas — never even entering a city except on rare and brief official business — we were faced with dislodging an obviously well-prepared enemy from a built-up urban community of considerable size. We had no experience at this kind of fighting, and the on-the-job training cost us heavily. A great many civilians must have died in the fighting. If you saw or heard — or thought you saw or heard — movement in the house next door, you didn't stop to knock; you just tossed in a grenade.

But along with a new kind of fighting came a new kind of opponent — one that was willing to stand his ground and fight it out until one side or the other won. Every house was a new battlefield, and the NVA were ferocious fighters, and we were ready to slug it out with them. After nearly a year of frustration, of stumbling around in the boondocks finding nothing — or worse than nothing: those maddening mines and snipers; of searching hooches and calling somebody's lunch Vietcong supplies; of beating up old men and women; of cowering down helplessly in the darkness and mud as mortar rounds fell out of the sky; of swinging away at an enemy without substance or form or being; of striking out time and time again; of getting a bucket of cold water thrown in your face every time you were about to come — we were ready to fight. We were dying to fight. We didn't give a damn.

It was exhilarating. I was scared utterly witless — but it was the greatest adrenalin high I'd ever experienced: to have real armed targets to shoot at; to be able to say, "We're going to go over there and take that house away from them," and then proceed to do it — and to stay there and hold it, instead of turning around immediately and going back where you came from; at last, at last, to be able to fight back!

And I fought back passionately, in blind rage and pain, without remorse or conscience or deliberation. I fought back at the mud of Con Thien, and the burning sand of Hoi An, and the alien blank faces in the marketplace at Dien Ban; at the Pentagon generals, and the

246

Congress of the United States, and the *New York Times*; at the Iron Butterfly, and the draft-card burners, and the Daughters of the American Revolution; at the murderer of Dorrit von Hellemond, and the son-of-a-bitch who had taken Jenny flying in his private airplane; at the teachers who had taught me that America always had God on our side and always wore white hats and always won; at the Memorial Day parades and the daily Pledge of Allegiance and the constant rumors of peace talks and the constant absence of peace; at the movies of John Wayne and Audie Murphy, and the solemn statements of Dean Rusk and Robert MacNamara; at the ghosts of Roddenbery and Maloney and Rowe and Basinski and Calloway and Aymes and Falcone and Stemkowski; at Jerry Dougherty and Lloyd Drescher and Jimmy Whitson; at freedom and democracy and communism and the monumental stupidity with which I had delivered myself into the hands of the nightmare; at the small boy with the terrible grenade in his hand, cocked and ready to be delivered into my lap. Power surged through the barrel of my rifle. Raw, naked, unmitigated power. It was a pure and simple purgation of the soul. A sacred rite. A necessity. I had no idea — had not the slightest inkling — what I was fighting for or against.

I was terrified.

Chapter 39

In the first few days, the fighting was confined to the area immediately adjacent to the MACV compound. Reinforcements, several companies from 1st Battalion, 5th Marines, managed to get through on the third or fourth day, and though we were still heavily outnumbered, we managed gradually to extend the tiny corner of the city that we held. As the rifle companies pushed farther and farther out from the MACV compound and the helicopter landing zone, resupply became increasingly difficult. The problem became acute after the Vietcong cut the highway between Hue and Phu Bai, blowing several small bridges and making the highway impassable. Already faced with a shortage of vehicles, which we'd been using for resupply runs out to the rifle companies, we could then no longer obtain any replacements for the vehicles disabled and destroyed in the intense fighting.

Finally, on the fifth morning, Colonel Glass called upon the scouts to solve the problem. "Must be vehicles all over this city, boys," he said. "Go get us some wheels." By noon, we had managed to lay our hands on two U.S. Army jeeps, two ARVN jeeps, a Volkswagen bus, a Peugeot, and a red Vespa motorscooter. The motorscooter wasn't much use for carrying supplies, but it was a whole lot of fun to putter around on, and soon became a regular sight among the tree-lined, pot-holed, rubble-strewn once-beautiful boulevards of Hue, jauntily motoring along at the head of our bastard supply columns.

The last vehicle we managed to obtain, however, was the best of the lot: a pretty blue Air Force jeep with its serial number and

248

"U.S. Air Force" neatly stenciled in yellow on either side of the hood. Hoffy and I spotted it parked behind the officers' quarters of the MACV compound, which we'd vacated several days earlier, having moved the battalion command group to a house across the street.

Duty with Military Assistance Command–Vietnam — MACV — especially in a cosmopolitan place like Hue, consisted largely of screwing beautiful women and drinking good whiskey while drawing combat pay and earning battle decorations useful for promotions. American personnel assigned to MACV were supposed to be advising the Vietnamese, but from what we could observe at the MACV compound in Hoi An and similar facilities, it was pretty much a matter of Sahib and the wogs. Thus, the MACV officers in Hue must have been very unhappy to find themselves in the middle of the heaviest fighting of the war.

One of these unhappy MACV officers was the pudgy little Air Force major who came waddling out of the officers' quarters, waving his arms frantically and screaming bloody murder as I held the light chain he'd wrapped around the steering wheel of his jeep while Hoffy blew the lock off with a shotgun.

"Hey! Hey, you! What do you think you're doing? That's my jeep!" the Major squealed. "You can't take my jeep!"

"Oh, excuse us, sir; we just wanna borrow it for awhile," Hoffy explained. "We were gonna leave a note. You weren't plannin' to use it today, were ya?" I stripped away the remains of the lock and chain, and attempted to give them back to the Major, but he didn't want them.

"That's Air Force property! I'll have you court-martialed!"

"Wait, listen, it's okay, Major," Hoffy replied. "We'll bring it right back. Just as soon as the war's over."

"Leave that jeep alone! Take your filthy hands off my jeep. I'm giving you a direct order!" the Major screamed as I swung into the driver's seat. "Who's your commanding officer? I'm placing you both under arrest!" With that, the Major began fumbling for his sidearm.

But he stopped abruptly, went rigid, and turned completely white when he found himself staring into the twelve-gauge barrel of Hoffy's shotgun. His lips continued to work frantically, but no sound emerged except a barely audible rattling deep in his lungs.

"You don't need this jeep, and we do," Hoffy stated flatly as he pumped the shotgun, ejecting the spent shell and chambering a fresh one.

"Now, Major," I intervened as I started up the Major's jeep.

"You don't understand. Private Hofstatter here has been promoted to corporal twice already, and both times he's been busted back down to private within a month. He doesn't like officers, he has no respect for authority, and he's not very smart. But he's loyal as all get-out to his friends, and he'll do anything they ask because he likes to make them happy. I'm a friend of his, and if you touch that pistol, I'm gonna ask him to blow your fucking face off. Now do you understand, sir?"

The Major's eyes widened into circles like two little saucers of milk, and his lips stopped working.

"Do you want the chain or not?" I asked. The Major didn't say anything, but he took hold of the broken chain when I reached out and handed it to him. Hoffy, all six feet and 200 pounds of him, was grinning from ear to ear.

"Get outta the way," said Hoffy as he climbed into the seat beside me. "We're in a hurry, and you're wastin' our time. Why don't ya go back inside where it's safe; jerk off or somethin'? Stay outta trouble, ya know?"

"Nice talkin' with you, Major," I said. We both popped him a proper salute, then I put the jeep in gear and pulled out. Hoffy never took the shotgun off him until we disappeared around the corner.

"Cocksucker's liable to shoot us in the back," said Hoffy.

"I hope he's not on our side," I said.

"Did you see that slacker's eyeballs pop?" Hoffy suddenly roared. We both started laughing uncontrollably. The jeep began to weave all over the street. "For chrissake, look out where you're going!" Hoffy laughed, waving the shotgun.

"Watch those buildings, will ya? Pay attention. Say, this is a hell of a nice jeep. Handles like a sports car. Watch this!"

"Just drive, goddamn it!"

That night, Colonel Glass asked the scouts if anybody had stolen an Air Force jeep while holding the owner at gunpoint. None of the scouts said anything. "Isn't that an Air Force jeep out there?" said the Colonel, pointing toward the doorway of the house we were using as the battalion command post. I looked at Hoffy, but he was looking down at his feet. "Ehrhart, didn't I see you driving that jeep today?"

"Uh, yessir," I said. "Sir, we were only kidding about the shotgun."

"Honest, sir," Hoffy volunteered, "and we told him we'd bring his jeep right back as soon as the war's over."

"Oh," said the Colonel. "Oh. Well. Well, see that you do—if there's anything left of it."

Chapter 40

The next morning, things were the quietest they'd been since the battle had begun six days earlier. Six of the scouts were out on a resupply run to the southeast section of the city, a job we'd pretty much taken over since we'd been the ones who'd scrounged most of the vehicles. The rest of us hung around the command group, providing security for Colonel Glass and generally waiting for something to happen. We could hear heavy gunfire coming from the southeast.

The command group had taken over a substantial three-story house just across and down the street from the MACV compound. From the looks of it, it appeared to have been the mayor's house, or the provincial governor's, or somebody like that with big bucks and power, but whoever had lived there was long gone. The house had taken a beating in the fight for its control, but it was a really nice house just the same: stone and concrete construction, high ceilings, canopied beds, a wine cellar, oil paintings on the wall, a big yard with a low stone wall around it, iron bars on the first floor windows to keep out satchel charges. Altogether a fine place to set up shop for awhile.

Which is exactly what we'd done, though not by choice. Our units had made progress over in the east and southeast sections of the city, but the NVA still held the area immediately to our west, including the block just across the street from us to the southwest. For two days, we'd tried to dislodge them so that we could push out our western perimeter. Two days in a row, we'd failed, taking heavy casualties. We'd expected to have to try again today, but this morning the Colonel

251

had decided, "Bullshit, this is crazy. Let's get some flame tanks and do this right." Flame tanks look just like other tanks, but instead of cannons, they mount giant napalm flamethrowers in their turrets. The Colonel intended to torch the whole block. That was fine with us.

Amagasu and I were in a second-floor bedroom, keeping an eye on the buildings fronting the street to the southwest of us; Wally and Hoffy were in the room directly above us. When I found out we were going to do nothing for awhile, since the flame tanks wouldn't be available until some time later that day, I just pulled a padded easy-chair over to the window and sat down to watch the war, every now and then firing a shot or two across the street just to keep them honest on the other side. Amagasu sat on the canopied bed cleaning his rifle. I hadn't had much sleep lately. After awhile, I began to get a little drowsy, so I decided to make some coffee.

Using C-ration cans to make a stove and cup, I boiled some water. I took out a packet of C-ration coffee. "Kenny, I'm makin' some coffee here," I said. "You want some?"

Suddenly the world was in pieces. I never heard the explosion. Only the impact registered.

Sprawled out on the floor in a silent confusion of dust and debris and shredded clothing, I couldn't understand why I hadn't heard anything. "I'm hit bad," I thought, "sonofabitch, they finally got me," while another part of my brain kept screaming, "Jesus fucking Christ, not now, not now, not after all I've been through, oh please not now!"

My stomach was down around my knees somewhere, that sinking feeling you get at the split-instant you wake up from a nightmare, but I knew this wasn't a dream and I wasn't going to wake up. I had no idea what had happened. I'd been hit by a wrecking ball or something. The back of my head was gone. I didn't want to die, and I knew I was going to. "It isn't fair," I thought. "Make it quick. Please make it quick. Jesus, it isn't fair."

Lying on the floor, or rather crouched over with my knees under me and what was left of my head between my knees, I waited for death. And I waited. And waited.

Finally, trembling all over, I carefully reached my left hand around to the back of my head. Slowly, tentatively, I patted and felt all over. "What the fuck?!" I thought. My helmet was gone, but my head was still intact. "It's all there!" I thought. I brought my hand around to the front of my face and stared at it: no blood. I hurt all over, but my head was in one piece and there was no blood.

Right about then, I noticed that I was bleeding from half a

dozen other places. "Oh, Jesus Christ shit!" I thought. I *was* going to die after all. Another nauseating wave swept over me. I began yelling at the top of my lungs: "Corpsman! Corpsman!"

But there wasn't any sound. I opened my mouth and formed the words, and I could feel the air rushing from my lungs and the vibrations of my vocal chords — but I couldn't hear a sound. I couldn't hear my own voice. "Oh, Christ, no! I'm deaf!" I hollered. Or thought I hollered. I couldn't tell which.

I started crawling for the bedroom door, but before I'd gotten halfway there, Wally and Hoffy and some guys from downstairs had reached me. They were talking and gesturing excitedly as they tried to stop the bleeding, but I couldn't hear them. Nothing but a tremendous rushing noise reached my ears, as though someone had clapped conch shells over both of my ears and then amplified the sound a couple of hundred times. I felt like I was under water. I was dazed and groggy, and I couldn't walk. They bundled me onto a stretcher and hustled me off to the little aid station set up in the MACV compound where a doctor plugged up the new holes in my body and gave me a couple of shots. Then I lost consciousness.

When I woke up, late in the afternoon, a corpsman came over and began talking to me. I couldn't hear him. I sat up on the cot. I gestured at my ears, and kept shouting for him to speak up, and he kept leaning closer and closer until he was about six inches away from my face and all the muscles in his neck were straining visibly as he worked his mouth in violent exaggerated motions. He reminded me of a drill instructor. By the time I finally managed to understand what he was trying to say, he realized that what he was trying to say was absurd, and we both burst out laughing.

Because casualties had been so heavy, and replacements light, the walking wounded were still not being evacuated out of the fighting. Every single rifle counted — and every man who could fire one. Men who would have been hospitalized under any other circumstances were still in the line. They were needed. The corpsman had been trying to find out if I'd had my bell rung too badly to continue fighting. Maybe I could at least sit around the MACV compound and take radio messages or something, he'd been trying to suggest.

"Radio messages?!" I shouted. The corpsman winced and gestured as though he were turning down the volume on a television set or stereo. "Are you kidding? Little far-away voices coming through static-filled headphones? I can't even hear *you*, Doc." The corpsman shrugged his shoulders and grinned sheepishly. "Never mind; I'll find something to do. Drive a jeep or somethin'.'" I stood up gingerly, as if testing an unsteady pair of sea legs. There were bandages on my right arm, right calf, and right hip. "See you later," I said, and I hobbled back across the street to the mayor's house.

Later that night, we managed to figure out what had happened to me: I'd been wounded by a bazooka-type antitank rocket known as a B-40 or RPG-10. Wally and Hoffy had actually seen the NVA soldier fire from a window across the street before either of them could react. They'd thought the rocket was headed right for them, but it entered the window where I'd been sitting. Judging from where the rocket had been fired, where it had impacted, and where I'd been sitting, it must have missed a head-on collision with my face by less than a foot, passing over my left shoulder and blowing up against a wall of the room about four and a half feet above and behind me.

The blast opened a hole in the six-inch thick concrete wall about two feet in diameter, splintered a four-inch thick solid wood table sitting against the wall just below the point of impact, knocked all of the paintings off the walls, collapsed and shredded the canopied bed, demolished the heavy stuffed chair I'd been sitting in, sent me flying half way across the room, broke my M-16 clean in half, and lifted Wally and Hoffy two feet off the floor of the room above me, knocking them both down.

But because I'd been crouched over at the time, attempting to pour the instant coffee into the boiling water, and was wearing a helmet and flak jacket that covered my head, neck and back, and was further protected by the overstuffed armchair, only my lower back, right arm and right leg had been exposed to the blast and the flying shrapnel and debris.

The back of my helmet was so badly punched in by shrapnel that I couldn't put it back on my head and had to get another one — which explained why it had felt like the back of my head was gone. We picked more than fifty pieces of jagged shrapnel and concrete rubble out of the back of my heavy nylon-mesh-and-fiberglass flak vest, the pieces ranging in size from a fingernail to a silver dollar.

But I received only a few small cuts, a mild concussion, and a loss of hearing. Even the hearing loss wasn't going to be permanent. The corpsman had managed to communicate to me that my eardrums had not been ruptured, and that, though my ears would ache for awhile, my hearing should begin to return within a week or so.

"I need a new piece," I told Sergeant Seagrave, holding up the two broken halves of my M-16. "You think we can find an M-14 around

254

somewhere?" Suddenly I realized that I didn't know what had happened to Amagasu. In the confusion and shock of my own injuries, and the groggy aftermath, I hadn't given Amagasu a single thought all day. And he wasn't here with the rest of the scouts. "Where's Kenny?" I asked. "What happened to Amagasu?"

Sergeant Seagrave tried to explain, but I couldn't hear him. He didn't want to shout. He dug out a piece of paper and the stub of a pencil. "Medevac out. Left arm gone below the elbow," he scribbled. I felt no terror now, but the same sinking sickness I'd felt that morning swept over me again.

"It's my fault," I said. "I drew the fire." Seagrave shook his head sharply back and forth. "The hell it ain't," I said. "I got fuckin' lazy. Sat in the same fuckin' place all morning, just askin' for it. I don't know *what* the hell I was thinkin'. Will he make it?"

Seagrave shrugged his shoulders. Then he scribbled on the paper again: "I don't know. I think so. It's not your fault. I'm glad you're o.k." He heated a large can of water, and poured in three packets of instant coffee. Then he poured half of it into another tin can. He held up packets of cream and sugar, giving me a questioning look.

"No, thanks," I said. "Just black." He handed me one of the tin cans. "This is all I wanted in the first place," I said.

Chapter 41

I pressed myself flat against the wall just inside the entrance to the building, my back to the wall, my head turned to the left. If I could have, I would have become a part of the wall itself—melted into it, so that nothing remained but the rough concrete.

Three hallways opened into the little entrance lobby of the building. I could see down the hallway that led off to the right of the entrance, and I could see down the hallway that went directly in from the entrance, where a bloated corpse lay like some hideous version of an inflated beach toy. But I couldn't see down the hallway that went off to the left of the entrance because my back was against the wall nearest to it; I would have had to lean out and look around the corner.

And the faint shadow creeping along the wall across from me was coming from that direction: someone was walking slowly toward me—but I couldn't tell if it was Mogerty, or a North Vietnamese soldier.

If I flipped a grenade around the corner, or turned quickly and fired, I might kill Mogerty. If I waited until I could see the man who belonged to the shadow, until he reached the end of the hallway where he could see me too, I stood a good chance of being killed myself. "You sonofabitch, Mogerty," I thought. "What the hell you run off and leave me here alone for? Serve you right if I blew you away, you goddamned bastard." I was sweating heavily, my pulse pounding in my temples and neck, my right index finger wrapped tightly around the trigger of my M-16. My knees were shaking.

It would have served him right, too. Mogerty should have known better than to leave me alone in a place like that. Since the moment I'd been hit, I'd heard nothing but the constant roar of a subway train going flat-out through a tunnel between my ears. In the days following, I'd had to keep one of the other scouts within sight at all times so I could follow his hand signals or see what I was supposed to do or know when to hit the deck because we were taking fire. I seldom had any idea what was going on around me or why we were doing things that we did. I just followed the leader, and did what everybody else did. I felt like a puppy that goes everywhere the kids are going simply because the kids are going. I had no business in a combat zone — but there were guys worse off than me, and I knew it. If you could see, walk, and fire a rifle, you stayed, and that was that.

Actually, if you put your mouth right up to one of my ears, and hollered real loud, some of what you were trying to say would eventually float through the roar of the train. But it was a lot of work for both speaker and listener, and you usually don't want to be shouting at the top of your lungs in the middle of a combat zone. So most of the time, the other scouts didn't bother trying to talk to me, and I didn't bother trying to listen.

I suffered one near-cardiac arrest after another in the week before my hearing slowly began to return. I tried never to blink, and I was constantly flinching and bobbing and ducking and flicking my head from side to side like a punch-drunk boxer.

So when Mogerty suddenly took off and left me standing there alone, I was more than a little uneasy. We had just run a load of ammunition and C-rations out to the grunts over on the southwest side of the city, an area where we'd finally managed to make some headway. Mogerty and a lieutenant had had a brief conversation which I couldn't hear, but I could see that the lieutenant kept pointing to a complex of three buildings about 400 meters or so behind us, back toward the center of the city, and as we drove back to the battalion command post, Mogerty had signaled for me to pull over to those buildings that had held so much interest for the lieutenant.

I'd stopped in front of the building he pointed to, and then he'd jumped out of the jeep, held up his hand in a kind of benediction, and mouthed what appeared to be, "I'll be right back." Before I'd had a chance to object, he disappeared into the building.

Sitting in the jeep in the middle of a courtyard surrounded by the multiple front windows of all three two-story buildings was a bit too much like sitting at the wrong end of a shooting gallery, so I'd left

257

the jeep and stepped just inside the building Mogerty had entered, wondering anxiously what he was up to, feeling extremely uncomfortable, and wishing he'd reappear ten seconds ago.

I couldn't holler for him to come back because I might alert any nearby NVA. I couldn't go in and look for him because I didn't dare go anywhere without another man to act as my ears. If Mogerty got into trouble, or called for help, or even got into a firefight, I'd never know; I wouldn't be able to hear it. All I could do was stand there and wait. The stench from the rotting corpse only a few feet away clawed at my nostrils, turning my stomach, but I couldn't go back outside because every time I looked at all those open windows facing the courtyard, I imagined an NVA sniper lurking inside each and every one of them. The anxiety mounted, my impatience growing into anger.

And then I'd noticed the shadow.

It was barely a shadow at all. There was a line of windows along the front of the building, and the windows let in enough light so that the moving figure in the hall to the left of me cast a slight blurred patch on the wall opposite the windows. That's when I'd plastered myself up against the left wall of the entranceway, the wall closest to the hall down which the figure was moving. My stomach, already queasy from the stench of the corpse, tightened violently. Was it an NVA soldier, or was it Mogerty? I tried frantically to keep my head and think clearly; I had only a few seconds, at most. "Goddamn you, Mogerty!"

If it was a North Vietnamese soldier, he'd know we were here because he'd be able to see the jeep from the windows he was passing. That would explain why he's moving so slowly and cautiously. Maybe he even saw us pull up. Maybe he's already killed Mogerty. He knows where I am. He's trying to sneak up on me. "Turn and fire. Turn and fire, you dumb shit!"

But what if it *is* Mogerty? What if he's seen the empty jeep and thinks something's happened to me? That would explain why he's moving so slowly and cautiously. Maybe it *is* Mogerty. What if I startle him? He could end up blowing *me* away!

But Mogerty can hear. He'd have heard gunfire, or even a struggle without gunfire, wouldn't he? He must know I'm okay; he wouldn't be sneaking. It *must* be a gook.

But how much noise does a man armed with a knife make? Mogerty wouldn't hear that if the man were good, quick and sure of himself, slitting my throat from behind before I could scream. Mogerty knows that.

The shadow crept closer. "You fucking sonofabitch, Mogerty; if I ever see you alive again, I'll kill you." I waited.

I'd stopped breathing. I felt for the safety switch on the left side of my rifle, just above the trigger; it was set for full automatic. My right buttock was twitching.

I waited.

Thick blood gushed through my veins; my whole body thump-thump-thumped, adrenalin-pumped muscles straining against the too-tight casing of my skin. Somebody somewhere was playing "Sergeant Pepper's Lonely Hearts Club Band"; I could hear snatches of it coming from an old gramophone. "You can't hear, Ehrhart," I reminded myself, "and people don't use gramophones anymore." But I could hear it.

I waited.

The rotting corpse seemed to be floating. The subway train was taking a long tight curve inside the tunnel, its metal wheels screeching and tearing at the metal rails. The Buddhist temple in the Horseshoe came crashing down in a roar of broken concrete and dust. Princess — my dog. February. How many days left? Jenny? Thump, thump, thump.

I waited.

The shadow reached the hall across from the entrance. My clothes were soaked. My crotch itched. I was getting dizzy. I wanted to throw up. I wanted to scream — I was screaming inside my head: "Come on! *Come on!* COME ON!"

A rifle barrel — just the tip:

AK-47.

Gook.

Waste 'im!

Now!

Do IT!

Turn, squeeze, full-automatic, the rifle bucking against my right hip, the man still staring at the corpse on the floor to the left, perhaps for a brief moment forgetting, the swift shudder crossing the mind like a dark wind, seeing himself lying there as I had done only a few moments ago, just for an instant distracted, all it takes to empty half my magazine into his belly, the man reeling and jerking long before he understands that the corpse isn't important, the enemy soldier three feet away is important, he finally looks up as he starts over backwards, dead already, squeezing the trigger, the AK splatters a few useless rounds into the ceiling, falls from his hands, the force of the bullets slamming into his chest and side driving him into the opposite wall where he stands pinned up by the bullets which just keep coming and coming, his blind eyes gazing at me in utter astonishment as my rifle clicks empty. He slumps to the floor with his back against the wall and his feet flopped out in front of him like a Mexican taking a siesta.

I was still standing over the dead NVA soldier with my empty rifle pointed down at him when I noticed Mogerty's boots and legs beside me. I drew the empty magazine from my rifle, and jammed in a full one. I was breathing hoarsely, my chest and shoulders heaving rapidly up and down, hardly aware of the acrid powder smoke and putrid air I was dragging deep into my lungs in huge quantities. My heart was still pounding, the way it does when you have a near-accident in an automobile.

"You sonofabitch, Mogerty," I said without looking up. "Cover me." I turned and walked out and sat down on the low steps in front of the building, laid my rifle across my drawn-up knees and put my head down on my rifle.

When I finally looked up, Mogerty was looking down at me as if to say, "What did I do? What happened?"

"You sonofabitch, Mogerty," I said again. I reached up with one arm, and Mogerty hauled me to my feet. Then I cuffed him around the back of the neck with an open palm, shook his head, and he smiled, and I smiled, and we both got into the jeep and drove away.

Chapter 42

Back at the battalion command post, we learned that Bannerman and Davis, two of the newer scouts, had been ambushed an hour earlier while on a resupply run similar to the one Mogerty and I had just completed. Bannerman was dead; Davis had already been taken to the landing zone to be evacuated out. Seagrave had to write the explanation down for me. In ten days, the ten scouts who had entered Hue had sustained one dead, two wounded and evacuated, and three walking wounded. We'd also lost our intelligence chief. We were doing better than some units. The days and nights wore on.

The scouts spent much of our time making the resupply runs from the supply dump in the MACV compound out to the rifle companies, and ferrying wounded Marines to the battalion aid station. The rest of the time we spent trying to clear out small pockets of resistance left in the wake of the rifle companies, and snipers who had infiltrated back through our lines — soldiers like the ones who had taken out Bannerman and Davis, and the one I had killed while waiting for Mogerty. The city presented a thousand places to hide. Racing along on resupply, we were shot at constantly, and the NVA snipers didn't limit themselves to rifles or even machineguns; often they were armed with B-40s, like the guy who'd gotten me and Amagasu, or with powerful little 57-millimeter recoilless rifles that could be operated by a single soldier.

With its tree-lined boulevards, its parks, its beautiful cathedrals and temples, and the broad River of Perfumes, Hue City must have been a breathtakingly magnificent city before the fighting had begun. But it hadn't taken long to reduce the city to smoking rubble. One afternoon, I watched an armored self-propelled twin 40-millimeter Duster topple a church, the gunner raking his fire back and forth along the base of the building while his two loaders jammed five-round clips of shells into the open breeches of the cannons one after another in an endless succession of stooping and lifting until the building's structural supports gave way and the church collapsed on itself.

Entering residential homes, it was not uncommon to find corpses lying under tables in corners where they had tried to find some protection from the fighting. Many of them were so badly distended by the gasses trapped in their decomposing bodies that you couldn't tell if they were male or female, civilian or soldier, or how they had died or who had killed them. They stank horribly.

The city's university, located near the river in the vicinity of the MACV compound, became a makeshift refugee center, its dormitories and classrooms jammed wall to wall with frightened hungry civilians, the halls and stairways filled as well.

On one patrol, we discovered an abandoned Catholic girls' school. We searched the place, finding nothing but clothes, books, school papers, Vietnamese fashion and movie magazines, and toilet articles. Very little had been disturbed. The students must have left in a hurry. I wondered where they had gone. In one room, I found a small fingernail clipper shaped like a guitar and covered with an orange enamel glaze. I put it in my pocket.

During those first two weeks, the Colonel moved the battalion command post four times. I had no idea why. Early on, we had moved from the MACV compound to the governor's mansion across the street. Later we'd moved to a house several blocks west. Then we'd gone back to the governor's, and finally we returned to the MACV compound. Hoffy and I wondered if the Air Force major was still around — both of us bursting into laughter as our eyes met, neither of us having to say a word — but if he was still there, he kept to himself. Captain Broderick took over Bravo Company when the previous company commander got killed, and a young supply officer named Lieutenant Casey became the acting S-2. The subway train continued to roar through the tunnel between my ears, and my eardrums ached constantly, but my hearing slowly began to return within a week or so. I was down to somewhere around nineteen or twenty days to go — and was actually shorter than that because I was supposed to be back in the States by the 395th day of my tour — but I didn't dare dwell on it. I'd been caught daydreaming once already. Anybody can make a mistake, but only a fool makes the same mistake twice.

Actually, it wasn't all that difficult to avoid thinking about home. I'd come to Vietnam with a vivid idea of how things would be thirteen months later: Jenny would be waiting at the airport in Philadelphia; I'd step off the airplane, wearing my dark green winter dress uniform, colored ribbons sparkling on my chest; she'd rush into my arms, and I'd pick her up off the ground and whirl her around and around, her golden hair flying, her skirt lifting away from her thighs like Ginger Rogers.

Blur the picture. Fade out. Everybody lives happily ever after.

But the movie had ended long before the camera had stopped running. As the distance from home had gotten wider and wider, beneath the fantasies that had slowly become ever more wild and grand, the vague lurking suspicion that home would never be any closer lay waiting like some dark object at the bottom of a pool. The closer I got to the fact of The World, the more frightening became the prospect of finally having to reach into the water. In those last few weeks, I still talked about that big silver Freedom Bird sitting on the runway in Danang — longed for it with unbroken intensity — but I seldom thought beyond it. I wanted out so badly that the wanting itself had become a permanent fixture, like a scar or a birthmark. The end of imagination was so incomprehensible, I turned away from it. The solid immediacy of survival made the turning easy.

Thurston was shot dead late one afternoon less than 200 meters from the mayor's house. We got the sniper who did it. A few hours later, Mogerty and Wally came bursting into the MACV building the scouts were calling home for the night, one of the smaller out-buildings in the compound.

"Anybody wanna get laid tonight?" asked Wally, grinning.

"Where?" asked Seagrave. "Here? In Hue?"

"Yeh," said Wally. "We found a whore over at the University. She'll take us all on — and it won't cost us a single piastre. All she wants is food."

"A fuck for a box of C-rations," added Mogerty.

"A case?"

"No. One box. One meal per fuck."

"Count me in," said Hoffy.

"Why not?" said Seagrave.

"All right!" Wally whooped. "Get some!"

"Where's all this gonna happen?" asked Seagrave.

"I got a buddy in the 60-mike-mike platoon by the river," said Mogerty. "It's all set up. He'll let us use his gun pit if we cut him in on it."

"Someone's gotta stay here on radio watch," said Seagrave.

I thought about volunteering. I wasn't sure I wanted in on a gang-bang. But I wasn't sure I wanted out, either. The idea repelled me, but it aroused my curiosity, too, and I didn't want the others to think I wasn't game.

"I'll keep an eye on the radio," said Morgan. "You guys go on."

The rest of us slipped into the darkness, moving cautiously in single file as though we were on any ordinary patrol. It was raining. Mogerty led us to the river, found his friend, and the two of them muscled the little 60-millimeter mortar out of the gun pit. "I hope to hell we don't get a fire mission," said the friend. Wally arrived a short time later with a Vietnamese woman wearing dark silk trousers and a light silk blouse. It was too dark to see how old she was or what she looked like. Wally and Mogerty counted heads — six — and paid for all of us: one-half a case. We sat in the rain, smoking and listening to the gunfire coming from the other side of the river, while each of us took his turn. No one said much.

When my turn came, I jumped down into the pit. The woman was sitting up on some cardboard, protecting her body from the mud. She was naked from the waist down. I didn't know what to say or where to begin. "Chow Co," I said. "Hello." She just grunted softly, and fumbled for my belt buckle. Her hands were cold. I undid the buckle myself, and dropped my trousers. Cold air and rain bit at my buttocks and tightened my thighs. I hadn't had much experience at this sort of thing — but even I knew that the woman's awkwardness and stiff body suggested either inexperience or deep hatred. "Probably both," I thought. My stomach felt sick. I finished quickly, pulled up my trousers, and climbed out of the pit.

"I don't think she was a whore," I said to Hoffy as we sneaked back through the rain toward the MACV compound. Hoffy said something that I couldn't hear. "What?" I asked.

Hoffy leaned into my ear. "So what?" he said. I shrugged my shoulders.

As we got close to the MACV compound, we could hear shouts of "Fire! Fire!" Even I could hear it, and I could see men running toward a flickering glow. We hurried up, coming out between two buildings into the open courtyard in the center of the compound. In one corner of the courtyard, the small shed that housed about a dozen NVA

264

prisoners was burning. The fire was already beyond control, the entire shed engulfed in flames. We could hear screams, and through the open door of the shed, we could see bodies covered from head to toe in fire. Some of them were still moving frantically. There was no way to reach them. They looked like Buddhist monks I'd seen on the television news when I was in high school, the ones who used to burn themselves in the streets of Saigon and Danang and Hue.

As I stood there watching, I noticed movement out of the corner of my eye. I turned toward the large pile of supplies in the center of the courtyard; several figures were rooting through the pile. Each of them shouldered what looked like a case of C-rations. They were ARVN soldiers! I couldn't believe it. Since the fighting had begun, I hadn't seen a single South Vietnamese soldier actually fighting for the South Vietnamese city of Hue. Yet now, here they were, sneaking into our compound amid the confusion of the fire and stealing our supplies.

"The fucking ARVN are stealin' our chow!" I shouted. The three thieves began running toward the opposite side of the compound, each still carrying a case of rations. "You goddamned gooks!" I hollered. I leveled my rifle and starting firing. "You fucking yellow cowards!" Two of the men crumpled to the ground before Sergeant Seagrave could knock the barrel of my rifle into the air and wrap me in a bear hug. The other three scouts took off after the third man, but he dropped what he was carrying and got away.

"Lemme go, Gravey!" I shouted. "Those goddamned gooks! It's their fucking city, for chrissake! It's their fucking war! And all the little cocksuckers do is steal our food!"

The courtyard was filled with people watching the North Vietnamese burn. When I'd started firing, men had scattered every which way for cover, having no idea what was going on. Now the crowd began to mill around again, their attention torn between the burning bodies in the now-collapsed shed and the two men lying in the courtyard. Lieutenant Casey ran up. "What's going on?" he demanded.

"Those gooks were tryin' to steal our supplies, sir," said Sergeant Seagrave, pointing toward the bodies on the ground. "They were takin' off with their arms full. Ehrhart fired on 'em."

Wally came over. "One of 'em's still alive, sir," he said. "What should we do with him?"

"Get him over to the aid station. Ehrhart, what do you think you're doing?"

"What, sir? You'll have to speak up, sir; I can't hear too good still."

"What are you doing?"

"They were stealin' our stuff, sir. They were right on top of the pile when I spotted 'em — them two and another gook. I hollered for 'em to stop, but they took off runnin'."

"You can't just — "

"The hell I can't sir. I been fightin' their lousy fuckin' war for 'em for twelve and a half goddamned months. They can't fight worth a fuck. They won't even try. And now they steal our stuff while we're out there gettin' taken to the cleaners. Fuck 'em, sir. I don't have to take this shit."

"They *were* tryin' to steal supplies, sir," added Sergeant Seagrave.

"They probably started that goddamned fire just to distract everyone," I said. "Goddamned NVA are worth more than these shitbirds."

"Settle down, Ehrhart," said the Lieutenant.

"Well, how *did* that fire get started, sir?" asked Seagrave.

"We don't know," said the Lieutenant.

An Army major, probably one of the MACV officers, came over to us. "How did those ARVN get shot?" he wanted to know.

"I don't know," said the Lieutenant. "Must have been a sniper."

"Well," said the major, "we'd better get this compound cleared. These men are sitting ducks out here."

Chapter 43

Early the next afternoon, the six of us scouts left were out along the south bank of the river half a mile east of the university. We were holed up in an abandoned national police station, trying to dislodge some North Vietnamese from a building across the street. On the other side of the river, propellor-driven A-1 Skyraiders of the South Vietnamese Air Force dove again and again at the Citadel of the ancient Annamese emperors, sending columns of black smoke high into the sky. During a lull in our own firefight, a jeep came flying up the road. The NVA started firing at it. We started firing at the NVA again. The jeep skidded into the little courtyard beside the station.

"Let's go, Ehrhart," Lieutenant Casey called from the jeep. "Your orders are in."

I didn't even bother to take one last shot across the street. I stripped myself of half my gear, giving it to the other scouts. Then I stood there for a moment, looking at Seagrave and Walters and Mogerty and Morgan and Hofstatter. I tried to think of something to say.

"Come on, Ehrhart!" shouted the Lieutenant. "Chopper's on the LZ right now. You wanna go home or not?"

"Give my regards to The World," said Sergeant Seagrave.

"Yeh," I said. "So long, you guys. Good luck." I jumped into the jeep beside the Lieutenant, and he took off. When I looked back, the other scouts were bent over their rifles, laying down covering fire for us. We roared back down the road, and as we got closer to the landing zone, I could see a helicopter sitting there, its blades turning.

"That's yours," said Lieutenant Casey. "Hurry up. Get on it." I scrambled out of the jeep before it had come to a stop, jumped aboard the helicopter, and a few seconds later we lifted off. As we gained altitude, the war fell away like dead flaking skin. The whole city lay spread out beneath me. I could pick out familiar streets and buildings: the mayor's palace; the complex of buildings where Mogerty had left me sitting alone in the jeep; the girls' convent school; Bannerman and Davis had been ambushed at that intersection. Already the memory was a kind of dream.

The helicopter beat noisily away to the south. I searched anxiously for the telltale orange muzzle-flashes that would indicate that we were taking fire. We passed out over the south edge of the city, the buildings thinning out until they mingled with garden patches and ricefields. There was the Shell gasoline station, now a collapsed wreck. Then there was nothing but green fields and treelines and hedgerows with clusters of thatched-roof huts spread among them. Only a few miles from Hue, a farmer and his water buffalo plodded through a flooded field. Women trotted along in conical hats, carrying baskets dangling from either end of long poles laid across their shoulders. Some of them looked up briefly at the passing helicopter.

When I got back to Battalion Rear at Phu Bai, the cluster of strongback hooches was nearly deserted. Almost everyone was in Hue, or dead or evacuated. Even the cooks, bakers and clerks from the motor pool and Supply and Admin and other support units had been thrown into the fighting.

"Every Marine's a basic rifleman," said the administrative officer when I commented on the ghost-town appearance of the compound. He handed me my new orders: the Marine Corps Air Station at Cherry Point, North Carolina, near Camp Lejeune. I'd been stationed at Lejeune for a few months in the fall of 1966, just after boot camp. Nine hours from Perkasie, if you drove fast; well within weekend range. I thought of Jenny. I hadn't heard from her since the middle of November. Not even a Christmas card.

"When can I leave, sir?" I asked.

"In a day or two. You've got to get checked out — get a physical, get your pay records. It shouldn't take long. Oh, I've got some good news for you, Sergeant."

"Sergeant?"

"That's right. You made the cut." He pulled out the promotion warrant, read it out loud, handed it to me and shook my hand. "Congratulations," he said. "One other thing — this just came through, too."

He pulled out another certificate. "Sorry we can't give you a formal presentation ceremony, but under the circumstances..." He shrugged his shoulders, then began to read aloud:

"United States Marine Corps Certificate of Commendation. The Commanding General, First Marine Division, takes pleasure in commending Corporal William Daniel Ehrhart, United States Marine Corps, for outstanding performance of duty while serving as an intelligence assistant with the S-2, 1st Battalion, 1st Marines, 1st Marine Division (Reinforced), Fleet Marine Force, in operations against insurgent communist (Viet Cong) forces in the Republic of Vietnam for the period 15 February 1967 to 16 February 1968. Throughout this period, Corporal Ehrhart consistently demonstrated exceptional knowledge and untiring devotion to duty while assigned as Assistant Intelligence Chief of a combat-committed battalion in the Republic of Vietnam. His tireless efforts and positive attitude contributed materially to the efficient collection and dissemination of combat intelligence. By his outstanding professional skill and dedication to duty, Corporal Ehrhart reflected credit upon himself, the Military Intelligence Service, and the United States Marine Corps. Donn J. Robertson, Major General, United States Marine Corps."

The Lieutenant handed the certificate to me. "Congratulations again," he said. "This seems to be your big day."

"Yessir, I guess so."

"I'm sorry the certificate says 'corporal.' We didn't know you were getting promoted till after we put in the paperwork for this."

"That's okay, sir; it doesn't matter anyway."

"I understand you've got a Purple Heart coming, too. You'll have to pick that up in the States, but the entry's already in your SRB; you're authorized to wear the ribbon."

"Seems like a silly award, sir. All you gotta do is get shot. Kind of like the booby-prize."

"You earned it. Listen, we got your replacement here; a Lance Corporal Jacobs. Try to break him in a little before you go, will you? We're sending him up to Hue in a day or two."

"Just in from Stateside, sir?"

"Yeh."

"You're gonna send a green kid up there, sir? He won't last a day."

"I've got no choice. Lieutenant Casey wants him up there. He's down to five men — you know that — and the rifle companies don't have anybody they can spare. See if you can teach him something before you leave. Here's your check-out sheet. I don't have to tell you, the sooner you get this completed, the sooner you can leave."

"No, sir. Sir, is Corporal Haller around here anywhere? The guy from operations. He didn't go into the city with us."

"Left for R&R yesterday. Australia. He won't be back till next week."

The new guy was sitting on his cot when I walked into the hooch. "You Jacobs?" I asked.

"Yeh."

"Sergeant Ehrhart," I said. It sounded strange. We shook hands. "Kinda lonely around here, huh? Where you from?"

"Maine. Near Portland," said Jacobs. He looked at me with a tight drawn expression. "You just come down from Hue, haven't you?" I nodded. "It's pretty bad there, ain't it?"

"Yeh, it's pretty bad," I said, "but it ain't as bad as it was a couple of weeks ago. They're gettin' it under control. When you get up there, find a guy named Sergeant Seagrave. He's the chief scout. You stick with him, he'll keep you out of trouble. You'll be okay."

"I hear the North Vietnamese are pretty good, too."

"Damn good. I gotta hand it to 'em; they're tough as nails, and they got balls. They ain't your run-of-the-mill dumb gooks." I gestured out the screened window toward a Vietnamese mama-san walking by on the road, her arms filled with dirty jungle utilities.

"I don't like that word," said Jacobs tentatively.

"What word?"

"Gooks. It's ugly."

I snorted. I suddenly wanted to punch Jacobs. I wanted to reach out and put my hands around his throat. "Yeh, I guess it is," I said.

"We're supposed to be helping these people," he said.

I let it go. "That your girl?" I asked, pointing to the picture on the shelf above his cot.

"My fiancée," said Jacobs, his face brightening. "Name's Melissa."

"Pretty."

"She's the sweetest." He picked up the photograph, looked at it, and sighed. "Man, you're so lucky to be goin' home. You got a girl back there?"

I didn't feel like explaining. "No," I said.

"Well, I guess you'll be glad to see your folks again; see your friends and all. Long time, ain't it?"

270

"Yeh. Real long." I thought of Mom and Dad; the thought hurt. What would I ever be able to say to them? Jacobs looked at the photograph of Melissa. "Don't worry," I added. "It passes. You'll get there. Guy named Jimmy Saunders told me that when I first got over here. He was the guy I replaced. Now you're replacin' me."

"I don't mind bein' here, really," said Jacobs. "I coulda waited till I got drafted. I coulda gone to college, you know? But I got an obligation, and I aim to do it. You know how it is; I don't have to tell *you* about it. I don't understand them draft-dodgers and hippies and all. I don't know how they can live with themselves. I guess that's why they never shave — can't look at themselves in the mirror. Your country gets into it, you got a duty to support your country, period. You want freedom and all, you got to be willing to sacrifice for it. Them creeps don't know how lucky they are, bein' American — "

"You want my advice?" I broke in. "Do yourself a big favor. Keep your mouth shut for awhile, and keep your eyes open, okay?"

Chapter 44

The taxi maneuvered through a thick white unbroken cloud that reduced visibility to the red taillights of the automobiles immediately in front of us. I had imagined the sparkling waters of San Francisco Bay dancing in the early morning sunshine and playing off the skyline of the City by the Bay. I had even been prepared to break down with joy and relief at my first daylight glimpse of America in thirteen months. But now I could barely see the heavy steel suspension cables of the Oakland Bay Bridge as we drove across it. I sat in the back seat absently measuring the empty space between my lower ribs, feeling puzzled and vaguely cheated.

"You just back from Nam?" asked the taxi driver.

"Huh?"

"You just back from Vietnam?"

"Uh, yessir."

"I guess you're glad to be home, huh?"

"You can say that again."

"Pretty rough over there?"

"Bad enough. I sure won't miss it any."

"Where you from?"

"Little town near Philadelphia."

"Oh, yeh? Where?"

"Perkasie. 'Bout thirty-five miles north of Philly."

"No, never heard of it. Must be pretty small."

"It is."

"I grew up near Philly," the cabbie explained. "Right across the river in Marlton, New Jersey. Got discharged out here after the war — right there at Treasure Island where I picked you up — just never got around to goin' back East."

"Which war?" I asked.

"World War Two," the cabbie replied, emphasizing the 'two' as though I had failed to recognize the obvious. "The big one. Vietnam and Korea, they ain't really wars. You know that? Congress never declared war. They're police actions, they call 'em."

"No kidding? Coulda fooled me."

"I was in the Navy. Pacific. Earned a Purple Heart at Midway. Jap dive bomber hit our tin can. Yeh, we didn't do none of this one-year-and-come-home stuff like you guys got nowadays. You went in then, you stayed in till the war was over. They oughta do that with this Vietnam thing. Make you guys fight a little harder, wouldn't it?"

"Thirteen months," I corrected. "Marines do thirteen months. I didn't make the rules. I just did what I was asked to do."

"Sure, buddy, sure. Don't get me wrong. You done your duty, and I appreciate that. I just don't understand how come this thing ain't over yet, that's all. I mean, what the hell, just a bunch of slope-heads with chopsticks. It's the damn politicians' fault, ain't it. They don't let you guys get the job over with. Bunch of bleedin' hearts, I'll tell ya; I don't know what this country's comin' to." The cabbie tossed his remarks back over his shoulder casually without turning his head, his attention riveted to the freeway ahead of him where the red and white lights of cars and trucks flashed in and out of the fog.

"You get to the airport, you go find a bar and have a drink on me," he continued. "Welcome home. You've earned it, that's for sure. Least you done your duty. I don't know *where* we'd be without fellas like you."

I thought about fellows like me. I thought about the six-year-old boy with the grenade, about the old man with his hands tied behind his back and the neat little hole in the back of his head, about the woman in the 60-millimeter mortar pit in Hue. I thought about my parents. What would I ever be able to say to them? I pretended to doze off so I wouldn't have to talk, or listen. We rode the rest of the way to the airport in silence. When we arrived, I paid the cabbie. He didn't mention the drink I was supposed to have on him, and didn't kick back anything on the fare. I didn't give him a tip.

Once inside the terminal, I immediately purchased a one-way ticket to Philadelphia and checked my heavy seabag. "Would you like to check that, sir?" asked the TWA clerk, pointing tentatively to the captured rifle I carried slung over my shoulder by a worn leather strap.

"No, ma'am, I'll carry it on if you don't mind. I've got papers for it. It can't fire. I took the bolt out. It's in the seabag." I showed her the empty space where the bolt should have been.

She looked at the rifle, then took the papers I was holding and looked at them carefully. "Okay," she said hesitantly. "Your flight leaves at eleven forty-three; concourse D. The gate should be posted about an hour before take-off. Have a good flight."

Eleven forty-three a.m. It was now just eight forty-five. I had three hours to kill. I'd arrived at Travis Air Force base before dawn on a military charter flight from Vietnam by way of Okinawa. From there, the Marines and sailors aboard the flight had been bussed to Treasure Island Naval Base in the middle of San Francisco Bay to await discharge or, as in my case, processing of their leave papers and travel orders to their next assignment.

The bus ride had been a nightmare. I'd ridden in nothing but jeeps and trucks for more than a year, bumping along pitted dirt roads at twenty-five or thirty-five miles an hour tops, and when that bus had hit the freeway and cranked up to sixty or sixty-five, I'd thought for sure we were going to crash. It felt like we were doing a hundred and ten. I'd ridden the whole way expecting to die like a crushed sardine at any moment, and by the time we'd arrived at Treasure Island, my uniform was drenched with nervous perspiration.

After two more hours of waiting in a transient barracks, I was finally able to get my leave papers and travel orders when the administrative office opened at 0800: twenty-five days' leave, then report to the Marine Corps Air Station at Cherry Point. But I couldn't get my travel money yet because the disbursing office didn't open until 0900. I didn't want to wait another hour. I didn't want to wait another minute. After thirteen months of waiting, my patience was at an end. I'd checked my wallet, decided that I had enough money to get home on, and hopped into one of the taxis waiting at the front gate of the base. Now I had three hours to kill.

I bought a magazine at a newsstand and sat down in the middle of San Francisco airport. It was bustling with people. Men in business suits carrying briefcases. Women in skirts and matching jackets, many of the skirts short like the ones Dorrit had worn in Hong Kong. And now here was an airport full of them. I sat there drooling.

There were also a number of people, most of them more or less my age, dressed in faded blue jeans and denim workshirts and pieces of green utility uniforms with rank insignia on the sleeves. A young couple sat nearby on the floor against the wall, backpacks and rolled-up sleeping bags gathered about them like a fortress. Both had very long hair held out of their faces with brightly colored headbands, and strings of beads hung from their necks. The man was bearded, and held a guitar lightly across his knees. When the woman moved, her breasts swung pleasantly beneath the loose-fitting workshirt. Her nipples poked at the faded blue material. She was obviously wearing no bra. I'd read about free love.

So these were the hippies, I thought. I couldn't remember ever having seen one before I'd left for Vietnam. Like the whole antiwar movement, the hippies and flower people seemed to have materialized out of nowhere during my absence from The World. In high school, I'd been reprimanded by the principal for allowing my hair to grow down over my ears and the collar of my shirt. There had been no hippies in Perkasie. It had never occurred to Jenny *not* to wear a bra, nor had it occurred to her to allow me to remove it, and the hem of her skirt had always reached her knees. When I'd enlisted, my picture had appeared in the local newspapers: the recruiter and I standing by the front door of Pennridge High School shaking hands. Nearly every teacher in school had taken the trouble to congratulate me, or pump my hand and wish me luck.

I wondered if there were any hippies in Perkasie now. All through the long scorching dry season of Vietnam and into the monsoons, I'd read about the hippies and their protest movement in almost every issue of *Stars 'n' Stripes* and *Time*: "Hippies Drop LSD at Haight-Ashbury Be-In"; "Black Panthers Shoot It Out with Cops in Berkeley"; "23 Draft Cards Burned at Yale Rally." As the months had worn on, the antiwar movement—like the Vietcong—had only seemed to get stronger: "Vc Flags Festoon Times Square"; "100,000 March on Pentagon"; "Actress Visits Hanoi."

"What the hell do *these* fuckin' people know anyway?" I thought, addressing myself to the hippies in particular and to everyone else in general. "What right do they have?"

Immediately, the other side of the question popped into my head: What right did *I* have? What had I done in the past thirteen months to be proud of? My stomach suddenly felt as though it was being squeezed by an iron fist. Hunched down behind my magazine, I watched the people in the airport coming and going, half-expecting a band of placard-carrying flower people to surround me at any moment, drowning me in flowers and chants of "Baby Killer."

I looked at my watch: nine a.m. "You oughta call Mom and Dad," I thought. My stomach wrenched even harder. In the two days I'd been at Battalion Rear in Phu Bai, I'd put off writing to let them know I was coming home until it had been too late to write from there. I'd had three more days of processing on Okinawa, but I still hadn't written. Every time I'd thought about it, I'd gotten scared. I'd see myself standing over the old woman at the edge of the ricefield; I'd see the old man with his hands tied behind his back going down in a lifeless crumple; I'd put the pen in my hand, but my hand wouldn't move across the paper.

And now I was only a few hours from home, and they still didn't know. "You better go call 'em," I thought, but I didn't get up. I tried to light a cigarette, but I couldn't hold the match steady and finally gave up, angrily crushing the unlit cigarette into an ashtray. "This is ridiculous," I thought. "It's over. Forget it. What about that Coca-Cola? I wonder if anyone drinks Coke at nine in the morning."

I thought of the vision I'd carried for months: me and a pretty American girl sitting at a booth drinking Coke, smiling and smiling, a simple welcome home from the alien ricefields and sand barrens and jungles of Asia. I'd rehearsed the scene a thousand times through the endless days and nights alone: the Coke, the smiles, perhaps a brief touching of hands before we went our separate ways. I looked around furtively at the women passing by, trying to determine which one might be safe to approach. "You chicken," I kept telling myself as opportunity after opportunity walked by. "How long you been waiting for this? If the guys could see you now, they'd laugh their asses off." I tried to screw up my courage, but the threads kept slipping.

And then I saw her: the lovely young blonde in a short pale green skirt and ruffled white long-sleeved blouse. She was walking right toward me; there was something in her face, in the magic twinkle of her mouth, that suddenly made it possible. "Looks kinda like Dorrit," I thought. She was almost in front of me. Was she looking at my uniform? At the three red sergeant's stripes on my arm? "Asshole," I thought. "Now's your chance! Get up and ask her."

"Excuse me, miss," I blurted out, popping to my feet directly in her path, "this must sound really odd, but would you have time to let me buy you a coke. I know it's kind of early, but I've been away for a long time and—"

The woman went white. You could see the color drain right out of her face like somebody had pulled a plug in the bottom of her stomach. She looked as though she was about to scream.

276

"Wait, please, you don't understand. I don't mean any harm. Really. I've been in Vietnam, you know? I just got back from Vietnam. I'd just like to celebrate with someone a little, you know? I mean, just drink a coke and talk a little. Coca-Cola, you know; it's so *American*. Like it means I'm back, you know? I'm finally home."

The woman backed up a few steps, and began to swivel her head nervously from side to side as though she were looking for an exit sign.

"Honestly, listen, wait," I went on, talking as fast as I could. "I don't mean to — it's just, you know, something I've dreamed about for a long time. Like a little fantasy, you know? I just wanna buy you a Coke, that's all; just sit and talk for a little — "

"I'm glad you're back," the woman stammered, interrupting me. "Look, I've got — "

"Sure. Just a minute or two, that's all I'm asking, okay?" I pointed to a nearby snackbar, and reached out to take her arm.

"Don't!" she almost shouted, pulling away sharply.

"Jesus, lady, all I'm asking — "

"*Please!* I'm sorry! Leave me alone!"

Abruptly, I was standing there by myself, the blood pounding in my temples. I could feel beads of sweat popping out along the hairline of my forehead, and I found myself almost unconsciously blinking hard against a rising wave of salt. People seated nearby were staring at me. I tried to smile as I sat down again. I accidentally knocked the captured rifle leaning against the chair, and it clattered loudly as it struck the bare tile floor. I picked up the rifle, opened the magazine, took out my cigarettes, dropped the pack, knocked the rifle as I reached for the pack, dropped the magazine as I grabbed unsuccessfully for the rifle, took a deep breath, picked up all three items and sat there staring straight ahead, the whole ungainly pile stacked up on my lap.

"Goddamn bitch," I muttered.

"Goddamn bitch. Couldn't even wait a lousy goddamned year. I'm puttin' my life on the line, and she's out flyin' around in private airplanes and goin' to proms." The thought startled me; I realized that I had been sitting there for some time thinking not about the woman in the green skirt, but about Jenny.

"I don't know; musta been tough on her. She's only eighteen; all her friends doin' stuff and all, goin' on dates and stuff. Once she sees me again — it's *me*; I'm really home — if I can just talk to her, touch her..."

"You're settin' youself up, pal. How long's it been since you heard from her? She tried to get her roommate to be your pen pal, for chrissake!"

"But she loved me, damn it! That just doesn't go away!"

"Just shut up. Don't think about it. Don't think."

Nine forty-five. "Jesus Christ, two more hours. Lemme outta here. I wanna be home." I opened the magazine and stared at the page: an article about Senator Eugene McCarthy, the Democrat bucking his own party to run against President Johnson on a promise of ending the war. American boys were dying in Asia for no good reason, he was saying; the war must be stopped. I thought about Rowe and Calloway, about Roddenbery and Aymes and Stemkowski and Frenchy and all of the others. How many? All for nothing? Was it possible?

Out of the corner of my eye, I noticed a skinny bearded young man in blue jeans and an embroidered denim jacket. He wore a headband, and carried a brightly colored shoulderbag. I glanced up. He seemed to be headed straight for me. "Oh, no," I thought, "please don't. Go away; just leave me alone."

"Peace, brother," he said, smiling broadly. He had freckles all over his face. "How goes it?"

"Look, I don't want any trouble. I'm just waiting for a plane. You come lookin' for trouble, you're gonna get it."

"Hey, be easy, friend," he said, lifting both hands gently away from his sides, palms facing me. "I noticed that rifle there. I'm kind of a gun buff; just wondered what kind it was."

"Oh."

"What kind is it?"

"Oh. MAS-36. French. It's pretty old; not in very good condition. I don't know why I kept it."

"Maybe you could clean it up; get it plated or something. My granddaddy used to have a whole wall full of old guns — rifles and pistols, all kinds — had 'em all fixed up really nice. He owned a ranch in Montana. That's how I know about guns. Used to spend every summer there with him. Punchin' cattle. Playin' cowboy. Used to have the neatest times — like starring in my own TV western. Great place for a kid, Montana. Yippee-i-o-cay-a!" He sat down in the seat next to me and stuck out his hand. "My name's Rex. What's yours?"

"Bill," I said, shaking his hand tentatively.

"You're just back from Vietnam, I guess."

"Yeh. That's where I got the rifle. I guess you could tell that."

"I figured. Well, I'm glad you made it back okay. I guess you are, too! How long were you there?"

278

"Thirteen months."

"Long time, huh?"

"Seems like forever ... Rex. I used to dream about today like you dream about bein' a millionaire or winning a gold medal in the Olympics." I shook my head slowly from side to side.

"You get drafted?"

I let out a short snorting grunt through my nostrils. "No. No, I enlisted. Right outta high school. I volunteered. Seventeen."

"Wow, that's heavy, Bill."

A small wild laugh escaped from my throat before I even realized it was there. "It certainly is, Rex," I said. We both smiled as if we were sharing a secret, though I wasn't sure what it was.

"Why don't you get lost, freak."

We both looked up to see two middle-aged men in business suits standing right in front of us. They were both glaring at Rex, as though I wasn't even there. "Beat it, freak," said the man on the left, who looked like a retired professional football player. "What are you bothering good people for? You want your slime to rub off on him?"

"He's not bothering me," I said as Rex stood up.

"It's okay," said Rex, addressing himself to me. "I've got a plane to catch, anyway."

"Go catch it," said the linebacker in the three-piece suit.

"He wasn't bothering me," I said.

"Nice talkin' with ya, Bill," Rex called back as he walked away, his body half turned to face us as he went. "I'm really glad you made it. Look out for yourself now, okay? Never know what you're gonna run into."

"You, too," I called, trying to wave around the bulk of the linebacker. The linebacker took a menacing step in Rex's direction.

"Peace, friend, peace," Rex laughed, lifting both hands in a Vee sign. "You're gonna give yourself an ulcer." He turned and skip-walked away, disappearing into the crowd.

"He wasn't bothering me," I said again. "We were just talking."

"They oughta lock up every last one of those scum," said the linebacker. "Makes me sick to see 'em on the same planet with you boys." He turned, finally, and looked at me. "You got time for a drink, Sergeant?"

I didn't think I liked the linebacker or his partner very much, but as soon as he mentioned having a drink, it occurred to me that I really wanted one.

"Yessir," I said quietly, "I've got time."

"No need to call me 'sir,'" said the linebacker as the three of us walked toward the nearest bar. "I'm just an old enlisted man, same as you. Corporal. Marines. Served in the Pacific. You know what they say: 'Once a Marine, always a Marine.'"

I'd heard the expression often enough; I wondered vaguely if it was true. "Maybe the cabbie sent 'em," I thought as we sat down. Both men ordered scotch on the rocks. I didn't like scotch. I liked sweet drinks like singapore slings and sloe gin fizzes and blackberry brandy. I'd only drank scotch because that was all Gunny Krebs had ever carried in his canteen. "Scotch on the rocks," I told the waitress.

"I'm sorry," she said, "but I have to ask. Are you twenty-one?"

"Of course, he's twenty-one," said the linebacker. "Can't you see those stripes all up and down his arm."

"May I see your ID, please?"

"He's old enough to drink, sweetie," said the linebacker, pulling a five-dollar bill out of his wallet and crushing it into her hand. "Just get the drinks; that's a good girl. How old are you, anyway?" he asked when the waitress was out of earshot.

"Nineteen — and a half."

"Goddamned crime; you're old enough to fight, then they try to tell ya you're not old enough to drink," the linebacker snorted. "Nineteen, and you're a buck sergeant — quite a rack of ribbons you got there, too." He pointed to the double row of decorations on my left breast. "You must be one hell of a good Marine." A surge of pride fought its way to the surface and emerged as a smile on my face. It made me uncomfortable. I looked down at the table. "My name's Barton," he said. "This is Davis. You just back from Nam, aren't you?"

"Yessir — uh, yeh. Just got Stateside this morning."

"Well, here's to you," said Barton, lifting his drink. "Take that weapon over there?"

"Yes."

"That musta been worth at least a stripe. You get the bastard that was carryin' it?"

"It was dark. I'm not sure who got him, me or Calloway." I was about to explain, then decided not to. I shrugged my shoulders.

"I know what you mean," said Davis, speaking for the first time. "Back on Iwo Jima — I was in the Marines, too — sometimes things got so wild you couldn't even keep score. Japs used to attack in human waves; suicide charges. Screamin' at the top of their lungs. All you had to do was lay there and mow 'em down. They just didn't care about dyin'. Die for the emperor and bow out smiling. The

280

Vietnamese are like that too, aren't they? Just don't value life, Orientals. One less face they gotta feed."

I tried to remember. It was true. I'd thought it was true, hadn't I? Kharma, nirvana, reincarnation, Banzai charges, Pork Chop Hill. Asians weren't like us. Even after I'd gotten to Vietnam: old women with black teeth and mouths full of betel nut; children with open running sores and flies all over their bodies; men with loose pajama legs pulled up, urinating in full view of the world; the strange clucking tongues; the empty faces.

Then one day on a patrol near Hoi An, we'd come upon a funeral procession: two men carrying a small ornately carved casket, obviously that of a young child; a file of monks with shaved heads and flowing saffron robes, playing reed flutes and tiny cymbals; a dozen peasants behind them, some of them crying, two women wailing as though their insides had been torn out. I'd watched them pass, and later that night, back at the battalion compound, I'd almost thrown up at the memory of it. Their grief had seemed so real.

Now the memory of it made me feel sick all over again. "I don't know," I said. "I really don't know." I wanted to be on the airplane. I wanted to be back home in Perkasie, in my own room, in my own bed. I tried to remember. I looked at my watch: ten twenty.

"They brainwash 'em," said Davis. "The Reds always brainwash their troops. Hop 'em up on dope and get 'em crazy for blood. I hear the vc go into a village and kill off everybody—everyone but the fighting-age men. Take the men and make 'em join the guerrillas. Isn't that right?"

"I never saw anything like that," I said. "I used to read about things like that before I enlisted, but I never saw anything like it while I was there."

"Well, it happens, believe me," said Davis, taking a gulp of his scotch and putting the glass back with a thump. "Happens all the time."

"You Americans are worse than the vc!" Sergeant Trinh had said the morning he'd told the battalion commander that he was through fighting for us. "Take your ignorance and go home!"

"What the hell do you know about it?!" I burst out, half rising to my feet. "You don't have the foggiest notion what's going on over there. None of you do! We're the ones who waste villages! They don't have to twist any arms to get recruits—we do their goddamned recruiting for them!"

The two men stared at me in disbelief. People at tables nearby turned to see what the disturbance was.

"Hey, Sarge, don't get riled," said Barton. "We're on *your* side, remember? There's no call to get mad. Come on; sit down and have another drink. Hey, we appreciate what you been through."

"The hell you say," I spat. "I got a plane to catch." I picked up my handbag and turned to go.

"Hey, your rifle," said Davis. I didn't stop. As I walked away, I could hear the two men talking.

"What'sa matter with him? Wha'd I say?"

"Christ, that kid's got a problem."

I looked at my watch: ten twenty-five. My head was spinning. I ducked into the nearest men's room, barely making it to the first urinal before I threw up. My stomach was empty: dry heaves. The retching tore at my guts like hot jagged steel.

"Are you all right, son?" There was a light touch on my shoulder. I spun around sharply. A stooped-over black man with curly gray hair took a quick step backwards, surprised by my sudden movement. He was dressed in coveralls and carried a pushbroom.

"I'm sorry," I said.

"Didn't mean to startle you. Are you all right?"

"Yeh. Yeh. I guess I ate somethin' bad or something."

"You want me to get a doctor?"

"No. I'm all right now. I'm just..." I flushed the urinal.

"You get yourself cleaned up; wash your mouth out. I'll go get you something to settle your stomach. You wait right here now; I'll be right back."

Chapter 45

In front of the Arrivals section of the Philadelphia airport it was crowded with cars and taxis and limousines, but I recognized Larry Carroll's beat-up DeSoto right away. I started waving. He spotted me and stopped, and I jumped in, tossing my seabag and handbag into the back seat. We shook hands.

"This old clunker's still running, huh?" I said.

"Like a champ." Larry eased out into the evening traffic.

"What took you so long to get here? Feels like I been waitin' in airports half my life."

"Well, you didn't give me much warning. 'Hey, I'm in Philadelphia; come pick me up.' "

"Yeh, well, sorry about that."

"How come your folks didn't pick you up?"

"They don't know I'm home yet. I was gonna call—I don't know. Thought it would be fun to surprise 'em. Geez, it's good to see you. Thanks for comin' down."

"What are friends for? Good to see you, too, Bill. I thought you might be gettin' home about now. You timed it just right."

"How long you home for?"

"A week. Term break."

"Anybody else around?"

"Jeff's around, but he's down in DC on the senior class trip till Friday. Eric Rogers is home. That's about it. Most of 'em don't get off till around Easter."

"Rogers," I said. "I wrote to him three times last spring — never wrote back once. Some friend."

"Yeh, well, I got a letter from Sadie Thompson back in January" said Larry. My stomach tightened at the sound of her name. "She wanted to know if I'd heard from you, if you were all right, when you were getting home, whole list of questions. Said she hadn't heard from *you* since last April or May. How come you haven't written to her?"

"I don't know, Larry. You know Sadie. Hell, you know what she said to me before I left? 'Try not to kill anyone.'"

"That's Sadie," Larry laughed.

"It ain't funny. That's been banging around in my head for thirteen fuckin' months. What am I supposed to say to her? What was I supposed to write? I'm havin' a picnic?"

"Pretty bad over there, huh?"

"Crazy, man. Jesus. Tell you all about it sometime. I'm *out* of it, that's all that counts. Somebody else's fuckin' problem now."

We rode a long way in silence, passing out of the city into the northern suburbs, and then into the rural country of central and upper Bucks County.

"Pretty shaggy hair you got there," I said finally. "Where's your beads?"

"Just keepin' up with the times," said Larry.

"Somebody oughta tell the commandant of the Corps," I said, running my hand over my bristly short hair. "He ain't heard yet. How do you like Penn State?"

"It's okay. Too much to do, though; I never seem to get around to the books. Damn good parties!"

"Everybody's in college but me," I said.

"Well, you gotta come up sometime — maybe some weekend. Where you gonna be?"

"North Carolina. Gotta report the end of the month."

We crested the long hill on Route 309 just south of Souderton, and Larry turned onto Fairhill Road. Familiar turf. Down in the wide shallow valley off to our left, I could see the lights of the small communities among which I'd grown up: Sellersville, Souderton, Telford, Silverdale, Blooming Glen, Dublin, Perkasie. Between the towns lay the dark patches of woods and the dark farm fields. The car glided along the dark two-lane roads, weaving a path down into the valley toward Perkasie.

"Never thought I'd be so happy to see Perkasie," I said.

"It's still Hicksville," Larry replied with a laugh.

"That's okay by me. I think I'm gonna enjoy a little Hicksville for a change. Hard to believe I couldn't wait to get out of here. God, that wasn't even two years ago."

Larry laughed again. "Hard to believe you're so glad to be back in the old dump."

"You don't know, Larry. Man, you don't know."

"I guess not," said Larry. "Don't think I wanna find—" He stopped abruptly in mid-sentence.

"What?"

"Nothin'."

The car slid up Chestnut Street over the bridge crossing Lenape Creek. We'd all grown up in that creek, storming through the lilly pads in our bare feet searching for turtles and snakes and catching golden carp with our bare hands, camping out, ice skating in the winter, a blazing bonfire making our wet skates steam. Just over the bridge, on the right, two three-story apartment buildings and a parking lot filled what had once been a swampy meadow.

"When'd they build those?" I asked.

"Last summer."

"Suburbia comes to Perkasie."

"Ugly, ain't they?"

The car approached the intersection of Chestnut and Third streets. I pointed up Third Street hill. " 'Member the time we trashed Old Man Bowen's garage?" I said. We grinned at each other, then laughed, each of us remembering back ten years.

"*You* got away—and then you came back! Sucker," said Larry.

"Least I didn't get caught red-handed—like you, sucker."

Larry turned the opposite way on Third Street. We passed the Third Street Elementary School. "Ah, the good old days," I said, nodding toward the school.

"Oh, yeh, swell. I always *loved* the nuclear bomb drills," said Larry. The fire bells clanging mercilessly, all of us scurrying out of the classrooms and into the halls where we'd sit facing the walls with our heads tucked between our knees and our hands over our heads, waiting for the Russian Sputnik to come through the roof, newsreels of the mushroom cloud over Hiroshima rising vividly behind my eyes. "I could never get it into my head that they were just drills," Larry went on. "Everytime we had one, I couldn't sleep for a month. Nightmare city. Hell of a trip to lay on a ten-year-old."

I thought of the small boy in the marketplace in Hoi An, and the trip I'd laid on him. My stomach rose, then sank sharply. "He had a

285

grenade, for chrissake," I thought. "What the hell else were you supposed to do?"

The car turned left onto Market Street. I could see a traffic light up at Fifth & Market.

"A traffic light?!" I said. "Apartment buildings. Traffic lights. Whaddaya mean, Hicksville? We're gettin' *civilized*. I go away for a year, and they turn the place into Levittown."

"We got two cop cars now," Larry boasted mockingly. "Two, folks. Count 'em."

We passed only two or three other cars on the way through town. The whole town lay on the edge of sleep, though it was only nine thirty.

"So where's the mayor?" I said. "Where's the majorettes? Where's my white Cadillac convertible? I thought you were gonna take care of everything, Larry. I feel like an ex-con sneakin' back into town in the dead of night."

"It's after six o'clock, buddy," Larry deadpanned. "Come back Memorial Day. You can be in the parade."

He turned the car onto Sixth Street. There was my father's church on the corner of the next block. We pulled up in front of the big stone house beside the church and stopped. Lights burned in the downstairs.

"Home, sweet home," said Larry.

"Yeh," I said. I blinked back tears, embarrassed. "Thanks, Larry. You be home tomorrow?"

"Yeh. Gimme a call."

"So, here I am," I said.

My mother, father, younger brother and I were sitting in the living room. It had taken quite a while to settle them down. My sudden appearance at the door had given them a start. Mom had screamed, almost fainting. I'd hugged my Dad for the first time since I'd been a little boy. Tom, now almost thirteen, had grown several inches.

"Why didn't you tell us you were coming?" Mom asked. "You said you wouldn't be home till the middle of the month."

"Well," I said, staring down at my shoes and fidgeting with my hands, "I figured the last few weeks would be the hardest on you, so I decided to let you think the last few weeks weren't here yet."

"What are the ribbons for?" Tom asked, touching my chest, his eyes wide.

"Nothin'. This one's the Sioux City, Iowa, Occupation Award,"

286

I said, pointing to the National Defense Medal. "This here's the Visit Vietnam Award. This one's the Thank-You-For-Visiting-Vietnam Award. This is the Booby Prize."

"That's the Purple Heart, isn't it?" Tom asked excitedly.

"That's what I said — the Booby Prize. All you gotta do is be in the wrong place at the wrong time." I couldn't help feeling the glow of my brother's admiration. It was confusing. "It's no big deal, Tom. I'm not a hero." I didn't want to say that.

"You were wounded?" Mom gasped.

"Just a little. In Hue City, last month. I got caught tryin' to paint the town red."

"Bill! Why didn't you tell us? Your letters said you were — "

"What was the point? You'd just worry. I imagine you did enough of that as it was." I reached into my sock and pulled out a pack of cigarettes. "Mind if I smoke?" I asked. I'd never been allowed to smoke in the house when I was in high school.

"Well, all right," said Mom, "but you know I don't approve."

"I know, Mom," I said, lighting one. "Mom, that letter you sent me..." I started laughing. "The one about getting lung cancer in twenty years. You'd have had a heart attack if you could have seen where I was when I got it. Twenty years?!"

Mom turned red, caught between laughter and tears. I looked around the living room. A portrait photograph of me in a dress blue uniform sat on the television set. A map of Vietnam hung on the wall. "Have you heard from Jenny lately?" I asked.

"We got a very nice Christmas card from her," said Dad.

"That's more than I got," I said. An awkward pause followed.

"People grow up, Bill," said Mom. "That's a long time to be apart at that age."

"Wasn't no longer for her than it was for me."

"It wasn't *any* longer," said Mom. "Just be thankful that you're home safe. Things'll get straightened out for the best. Give yourself some time. You just got home."

"I am, Mom. It's good to be here. Man, I never knew thirteen months could be so long."

"Well, it's good to have you home, son," said Dad. "We're very proud of you."

I winced involuntarily, immediately hoping he hadn't noticed. I wondered if I would ever be able to tell them what had happened in Vietnam. I wasn't sure myself what had happened. Now wasn't the time to try to explain, I decided. I let it go.

287

"Can I borrow the car for a little while?" I asked. "I'm gonna buy one tomorrow, but I'd sort of like to go somewhere tonight."

"Where?" asked Mom. "You just got home. It's ten thirty."

"Well, I just thought I'd drive over to Trenton."

"Tonight? To see Jenny?"

"If I can just talk to her, Mom," I said, lifting my shoulders in an unfinished shrug. "You know? Once she realizes that I'm home..."

"It'll take you an hour to get there," said Dad. "It'll be midnight. You won't even be able to get in the dorm."

"They'll let me in. I'll explain. I'll wear my uniform."

"Why don't you just get a good night's sleep," said Mom. "You've had a long day."

"Mom, I've waited a long time already. Maybe too long."

"At least call first," said Dad. "She'll be asleep by the time you get there."

I went to the telephone in the dining room, then decided to go upstairs instead. I got the main number for the nursing school from the operator, and finally managed to get through to the right dormitory.

"Just a minute," said a sleepy voice, "I'll see if she's up." I hadn't heard Jenny's voice since I'd called her from Pendleton the day before I'd left the States. I tried to remember what it would sound like. The receiver scraped against my ear. I tried to think of a good first line.

"Hello?"

"Jenny?"

"Yes."

"It's me. Bill."

"Oh. Uh, hello. I was asleep."

"Jenny, I'm home. I'm in Perkasie."

"That's wonderful, Bill." There was a pause. "It's good to hear your voice again."

"Yours, too, Jen. Gosh, it sounds good. Just like I remembered."

"How are you?"

"Okay. Fine. I, uh, I got wounded last month ... but it wasn't too bad." Another pause. "Listen, can I come over to see you?"

"When?"

"Tonight."

"Tonight?"

"Sure. I can be there in forty-five minutes."

"Bill. Uh. It's awfully late. The dorm's locked. They don't allow visitors after ten."

"Oh. Well, look, how about tomorrow? I can drive over first thing in the morning."

"Bill, I've got class all day—"

"Well, tomorrow night then. I'll take you out to dinner; someplace fancy—"

"Bill, I'm sorry, I've got a big test Thursday. I've just got to study for it. I just can't—"

"Well, when then?!" Another pause. "Are you ever gonna see me, for chrissake?"

"Don't swear at me, Bill—"

"I'm not swearing! Don't you even want to *see* me?" There was another long pause. "Jenny?"

"Bill, I just don't think it's a good idea to see each other right now."

"You won't even let me *talk* to you?! Jenny, it's me, Bill! You were gonna *marry* me. Doesn't that count for anything?"

"I'm sorry. I don't want to hurt you. I tried to explain when I wrote. I *tried* to explain. It's not you. I'm just—"

"You can't even *see* me? You can't even *talk* to me?!"

"Bill, please try to understand; it isn't easy—"

"Oh, I understand, all right—"

"—I just don't think it would be—"

"—I understand! You sucker me in; then when things get tough, you dust me off just like that! I'm over there gettin' my ass shot at every goddamned day, and you're back here spreadin' your legs for every rich draft-dodger that comes down the pike! You goddamned whore! You think you can just—" The phone went dead. "Jenny?! Jenny, I'm sorry; I didn't mean to—" I lifted the receiver away from my ear and held it at arm's length. "You don't understand," I said softly. "Jesus fucking *Christ*!!" I slammed the receiver down so hard that the cradle cracked.

I didn't go back downstairs again. I couldn't. I went into my room. On top of the dresser, and on the night stand, and hanging from the ceiling on strings, were the dozens of plastic model airplanes I'd made while I was growing up: P-38 Lightnings; P-51 Mustangs; Spads; Sopwith Camels; B-17 Flying Fortresses; F4U Corsairs with their graceful gull-like wings—each plane carefully hand-painted and carrying the proper military markings. I knew all about each one: its armament, powerplant, top speed and rate of climb and range; which ones could turn tightly in a dogfight; which could take a beating and keep flying. I even knew about the men who'd flown them: Pappy

Boyington, Richard I. Bong, Frank Luke, Billy Bishop, Eddie Rickenbacker. Aces. Knights. Heroes.

I took off my uniform and hung it up carefully on the back of the door. I turned out the light, and stretched out face up on the bed, my hands behind my head. Every fifteen minutes, the clock downstairs in the living room chimed. Every fifteen minutes. Far into the night.

Chapter 46

"Are you sure you want to buy a car?" my mother asked the next morning at the breakfast table.

"I've got enough money, Mom," I said. "Over two thousand dollars."

"But it'll take all your savings. What about college?"

"I've got another fifteen months before I can even think about college. I'll save what I make from now on — I'm gettin' sergeant's pay now, you know — and I'll have GI Bill money, too. Who says I'm goin' to college, anyway?"

"Bill!"

"Well, heck, all they do is protest and demonstrate anymore. Some education. Look, I'll worry about college when I get to it. I got nothin' else outta Vietnam; least I oughta be able to spend the money on somethin' worth havin'."

"Something worth *having*," Mom corrected. "Honestly."

"I'll have to go along with you," said Dad, who had entered the kitchen in the middle of the conversation. "I don't think you can buy a car in Pennsylvania until you're twenty-one."

"What?"

"I think that's right," said Dad. "I'll call Justice Hunsicker and check, but I think the title will have to be in my name."

"Oh, that's really swell. I can fight their war for 'em, but I can't buy a car with the money I earned fighting it. Geez, I can't vote. I can't drink."

"Well, you shouldn't be drinking, anyway," said Mom.

By the middle of the afternoon, I was the proud owner of a 1968 red Volkswagen bug with black interior—or at least, I was the owner in all but name. No more asking Mom and Dad for the keys: "Be back by four, I have to go shopping." Just gas it up and go, any place I wanted, whenever I felt like it. My own car. For the first time in ages, I felt like a million bucks.

All I needed was the insurance. So I walked the two blocks from my house to McGilvery's Insurance office.

"Well, hello, Bill!" said Mrs. McGilvery when I walked in. "It certainly is good to see you again. What can I do for you?"

"Is Mr. McGilvery in?" I asked.

"He's out right now. Is there something I can help you with?"

"Well, I just bought a new car, and I'd like to get insurance for it."

"I think I can take care of that for you. Let me just get your parents' policy."

"No, I want my own insurance policy. It's my car."

"But you're not twenty-one, are you?"

"No, but—"

"Then the car's in your dad's name, isn't it?"

"Well, yes, but—"

"Well then the car will have to be added to your parents' policy. There's nothing to it. All we do is enter it as a third family car."

"I really don't think I need to be dependent on my parents anymore, do you?"

"Well, that's the law in this state—"

"I don't care about the law. I just want my own policy."

"I'm sorry, Bill, but we have to—"

"Do you know where I just been, Mrs. McGilvery?"

"I understand—"

"No, you don't understand! Nobody made my parents come along and hold my hand in Vietnam!"

"Please, don't get upset. There's nothing I can do about it. You're underage."

"Underage?!" I snapped. "I wasn't underage when you asked me to fight your lousy war for you so you could sit around here getting rich off suckers like me! I'm a goddamned Marine sergeant, Mrs. McGilvery! I'm a combat veteran!"

"What do you think you're doing, talking to me like that?" Mrs. McGilvery said sharply. "What's gotten into—"

"I'll tell you what I think I'm doing," I said, banging my fist down on the counter between us, my voice rising. "I didn't go through all that crap just to get this kind of crap! I can't buy a car! I can't buy a beer —"

"Bill Ehrhart, you just settle —"

"— I can't go to the bathroom without my mommy! Settle down, my ass! What *is* this?! I got a right to that insurance policy! I earned it!"

Mrs. McGilvery suddenly burst into tears. "You have no *right* to come in here and behave like this!" she cried. "Your parents raised you better —"

"I got a right to somethin' better than *this*! I got a *right*! You gimme that insurance —"

"Get out of here *this minute*," Mrs. McGilvery wailed. "You just get out of here this minute, or I'll call the *police*!"

"Call the police?! Call the fuckin' police! Call the goddamned National Guard, for chrissake! I don't give a big rat's —"

"*Get out of here!*" Mrs. McGilvery shouted. She was crying hysterically. "*Get out of here! You get out!*" She fumbled for the telephone, and started dialing.

"*All right!* I'm goin'! But I won't forget this." I slammed the door hard behind me.

Chapter 47

"Probably blow this sucker right straight out my ass," I said, hefting the fat cheeseburger and shaking it at Larry like a meaty fist. I took a huge bite of it, talking and wiping my chin as I chewed. "Ummm. Ummph! Wunnerful!" I swallowed hard. "I got a system full of fortified canned food — even the cans are green — my stomach ain't used to this stuff anymore." I took another bite, stuffed in a couple of French fries, and washed it all down with a gulp of Coke. "Last time I ate cheeseburgers — back at China Beach in August — I was up half the night, sittin' on the can." I thought about Gerry; I hadn't heard from him since he'd been evacuated out.

At three a.m., the R&S Diner was almost deserted and very quiet. Earlier in the evening, Larry and I had gotten some beer from his older brother, and had spent the whole night cruising every square inch of upper Bucks County. Larry had let me drive his car since I couldn't drive mine; it felt incredible to sit behind the wheel, just hit the key and go. "Let's go here; let's go there" — and off we'd roar without having to ask permission or wait for orders. We'd finally ended up at the R&S.

"I still can't believe that bullshit with my car today," I said.

"Yeh, well, it wasn't Mrs. McGilvery's fault," said Larry. He let out a short laugh. "Man, you musta freaked her right out of her drawers."

"Aw, fuck 'er. Jesus, were my parents ever pissed at me. Mr. McGilvery called up Dad, really gave him an earful. Cancelled their policy and everything. Now they gotta find another insurance company. You know what that asshole said? Said they wouldn't insure anybody with a *maniac* in the family! The World! Welcome back to The World. I oughta go burn that fucker's place to the ground."

"So, what's the story on Jenny?" Larry asked. "You two still, uh..."

My stomach tightened. "She won't even see me," I spat. "Aw, what the hell; who needs the aggravation, anyway? Just a goddamned kid. I got no use for fair weather friends." We both ate in silence for awhile.

"You know about Kenny, don't ya?" asked Larry.

"Yeh. Mom wrote me when it happened. It was weird, man. He'd just written to my parents to get my address, you know? Mom said they got his letter, sent him my address and a box of candy. About a week after I got Mom's letter, I get a letter from Kenny." I shuddered involuntarily, my stomach fluttering. "Readin' his letter — knowin' he's already dead."

"You two anywhere near each other?"

"No. I was way up north; he was out in the central highlands somewhere. Jesus, what a waste. Mrs. Wommack called my Mom a couple of weeks ago, asked her to make sure I stopped by to see her when I got back. I oughta do it — she was always real nice to me; you know how she used to be; just like Kenny — but Jesus, I don't think I can deal with it. You know she's gonna be lookin' at me, askin' why, even if she doesn't say it. 'How come my son instead of you?' What am I supposed to tell 'er? He died for his country? I don't think I can deal with it. Maybe after awhile."

"Hey, this is supposed to be a party!" said Larry. "Let's lighten up here. Where to now? Walt Whitman, which way does your beard point tonight?"

"Home. To bed. I've hardly slept in two and a half days. I'm runnin' on fumes."

"Nonsense, my man. The night is young. Let's go see Jeff Alison."

"He's in Washington, for chrissake," I groaned. Though Jeff was our age, he was two years behind us in school, and the Pennridge High School seniors were on their annual trip to the capital.

"So what?" said Larry. "Whaddaya think that machine's for?" He flipped his thump toward the beat-up DeSoto outside. "We can make it just in time for breakfast."

"I'm *tired*, Larry."

"Here, eat these," he said, handing me two white tablets. He popped two into his own mouth. "Make you feel like a new man."

"Speed?"

"Not so loud, buddy. Go on, eat 'em."

I'd never taken speed before. Aside from the little marijuana I'd smoked at Con Thien, I'd never taken illegal drugs of any kind. That was for hippies and freaks — the one's I'd read about in *Stars 'n' Stripes* and *Time*. I shrugged my shoulders, popped the pills into my mouth, and swallowed. "Let's cruise, Dr. Watson," I said. "I didn't get to see much on our trip, anyway. Maybe I'll do better this time."

We both laughed, remembering our own senior class trip two years earlier. I hadn't lasted through the first day. I'd been caught smoking a cigarette in the men's room of Scholl's Cafeteria — a violation of school and trip rules — and when I'd been told that I could remain on the trip only if I apologized to the entire class for breaking the rules and henceforth never left the tour bus without a chaperone, I'd taken the Greyhound instead.

Not that I'd been a troublemaker or a bad student. I had a rowdy streak in me, to be sure. I'd partied heavily on weekends, and in the close atmosphere of Perkasie, my reputation had quickly exceeded even the facts. But I had also been an honor student for four straight years; I'd been elected to the National Honor Society, and was vice president of student council my senior year. I'd lettered in track and soccer, won the Pearl S. Buck Literary Achievement Award, and had been one of three student commencement speakers.

But rules were rules, and I'd been sent home from Washington before the first day was over.

Year after year, the school rented rooms at the Chevy Chase Motor Lodge. Larry and I cruised into the parking lot a little after seven a.m. "Here," said Larry, reaching into the glovebox and pulling out an assortment of ties. "Put one of these on. Don't wanna look like ruffians." We went into the restaurant; it was packed with Pennridge students. I knew many of them — they'd been sophomores when we were seniors — and when they saw us, a grand palaver of hugs and handshakes erupted. For the first time since I'd gotten home, I felt like somebody special. We found Jeff and sat down at the counter to eat.

In one corner of the restaurant sat the chaperones, all of them former teachers of mine. They just sat there. They were staring at us. I waved cheerily. None of them blinked.

"What's their problem?" I said, nudging Larry.

"Maybe they think you're supposed to be dead," he replied.

"You think they could say hello or something."

"Constipation. Let's eat."

About the time we were finishing, Mr. Ettison, one of the school guidance counsellors, approached us.

"Hi, Mr. Ettison!" I said. He'd been my soccer coach.

"Hello, Bill," he replied gravely. "What are you doing here?"

"Eating breakfast. We were in the neighborhood...," I joked. Mr. Ettison didn't smile. "No, you know, I just got back from Vietnam. I haven't seen Jeffrey here in more than a year. We just thought we'd come down and say hello."

"You boys had better leave," he said. "We don't want any trouble."

"We're not going to give you any trouble, Mr. Ettison; we just—"

"Good. I'd appreciate that. Why don't you just finish up here and go?"

"Hey, whatsa matter with you, Mr. Ettison? What did we do? We haven't done anything wrong."

"We've got three hundred students here, and we don't want any trouble—"

"I can't eat breakfast in a public restaurant?"

"—I've already told the management if they rent you fellows a room, we'll cancel our contract with them—"

"We're not stayin'! We just—"

"—if I see you anywhere in the motel, I'll call the police."

"Call the police?!" I said loudly. "Why the hell's everybody tryin' to call the cops down on me all of a sudden? What, I go to Vietnam, do my duty, suddenly I'm a criminal or something?! What's your problem, man? Wha'd I ever do to you?"

Mr. Ettison's bald head glistened with perspiration. "I won't argue about this," he said.

"Hey, you ain't my teacher anymore!" I shouted. "You ain't shit! I don't have to take this kind of crap from you!" I started to cock my fist, but Larry grabbed me by the crook of the elbow.

"Come on," he said, "it ain't worth it." He turned to Mr. Ettison: "The man goes off, fights your dirty little war for you, you can't even be nice to him. You oughta be ashamed of yourself." Then he turned to the waitress behind the counter. "He's payin'," he said, flipping his middle finger at Mr. Ettison.

When I woke up, we were just south of Wilmington, Delaware. "I musta dozed off," I said. "How ya doin'?"

"I'm still wide awake," Larry said. "I took some more speed around Baltimore."

"You're gonna kill yourself on that stuff."

"You should talk," he laughed, "after what you've just been through."

"Yeh, I guess so," I said. We rode along in silence for awhile.

"Was it worth it?" Larry finally asked.

"What?"

"Joinin' the Marines. Goin' over there."

"Well," I said, "I guess so. Just somethin' I hadda do, I guess."

"The hell it was. Don't gimme that civics class stuff. You coulda gotten deferred; you were accepted at college."

"What the fuck you gettin' on my case for?" I said sharply.

"Hey, Bill, we go back a long way, remember? I'm not gettin' on your case; I just need some straight answers. I keep thinkin' about Kenny — gone, you know, just like that. And for what?"

"I'm sorry, Lar; guess I'm a little wired up these days. I don't know. Everything's all — I been thinkin' about a lot of guys like Kenny. Been thinkin' about 'em for a long time. How do you go through all that, and then tell yourself it wasn't worth it?"

"Well, was it? Either it was or it wasn't."

"It just ain't that simple."

"Only as complicated as you make it, buddy."

"You don't understand, Larry — "

"Well, I'm tryin' to. That's why I'm askin'."

"Why the hell's it so important? I don't feel like talkin' about it right now."

"Because I'm thinkin' about goin' to Canada, that's why it's so important." Larry's words hit me like a brick in the stomach. The draft-dodgers went to Canada. The cowards and traitors. Larry was my friend; we'd known each other since we were eight years old. "Bill, you still there?" asked Larry.

"Yeh. Yeh. Wow. That's heavy, man."

"Ain't it, though?"

"What the fuck you wanna go to Canada for?"

"Cuz I don't think there's anything goin' on in Vietnam that's worth dyin' for."

"You got your deferment. What's the problem?"

"I ain't gonna have it for long. I'm about to be flunked out."

"What the hell, man; you ain't stupid. You got no business flunkin' outta school."

298

"It ain't that simple —"

"Well, it seems to me I've heard that somewhere before."

" — there's so much goin' down, Bill. I just can't seem to put my nose to the books. There's something big happening; the whole country's gone crazy —"

"You're tellin' me?! Thirteen fuckin' months, all I did was dream about gettin' back to The World. So I finally get here, and everything's bass-ackwards every which way to Tuesday. It's *worse* than Nam — I can't even put up a short-time calendar."

"A what?"

"A short-time — never mind; you hadda be there."

"That's just the point. Once I flunk out — and I don't think I'm gonna make it past this term — I'm gonna be 1-A. And I'm fit as a fiddle. They're gonna draft me so fast it'll make your head spin."

"Why don't you apply for a CO?"

"Are you kidding? With *our* draft board?" I wouldn't stand a snowball's chance in hell. Besides, I'm not a conscientious objector. I'll fight for my country; it's just that bullshit in Vietnam I object to."

"Christ, Larry, I don't know. What am I supposed to say?" We both sat there for awhile, riding along to the sound of the engine. "Why don't you get your radio fixed?" I asked.

"Can't afford it," said Larry. We lapsed into silence again.

"I used to have this buddy over there," I said, "guy named Randy Haller. He got busted for burnin' his draft card, and the judge gave him a choice: jail or the Marines. One night, he told me if he had it to do again, he'd have gone to jail. Sometimes I think he meant it." I sighed deeply. "I don't know, Larry. It just hurts like hell most of the time."

"That's what I thought," said Larry, putting his right arm across the back of the seat and patting my neck. We were north of Wilmington now, almost to the Pennsylvania line near Kennett Square.

"Pretty big step," I said, "goin' to Canada."

"I know. Don't think I ain't thought about it long and hard. But I ain't goin' to Vietnam. And I've never heard nothin' good about prison. And that don't leave much else."

"When you figure on goin'?"

"End of May, when the term ends. I wanna leave before they come lookin' for me; make it easier to get across the border," said Larry. He paused for a few moments. "You wanna come along?"

I didn't say anything for awhile. "I almost deserted in Hong

Kong, while I was on R&R. I met this girl there—Danish girl. I was all set to pack it in. I think I was really gonna do it. Maybe she'd still be alive if I had."

"What happened?"

"She got murdered in January. I hadda read about it in the newspapers."

"That's too bad."

"Yeh," I said, shrugging my shoulders. "Anyway, it's too late now. I've already paid my dues. All I wanna do now is forget the whole fuckin' thing." We both stared straight ahead up the highway. "What are you gonna do when you get there?" I asked.

"I don't know. I'll figure somethin' out. I heard there's groups up there that'll try to help ya out; find you a place to stay, maybe a job. I'll make out."

"Write me a letter, will ya? Lemme know how you're doin'?"

"Sure."

Chapter 48

The next afternoon, I was sitting in the living room watching soap operas when the doorbell rang. It was Eric Rogers. He sported a scraggly beard, a Mexican serape, and tennis shoes with no socks. "I saw your mom up town yesterday," he said. "She told me you were home."

"Yeh."

"Just thought I'd stop by."

I stood there for a moment, not knowing quite what to do. "Come on in," I said. We sat down in the living room, and an awkward silence descended.

"What are you watchin'?" asked Eric.

"*Love of Life. As the World Turns.* I don't know; one's the same as the next. Just passin' time." Another awkward pause. "You want some coffee or somethin'? Soda?"

"Yeh, sure. Coffee."

I got up and went to the kitchen to heat water, relieved to have something to do.

"How are you?" asked Eric when I came back.

"Still in one piece. You want sugar or somethin'?"

"No." Another pause.

"I wrote you a couple of times," I finally said.

"Yeh, I got your letters."

"How come you didn't write back?"

"I wanted to. I didn't know what to say. I don't know."

"You couldn't say 'hello; hope you're okay'?"

"Geez, Bill. I didn't know what to say. It's all, you know, uh; I've applied for a CO and all. What was I supposed to say to you?"

"So you think the war's wrong, you gotta turn your back on your friends? How long we know each other, eight years? I mean one lousy letter? You couldn't even tell me what the weather was like?"

"I'm sorry, Bill. I was havin' a tough time, you know? I hadda get things straightened out in my head. There you were, right in the middle of all that, doin' all that —"

"You don't know what I was doin'! You don't know what tough times are, Eric! You're damn right, there I was right in the middle of all that. You don't think it woulda been nice to get a letter from you? I wrote you three goddamned times! You think it didn't matter to me?"

"Look, Bill, I'm really sorry —"

"Yeh, I'm sorry, too. I got no use for fair weather friends."

"I guess I'd better go," said Eric after another long pause.

"Yeh, I guess so."

Chapter 49

"Hello," I said, picking up the telephone.

"May I speak to Bill, please?"

"This is Bill."

"Oh, hello, Bill! I didn't recognize your voice. This is Mr. Jones. I was wondering, if you're not too busy, maybe you'd be willing to come and talk to my history classes while you're home."

"What about?"

"About Vietnam. I think it'd be good for them to talk to someone who's really been there. By the way, I'm very pleased that you're back safe and sound. That was a real shame about Ken Wommack."

"How come it's okay for me to talk to 'em in class, but I can't go near 'em in Washington?"

"Well, gee, Bill, I just thought — "

"How come you weren't so pleased to see me safe and sound then? I saw you there, sittin' there with the rest of 'em starin' at me like I was some kind of freak or somethin'. You couldn't even be bothered to say hello to me. 'We'll call the *cops* on you!' Now you want me to do you a favor? Jesus!"

"Now wait a minute, Bill, that was different. We had to think of the — "

"What kinda sucker you take me for? Stuff your history class up your ass," I said, hanging up.

Chapter 50

"Mom, I think I'm gonna go down to Cherry Point tomorrow."

"Bill. Why? You've hardly been home a week yet. We *like* having you home."

"Yeh, I noticed," I laughed. "You don't even holler at me for not makin' my bed."

"Ma-*king* your bed," she corrected. "Honestly, you shouldn't be so lazy when you talk. You know better."

"Aw, Mom."

"Bill, you've got more than two weeks yet. Why don't you just rest for awhile? It's *nice* to have you around."

"I know, Mom. It's nice to be home. I'm really glad to see you. You don't know. I really am. But there's nothin' to do. I'm just sittin' around."

"Well, go out and do something, then. Have you seen Mrs. Wommack yet?"

"Mom, I told you, I just can't."

"You really ought to. Kenny was your friend."

"I know, Mom. I just can't. You know what she's gonna be thinkin'. I went to Kenny's grave. I'll write her a letter. Please, Mom, can you understand?"

"Yes, I can," she said. "At least go out and see your friends. You can do that."

"Most of 'em are at school."

"Larry's home."

"Larry's — he went back yesterday."

"Well, Jeff's not in college. Isn't Scott Stevens living at home? I saw Eric Rogers last week."

"I know. He stopped by. We didn't have much to say. Mom, I don't have much to say to any of them. I can't explain. Everything's, well, just different. It's not the same anymore. I went to see Scott the other day, you know? It was nice to see him again, but then there was nothin' to say. We just kind of sat there for awhile, and then I left. I felt worse when I left. I don't know what happened, Mom. It feels like I finally managed to escape from Jupiter — and I've ended up on Mars. 'Ehrhart to Earth, Ehrhart to Earth' — and nobody answers."

Mom's eyes filled with tears. It was obvious she was struggling hard. I wanted to put my arms around her, but I couldn't.

"Hey, Mom, it's okay. It's not like I'm goin' back to Vietnam. I'm just goin' to North Carolina. Be close enough to come home weekends, sometimes, even. And I won't lose the leave time. What I don't use now, I can take later. That'd be even better. I can take it this summer when everybody's home from school, you know? Be lots more to do then. I can take a whole month off. Maybe July."

305

Chapter 51

According to any Marine you stop on the street, the Army has no function at all; the function of the Navy is to transport Marines over large bodies of water; and the function of the Air Force is to provide a home for wayward cowboys and gunfighters. The Marine Corps has its own air force. It maintains fighter planes for close air support of infantry operations, helicopters for hauling the infantry short distances, and transport planes for hauling them longer distances. There are three Marine Air Wings, one for each of the three ground divisions.

Back in the fall of 1966, my first duty assignment after basic training had been New River Air Facility, a helicopter base supporting Camp Lejeune. I'd arrived there with only a basic military occupational specialty (MOS) of 0200–intelligence, and I'd only spent a few months there — part of which I'd actually spent on temporary assignment at the Amphibious Intelligence School at Little Creek, Virginia. But when I'd left for Vietnam, even though I was due to go overseas on orders to a Marine ground unit, I'd been assigned the more specialized MOS of 0221–air intelligence, rather than 0231–ground intelligence.

I never thought about it much in Vietnam. What difference did one digit make? And besides, it was kind of like a little joke to have an air wing MOS in the infantry. People would ask, "What are *you* doing in the infantry?" And I'd reply, "My plane crashed." But when I finally left Vietnam, whoever cut my new orders looked at my air wing MOS, and ignoring the fact that all of my experience and knowledge was confined to ground intelligence, had assigned me back to an air unit.

Even after I'd gotten my new orders, I hadn't thought about it very much. But when I reported for duty at the Marine Corps Air Station, Cherry Point, North Carolina, I found myself assigned as the assistant intelligence chief of the entire 2nd Marine Air Wing. It was a matter of the blind leading the unwilling. I had half a dozen junior enlisted men under me, and I was supposed to supervise their work, only I had no idea what they were supposed to be doing. I was forever having to go around asking privates and lance corporals what they were supposed to be doing, so that I could see that they did it. I suspected that they were conning me silly — which any sensible Marine would have done under the circumstances — but I had no possible way of knowing. I would have given a month's pay for something familiar like a cartridge belt or a map and compass or a field radio, but there were none to be had in the Air Wing.

The only enlisted man senior to me at Wing Intelligence was an old master gunnery sergeant named Berger. He'd been the top sergeant down at New River when I'd been there as a lowly PFC. "Well, Ehrhart, you've done all right for yourself in a year and a half," he said the day I reported for duty.

I hadn't been there two hours before I pulled Berger aside. "Get me out of the Air Wing, Top," I said. "I'm a fish out of water here. I'm lost."

"You don't know a good thing when you see it, Ehrhart," said the Top. "You've done your time with the grunts. Relax and enjoy yourself. You'll catch on soon enough."

"Please, Top, I'm serious."

"Go pick up the message traffic, will you?"

Top Berger and I had this conversation every morning at 0800. He couldn't be budged. He liked me. He thought he was doing me a favor.

To compound the problem, the peacetime military in general is ruled by King Mickey the Mouse. After thirteen months in Vietnam, where polished boots and starched trousers and crisp second lieutenants had gone by the boards in favor of trying to keep dry and stay alive, I'd forgotten what real Mickey Mouse was. Immediately upon arrival at Cherry Point, however, I had my memory jogged soundly.

I had to wear a clean pressed dress uniform to work every day, complete with tie and jacket. I had to polish my shoes every day. I had to shine my brass belt buckle and tie clasp every day. Every time you turned around, there was some kind of rifle inspection or clothing inspection or work inspection or equipment inspection, presided over by a glaring major and a somber colonel, both of them walking up and down the ranks nodding grimly with their hands behind their backs and followed by a gunnery sergeant with a clipboard like a puppy on a leash keeping score.

And if you got to work five minutes late, somebody wanted to know why. And if you left work five minutes early, somebody wanted to know why. And if you had a little scuff on the tip of your left shoe, some second lieutenant right out of Officer Candidate School, his new gold bars gleaming in the sun, wanted to know why. Mickey Mouse. And it went on day after day after day.

Chapter 52

Only the weekends provided some relief. I never went off base, except on weekends. Almost every weeknight, I went to the NCO club on base, got drunk, staggered back to the barracks when the club closed, and passed out. But on weekends, I'd jump into my red VW and drive as far and as fast as I could before Monday morning.

The first weekend, I drove to Pembroke, North Carolina, to visit an old high school chum named Ron Charles who was going to college there. "At least I can drink legally in this state," I said to Ronnie. We had nothing else to say to each other. He set me up with a date, and we went to the beach. I got drunk and passed out, and when I woke up, it was dark and I was lying alone in the back seat of my car in the parking lot outside Ron's dormitory. I climbed into the driver's seat, turned the engine over, and drove back to base.

The next weekend, I drove to New York City to see another high school friend named Sheryl Brigham. I got drunk and kept her up half the night pouring my heart out about Jenny and God knows what all else, and in the morning she told me her boss called and she had to go in to work. I got in my car and drove back to base.

The next weekend, another Marine invited me to go with him to visit a friend of his at the University of Virginia. We went to a fraternity party, and I got drunk. A long-haired fellow wearing beads and a jungle utility jacket started hassling me about my short hair, so I pulled a switchblade knife on him, and while he was staring at the gleaming blade, I stepped into his knee and hinged it the opposite way for him.

We had to beat it out of there in a hurry. We went back to the friend's apartment, and I kept drinking until I passed out, and when I woke up in the morning, the other Marine and his friend asked me to leave, so I got in my car and drove back to base.

The next weekend, I went to Myrtle Beach, South Carolina, with three other Marines from base. We rented a beach cottage, and I got drunk and never made it out the door of the cottage until it was time to go back to base. About fifteen miles out of Cherry Point, we got stopped by a cop.

We were coming down a long steep hill on a two-lane road. At the bottom of the hill, the road turned sharply to the right. Just around the curve, out of sight until you were almost on top of it, was a sign reducing the speed limit from 55 to 35. Not ten yards beyond the sign was a cop with a radar unit. He flagged me over. He'd clocked me at 43 miles per hour. He took us straight to the nearest Justice of the Peace, and the JP fined me $65. Cash. When I asked the JP for a written receipt for the money, he threatened to throw us all in jail until the circuit judge came around. "He oughta be here in about three weeks," the JP drawled. "You wanna argue, boy? You can argue with the circuit judge."

Chapter 53

The next weekend, we had a Saturday morning inspection, making it impossible to travel any distance that weekend. So on Saturday night, I decided to check out the local action. I went to a dance-bar in a town near the base. The joint was jumping, as they say, and I was quickly in the mood to bogey.

I sidled up to a young woman and asked her to dance. She declined sharply, looking at me as though I'd just asked her to suck on my penis. It was startling. I had another beer. After awhile, I got up enough nerve to ask another girl to dance. She said no. I had another beer. In the next two hours, the sequence repeated itself a dozen times with the same result, my frustration and anger mounting with each attempt. Was it my accent, which marked me as a Yankee? Was it my short hair, which marked me as a serviceman? Was is my breath? What the hell's the matter with *me*?!

I thought of Dorrit von Hellemond. I thought of the young woman with the AK-47, the one in the photograph I'd taken off the dead Vietcong. I thought of the woman in the gun pit in Hue. After awhile, the beer made thought impossible. My stomach heaved up and down. I went to the men's room and threw up. I left the bar. I called Jenny from a pay phone and begged her and begged her to love me, running out of change about the time I realized that I was talking to Jenny's dorm counsellor. I went back to the base and masturbated in the shower, passing out beneath the warm stream of water before I finished.